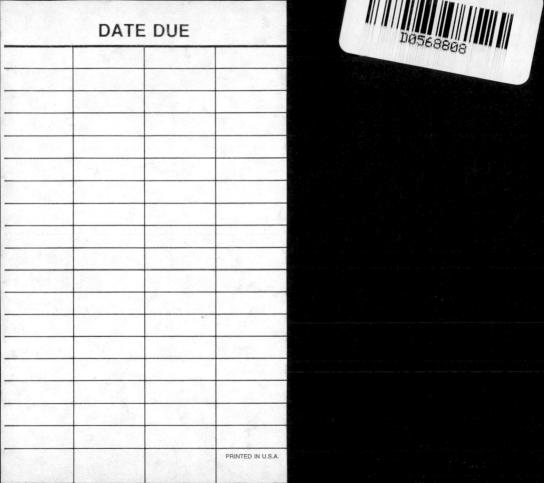

DATE DUE

			PRINTED IN U.S.A.

D0568808

Ancient Wisdom and Secret Sects

Ancient Wisdom and Secret Sects

By the Editors of Time-Life Books

TIME-LIFE BOOKS, ALEXANDRIA, VIRGINIA

CONTENTS

To belong, to have status, to know secrets, to understand mysteries: These promises have lured people to secret societies since the dawn of humankind. They are answers to the nearly universal thirst of men and women to be accepted by their peers, to be among the select, the chosen —the initiated.

Initiation is the rite in which the outsider is admitted in. He proves himself worthy of inclusion in the elite group he aspires to, and having done so, he learns the lore and secrets that give it its special character and lie at its heart.

The initiate may be a college sorority pledge, an Australian Aborigine on the verge of manhood, or a candidate for membership in the Freemasons, as depicted in the illustrations on this and the following pages. He may be favored with keys to purported magic and cosmic riddles, or merely with a secret handshake that links him to his newfound brothers. But however greatly the rituals differ in particulars from sect to sect, the salient features of initiation are much the same.

An oath of secrecy is usually a key part of the ceremony, for the group's existence and identity are defined by what it hides. Indeed, the strength of the knowledge revealed to the initiate is often seen to depend upon its secrecy, as a saying of the Zuni Indians of the American Southwest suggests: "Power told is power lost."

In initiation ceremonies both primitive and modern, the initiate typically becomes the central player in a pageant that dramatizes his transition from outsider to group member. During this drama, he is generally treated as a stranger or spy while he undergoes a series of challenges or tests to prove himself fit for the honor of belonging. The rigors may be metaphorical or actual. There may be discomfort, deprivation, the threat of injury—real or symbolic—or even the threat of death.

Another common part of initiation rites is the allegorical journey a candidate takes, representing the distance from his old benighted state to his enlightened one as a group member. This journey, particularly in more primitive ceremonies, often takes the form of a ritual death and rebirth. In certain tribal puberty rites, for example, boys endure long separation from their families, along with tests of strength, stamina, and the ability to endure pain—stringent constituents of the ritual "death" they experience before their rebirth as men. Far from tribal life, modern Masons also undergo challenges and an allegorical death-rebirth, though without the physical tests imposed on the aboriginal adolescents.

Many groups' trials of initiation are meant to purify the outsider and ready him to receive the treasured secrets of the organization. In some sects, the initiate does not receive the full body of wisdom all at once, but in stages. He begins his spiritual growth at the bottom rung of a hierarchy, sometimes symbolized by a ladder that extends past earth and into the heavens—his ultimate goal. Each step up is accompanied by new initiation ceremonies and more profound revelations.

Masonic ritual, for example, works through three basic degrees of membership—those of entered apprentice, fellow, and master—followed by a panoply of higher degrees for the dedicated seeker. Many of the thematic motifs outlined

In a depiction of an eighteenth-century Masonic initiation (above), an officer called the tyler knocks at the lodge door, requesting entry for the blindfolded candidate for the entered apprentice degree. Inside, an inner guard challenges him with a sword point at his breast, as a test of courage (right).

above may be seen in the three illustrations here, which represent the first two initiation steps for the first-degree and a key stage in the third-degree initiation ceremonies of eighteenth-century Masonry. (See chapter 3 for a detailed discussion of Freemasonry.) In the first painting *(page 6),* the candidate stands before the door of the lodge as the tyler, or guard, knocks on the outsider's behalf to request entry. The candidate has relinquished his worldly possessions and wears a rope noose loosely around his neck, symbolizing the bond between every Mason and his lodge. He is blindfolded, both as a reminder of the sect's shield of secrecy and to signify the darkness that precedes the spiritual illumination he will experience from learning the Masonic mysteries.

The next picture *(page 7)* depicts a physical challenge put to the initiate—a member's sword point pressed against his chest—as a test of his courage and spiritual readiness. The significance of the single slipper he wears is known only to initiates but is interpreted several ways by outsiders. Some say it derives from the biblical tradition of removing one sandal to indicate a willingness to enter into a commitment. The blindfold will ultimately be removed to signify the initiate's passage from darkness into enlightenment.

The final painting *(page 8)* illustrates the symbolic death and rebirth that candidates experience at later stages of initiation. This particular rite reenacts the saga of a Masonic hero named Hiram Abiff, who, some say, suffered a martyr's death at the hands of villainous subordinates

when he refused to reveal the secrets of the master mason degree. In the painting, the initiate undergoes a symbolic reenactment of suffering and death; when the ceremony is completed, he will have earned the high position of the master mason through spiritual endurance.

Although such initiation rites may teach complex truths, they work at their simplest level to create a powerful bond of shared, private experience among members. Veterans of the group often find the emotions of their own initiation ordeals revitalized when a new member is initiated; the common experience of fear, pain, and revelation unifies those who have been through it, setting them apart from others. Thus the ceremonies reinforce the group's traditional values even as they are handed down to a new generation.

There are those who say that the emotional experience of initiation into certain mystical sects is indescribable, so potent is the ritual at tapping some deep wellspring of human need and aspiration. This opaque, ineffable quality seems to have suffused the rites of the Eleusinian mysteries, the most famous secret sect of antiquity, one that celebrated the mother-goddess Demeter. Its initiates, said the Greek philosopher Aristotle, discovered in the ritual no particular facts or concrete answers. Rather, they experienced truths emotionally, intuitively, and directly. Almost 300 years later, the Roman statesman Cicero left only this enigmatic statement about his own initiation into Demeter's cult: "We have learned to live and die with better hope."

Surrounded by Masons holding drawn swords, a candidate lies on a canvas representing the coffin of a mythic hero who died defending the Masonic secrets. The lodge master, sitting at the altar with an open Bible, presides over this ritual death and rebirth—the climax of initiation rites for the master mason degree.

CHAPTER 1

Brotherhoods of Old

ugust 1, 1984, began as a routine day for English laborer Andy Mould. He had been cutting peat with a crew at Lindow Moss, a 150-acre peat bog in Cheshire, and now he was at the mill, watching an elevator carry the freshly cut blocks to a shredding machine. As his eye scanned the elevator's platform, he noticed what appeared to be a chunk of wood. Mould picked the block up and playfully tossed it toward a co-worker, who dodged it. As the object hit the ground with a thud and loose peat fell away, the two men found themselves staring at what looked to be a human foot.

Local police were immediately called to the scene, as was county archaeologist Rick Turner. The authorities quickly determined where the foot had been unearthed and located the rest of the body, which had only barely escaped the blades of the peat-cutting machinery. The remains appeared to be ancient—not those of a recent murder victim, as had been feared—and the police withdrew, leaving the painstaking job of removing the corpse intact to Turner and a crew of specialists.

The body, a male called Lindow Man by those who studied it, had been remarkably well preserved by the acidic, airless conditions of the bog. Scientists were able to determine that Lindow Man had died in about the second century BC and that he was between twenty-five and thirty years old at the time of his death. He was of medium height and was powerfully built, although he lacked the pronounced musculature peculiar to a warrior. He had the smooth, unroughened hands of someone belonging to an elite social class. His body offered many clues about his life but none as startling as the evidence it revealed about the nature of his death: Lindow Man bore distinct signs of ritual murder.

There was no evidence of a struggle. He had been knocked unconscious by two blows to the head, scientists concluded, then garroted, and finally bled from an incision made at the throat in the carotid artery. As far as the experts could determine, Lindow Man had been in perfect health until his grisly end.

Who was Lindow Man, and how did he arrive at such a fate? Some experts studying the remains believe he was a Druid, a member of the pagan, priestly sect of the Celts, a people who populated much of the Continent and Britain perhaps as long ago as the eighth century BC. Said to govern the spiritual, intellectual, and ritual life of their people, Druids were also believed to practice human sacrifice as part of their religious ceremonies. Food remains that are thought to be from just such a ceremony were discovered in Lindow Man's stomach, and it was this evidence that convinced some researchers of his Druidic connection. Lindow Man had apparently received as a last meal a charred piece of bannock, a barley cake traditionally served at Celtic festivals celebrating the advent of spring. An ancient Druidic custom allegedly performed at the celebration involved distributing portions of a special bannock to all those present. One piece of the cake was blackened, and the person who received this burned morsel was marked for sacrifice to the gods.

As is the case with many other secret sects, what is known of the Druids seems to be an intricate weave of fact and fancy. They left behind no written descriptions of their rites and beliefs, choosing instead to protect their tradition by committing all learning to memory and transmitting it orally. Modern knowledge of the Druids is thus based on a smattering of Greek and Roman accounts that were usually second- or third-hand at best, and on some Irish epic poems passed down orally through the centuries and eventually transcribed by medieval monks. By keeping their esoteric lore unpenetrable, the Druids conferred on their followers a sense of exclusivity, of being the sole possessors of a special knowledge handed down through the ages.

Although the term "secret sect" may mean that both a group's membership and its activities are concealed from the outside world, more generally it refers to a group whose membership is known but whose doctrines and rituals are meaningful only to initiates. In its secrecy it confers a feeling of uniqueness, of having entered an inner circle and shared a common experience, of having been spiritually uplifted through the revelation of a special wisdom or philosophy. This idea of special, hidden knowledge has been central to secret organizations from the earliest times. It endows a fraternity with a certain glamour—and, in the cases of sects with evil intentions, a sinister appeal—that draws people to the group and speaks to some deeply felt human need.

Secret sects exist both in primitive and in technologically advanced cultures. They almost certainly predate recorded history; one interpretation of prehistoric cave paintings is that they were part of special Stone Age tribal rites meant to summon game animals by sympathetic magic. Tribal secret sects were generally concerned, however, with rites of passage into adulthood for young boys and girls and with preserving the cultural traditions of the tribe. Other groups through the ages banded together for religious and political purposes, as did the Druids and the twelfth-century Knights Templars. Some came together as, or evolved into, ritualistic brotherhoods. Groups of this sort include the Freemasons, the Rosicrucians, the Theosophists, and the Hermetic Order of the Golden Dawn. Each of these societies had its special beliefs and rituals, its arcane totems and customs. But all of their members sought enlightenment through religious teachings based on mystical insight.

Common threads run through every group. Indeed, it is startling to note the underlying similarities among such organizations, which on the surface can be as different as the Assassins (a medieval Muslim sect who murdered Christian Crusaders) and a modern-day fraternal organization such as the Benevolent and Protective Order of Elks. Secret societies typically choose their membership according to particular criteria and require the novices to undergo an initiation ritual. The ceremony usually includes the recounting of a myth, legend, or belief about the origins of the sect, the introduction of meaningful signs or symbols, and

This first-century-AD wall painting, thought to be from a villa in the ancient Roman city of Herculaneum, depicts priests of the Isis cult performing a water ceremony. The Egyptian goddess Isis was associated with the land, and her husband, Osiris, with the life-giving waters of the Nile.

an oath of allegiance. Initiates generally advance to a position of importance within the society over time, through an elaborate, hierarchical system of ranks or degrees.

Another link among many secret sects, past and present, is the tradition of tracing their ancestry back to the so-called mystery cults, or religions, that thrived in the ancient Mediterranean world. These cults—of Eleusis, Dionysus, Isis and Osiris, and others—were religious in nature and grew out of a widespread desire for an individualized faith that could assure its followers of immortality. In ancient Greece, religious festivals were often combined with official functions of the city-states, such as agricultural observances. This blending of religion and politics forged a strong sense of cultural solidarity, but it left the spiritual needs of many unfulfilled. The mystery cults attended to those unsatiated needs.

The term *mystery* derives from the Greek word *musterion,* meaning "that which is reserved for initiates only." And what apparently drew many people to the mystery cults was the ecstasy and sense of renewal provided by elaborately staged induction rites. Festivals of initiation usually went on for days and culminated in a secret drama of sacrifice and rebirth. At their most sophisticated, the cults embodied ideas such as the resurrection of the dead and the promise of eternal life—concepts that later religions, including Christianity, would incorporate and refine. Unlike Christianity, Judaism, or Islam, however, the mystery religions usually lacked any fully developed theology or moral code to guide their followers in day-to-day living; they operated on an emotional rather than intellectual level. As the Greek

A priestess playing the role of Isis leads a ceremonial procession in this Roman marble relief dating from about AD 100. The snake wound around her left arm was believed to bring good fortune.

philosopher Aristotle observed, initiates "do not so much learn anything, as experience certain emotions, and are thrown into a special state of mind" *(see pages 6-9).*

A number of the mystery religions had origins in fertility cults or grew out of local agricultural festivals. One of these was the cult of Eleusis, which flourished in Greece from about the sixth century BC until about AD 395. Centered west of Athens in the town of Eleusis, the sect honored Demeter, goddess of grain, and her daughter, Persephone. According to Greek mythology, young Persephone was abducted and forced to marry Hades, lord of the underworld. To reclaim her daughter, Demeter prevailed upon Zeus, king of the gods, to intervene. Zeus persuaded Hades to allow Persephone to live on earth eight months of the year, a period suggesting the growing season. For cult followers, Persephone symbolically died each year with the harvest, and her goddess mother created winter from grief. Persephone was reborn each spring with the new crop, and Demeter rejoiced by making the land fruitful again. This allegory of death and resurrection was the basis for the initiates' hope of eternal life.

Worshipers celebrated the Eleusinian mysteries, or rituals, three times a year. Every Greek, regardless of social class, became eligible for initiation into the cult by joining in the "lesser mysteries" held in winter and spring. The initiates fasted and took part in other ceremonies designed to help them attain a proscribed level of moral and physical purity, all in preparation for the "greater mysteries" to be staged at the harvest in September. At that time, all the Greek city-states were called on to join in honoring a holy truce of fifty-five days, and neophytes from throughout the Hellenic world gathered in Athens to ready themselves for the great initiation. As part of the ceremony, each participant bathed himself and a small pig in the sea, then offered the pig as a sacrifice. Next, the initiates, bearing branches of myrtle, walked the more than ten miles between Athens and Eleusis in formal procession, escorting statues of De-

effect on Greek religious life. Followers of Dionysus achieved union with their god through drink and dance, the indulgence of base impulses, and freedom from inhibitions. Cult rituals included orgiastic festivals, along with prayers and sacrifices to the god of license. As a means of neutralizing its ecstatic bent, the sect was apparently incorporated into a number of existing state cults—the one at Eleusis and also an ascetic religious movement called Orphism.

Orphism's inspiration was the musician-hero Orpheus, of Greek myth, whose lyre was so eloquent it tamed

A whirling maenad with tambourine and torch engages a satyr in the orgiastic dance practiced by the followers of Bacchus, the Roman wine god associated with Dionysus. The small slate panel, inlaid with marble, dates from the first century AD. It was salvaged from the rubble of a house in Pompeii.

meter and Persephone and other sacred objects. All was joy and merriment until, just before reaching their destination, the procession was met by a group of men who hurled insults at the celebrants. This scene, according to historians, was planned to humble the exalted worshipers.

At the end of the march, when the initiates reached Eleusis, there was more revelry and dancing, followed by a night of rest. The next day included fasting and more sacrifices to the gods. Then, as night drew near, the initiates gathered outside the temple of Demeter and waited for a torchbearer to appear at the door and bid them enter. Inside, a ritual meal was eaten and sacred dramas were performed, reenacting Demeter's search for Persephone. The ceremony culminated in a display of sacred objects bathed in a dramatic blaze of light.

The Eleusinian mysteries enjoyed great status among the Greeks and eventually the Romans. Over time, new rites were added, and Dionysus, the god of wine, revelry, and fertility, was incorporated into the ritual. The Dionysian cult had appeared in northern Greece about the beginning of the seventh century BC and gradually penetrated southward. The nature of the cult, however, had produced a disturbing

savage beasts and once even caused Hades, the saturnine god of the underworld, to weep. Orphic beliefs—which included the idea that the body was a hindrance to spiritual life and should be transcended—contrasted sharply with those of the Dionysian cult, yet the ascetics made good use of the grim legend surrounding the playful god. According to one version of the myth, Dionysus, son of Zeus, was killed and eaten by Titans, the giants that made up the oldest generation of Greek deities. In response, an enraged Zeus, king of the Olympian gods and lord of the heavens, launched a hail of thunderbolts against the attackers, setting their bodies ablaze. Yet neither Dionysus nor the Titans were completely lost: Dionysus's undigested heart was retrieved from the flames and fed to Zeus. He then impregnated the earth goddess Semele, and Dionysus was reborn. From the ashes of the Titans, so the story goes, sprang the human race. To the followers of Orphism, this myth confirmed the belief that human beings had an intrinsic capacity for both good and evil, and that as Dionysus was reborn, so could his faithful worshipers be.

Orphism greatly influenced the followers of Pythagoras, the sixth-century-BC mathematician and philosopher

*Wild animals sit transfixed by the melodies of the
legendary musician Orpheus in this third-century-AD Roman mosaic.
By the fifth century BC, Orpheus had become linked with a
mystery religion dedicated to purifying the soul through self-denial.*

who founded a sect based on his own metaphysical system. The Pythagoreans were a kind of intellectual secret brotherhood dedicated to a life of the mind. Like the Orphists, the Pythagoreans regarded the body as an impediment to the spiritual life and believed the exercise of ritual and ascetic practices, such as avoiding food from animals, could aid in the attainment of higher knowledge. Initiation into these cults and the

The Persian god Mithra slays a wild bull, symbolizing rebirth, in this second-century-AD sculpture. A dog, sacred to the Persians, and a snake, representing evil, vie for the animal's blood, which supposedly generated all living things. Sacrificing a bull was central to Mithraic cult initiation.

ing notions of resurrection and immortality.

The Roman writer Apuleius was probably describing his own initiation into the mysteries of Isis and Osiris in *Metamorphoses,* his famous second-century-BC treatise. The hero of the story, Lucius, commenced his induction with priestly instruction from the Egyptian *Book of the Dead.* After a ritual bath and head shaving, Lucius was led by a priest into the temple of Isis,

knowledge of their secret doctrines supposedly set the neophyte on a path toward a cleansing series of reincarnations. When the soul was completely pure, they believed, it would be set free and made fully divine.

The cults of Dionysus and Orpheus enjoyed their greatest following in Italy, where they and other imported sects vied for the Roman soul. By the first century BC, Rome had become the commercial center of the Mediterranean, a cosmopolitan capital teeming with people and ideas from the far reaches of the ancient world. The mystery cults captured the imagination of the empire. Particularly compelling was the cult of Isis and Osiris, an Egyptian sect that dated from the time of the Pharaohs.

The story of Isis and Osiris was as grisly as that of Dionysus, and like other ancient myths, it embodied the concept of death and rebirth. Osiris, rulcr of Egypt and son of the sky and earth gods, was murdered and dismembered by his evil brother, Seth. Osiris's body, such as it was, was cast upon the river Nile. Isis, the god's grieving widow, collected the remains, and the ruler was restored to life by their son, Horus. To the Egyptians, Osiris symbolized the Nile itself: His death represented the advent of drought and his resurrection the great river's annual restorative flood. To the Romans, the story of Osiris embraced the exhilarat-

where he stood at the feet of the goddess and was told "secret things unlawful to be uttered." For the next ten days, the initiate abstained from meat, bread, wine, and sex. Then, on his initiation night, Lucius was taken to the most sacred part of the temple to participate in a mystic drama reenacting the search for Osiris's body. Apuleius goes on to tell how, at midnight, the neophyte was struck speechless by a shaft of light that seemed to appear out of nowhere. "I saw the sun brightly shine," Lucius recalls in awe. "I saw likewise the gods celestial and the gods infernal, before whom I presented myself, and worshiped them."

Like the mysteries of Isis and Osiris, the Persian cult of Mithra had its greatest flowering among the Romans. The emperor Nero was initiated into the Mithraic mysteries, and Mithraism became the semi-official religion of the Roman army, whose legions spread it to the ends of the empire. According to ancient myth, Mithra, the Persian sun god who represented good, was locked in eternal battle with the forces of evil. As part of the battle, Mithra killed a great bull. Some scholars claim that the beast embodied the spirit of evil, others that it was a sacred bull whose death was a sacrifice. In any case, from the bull's blood sprang all the herbs and plants useful to humanity. This miracle revealed Mithra as the regenerator of the earth and the creator of life made richer and more fruitful.

As with other early cults, Mithraism had its roots in an agricultural rite, and it placed great importance on the secret ritual of initiation. At the heart of the Mithraic ceremony was the sacrifice of a bull and the initiate's baptism in its blood. Mithraism recognized seven degrees of divine knowledge. Members could advance from one degree to the next by undergoing a special initiation, tests of courage and stamina, at each stage. The seven ranks corresponded to the seven known celestial planets, and scaling them was a metaphor for the passage of the soul through the planetary spheres toward heaven.

There were parallels between Mithraism and Christianity, and the two religions competed for dominance in the Roman Empire. The setting and rising of the sun, symbol of the sun god Mithra, recalled Christ's death and resurrection. Moreover, the Mithraic festival in celebration of the sun god's birth was held on December 25, recognized as Jesus' birthday. Both religions included a baptism and a sacrament of bread and wine, and both guarded their central rites from nonbelievers: The Christian Eucharist, in which the worshiper takes bread and wine as the body and blood of Christ, was itself a ''mystery'' originally performed only for those instructed in the Lord's ways.

At the same time the Romans embraced the Mediterra-

The Mithraic figure Aion was said to represent time and to hold the keys to the world beyond. The lion head allegedly denotes summer and the god's fierce temperament. The snake around his body represents the underworld and is symbolic of the cold aspects of Aion's nature. Aion's menacing countenance, scholars believe, reveals that Mithra's followers recognized the power of time and looked to their god for salvation.

nean mystery cults, they were seeking to quash a pagan sect holding sway at the northern fringe of their empire. In the forest of Gaul (now France) and in the mist-shrouded British Isles, Celtic tribes were worshiping a pantheon of rough-hewed gods and woodland spirits. The keepers of these faiths were the Druids. Druids appear to have played a pervasive role in Celtic society. According to the few Greco-Roman literary sources that survive from that time, the Druids were priests and philosophers, educators, arbiters, and healers. They not only oversaw all religious and ritual observances, but, according to Julius Caesar in his 51 BC work *Commentarii de Bello Gallico* (Commentaries on the Gallic War), they studied ''the stars and their movements, the size of the universe and the earth, the nature of things, the power of the immortal gods.'' As repositories of cultural knowledge in a society without writing, Druids spent lifetimes memorizing Celtic laws and epics. Their political powers were at least equal to those of the king, whom they personally chose from the royal family and advised on matters of state and war. Druids occasionally served as commanders in battle, although they were not required by law to perform military service or to pay taxes. They knew the herbs and plants used for treating various ailments and practiced numerous methods of divination; it was claimed of an Irish Druid named Fingen that he could diagnose a man's illness by the smoke from his chimney. Druids also reportedly instructed young children in cultural traditions and the ways of the Druidic order so that some day they too might join the sect.

Druids were apparently recruited from the upper classes of Celtic society and passed through three levels, or degrees, of authority: *vates,* those who practiced divination; *bards,* the reciters of sacred poetry; and *druids,* the priests in charge of ritual ceremonies. All came to be known generally as Druids. The Druids set aside one day each week for religious observance and presided over four seasonal festivals every year. Like the followers of Mithra, the Celts were said to celebrate the winter solstice on December 25; during that ceremony and those celebrating the summer solstice

This skull, set in the doorpost of an ancient Celtic temple, was thought to lend power to those inside and to protect them. Ancient Celts not only hunted their enemies' heads, they also worshiped the human head, believing it contained the soul.

and the autumnal and vernal equinoxes, initiation rites were allegedly performed. The great annual celebration of Beltane, or May Day, commemorated the sun's resurrection. Ritual feasts were held and dances were performed; and at midnight, according to one source, in a sacred grove of trees illuminated by bonfires, an initiate reenacted the symbolic death and resurrection of Hu, the sun god of the Druids.

According to Pliny the Elder, the times of some Druidic ceremonies were determined by observing the rare appearance of mistletoe growing on an oak tree. A white-robed Druid would scale the tree and, with a golden sickle, free the parasitic plant, believed to embody the spirit of the oak, a sacred tree. A great feast ensued, and two white bulls were sacrificed.

Many Druidic festivals were agricultural fertility rites, and animal sacrifices were undoubtedly involved. But it is almost certain that during some rituals—on the eve of battle, it has been said, or when a highly placed person fell ill—the Druids sacrificed humans as well. Caesar claimed that the pagans constructed huge, human-shaped wicker cages, crammed them with victims, then set the twigs ablaze. Although convicted criminals were usually the ones offered to the gods, he explained, innocent victims were substituted if malefactors were in short supply. Some sources claim the Druids even sacrificed their fellow members if the need to do so arose. The classical author Diodorus Siculus also reported scenes of human sacrifice. "When they attempt divination upon important matters they practice a strange and incredible custom, for they kill a man by a knife-stab in the region above his midriff." After the sacrificial victim fell dead, Diodorus went on to say, "they foretell the future by the convulsions of his limbs and the pouring of his blood."

Some historians doubt the accuracy of these lurid tales: Caesar most likely embellished his description of the Celtic savages in order to justify his Gallic Wars, and the other accounts were probably not those of eyewitnesses. Still, other authorities believe that the old historical narratives do not stray very far from the truth. Certainly, the 1984 discovery of the Lindow Man's remains in the Cheshire peat bog bolstered the case that the Druids did indeed practice human sacrifice. Roman au-

thorities in Gaul and Britain tolerated this and other Druidic religious rites, but they feared the Druids' political power among the subjugated Celtic tribes. In AD 54, a decree was issued abolishing the Druidic religion, and seven years later a campaign was launched to stamp out the last vestiges of the pagan sect. A final confrontation took place at Anglesey, an island off the northwest coast of Wales and a stronghold of Druidism. According to the distinguished Roman historian Tacitus, as the Roman boats came ashore, long-bearded Druids and black-clad women raising torches leaped from the woods, shrieking and howling and hurling curses at the invaders. Alas, this verbal fusillade proved powerless against the steel of Roman short swords; the warriors cut down everyone and everything they found in their path. Not even the trees in the sacred grove—which Tacitus described as stained with the blood of captives—were spared.

The slaughter at Anglesey, as well as the eventual conversion of the Celts to Christianity, effectively ended Druidic influence in the ancient world. Only in Wales and Ireland did Druidism survive into the Middle Ages as the bardic tradition of memorizing epic poems. Modern times, however, have seen a revival of the sect. Today most followers simply strive to promote the ideas and principles of Celtic civilization. Some splinter groups, however, maintain what they construe to be the mystical traditions of the Druids. Garbed in white robes, these contemporary druids, bards, and vates reenact initiation ceremonies and seasonal pageants—minus, of course, any human sacrifice—at Stonehenge and similar sites throughout Britain. The modern sects seem to be drawn to these megaliths, and many of them believe ancient Druids were the ones who erected the columns at Stonehenge. But Stonehenge predates by about a thousand years the arrival of Druids in Britain. And although the Druids almost certainly used the monument as an observatory for marking the arrival of the seasons, this ancient sect seemed to prefer the privacy of sacred groves in which to conduct the clandestine rites of its pagan faith.

This detail from a Celtic ceremonial cauldron may depict human sacrifice, often accomplished by drowning or suffocating the victim in just such a vessel.

By about AD 300, Christianity had supplanted Druidism and the ancient mystery religions as the officially sanctioned faith of the Roman Empire. The Britons seemed to embrace the new system of belief with more alacrity than other nations, perhaps because early Christianity shared with Druidism some common tenets: the immortality of the soul, a belief in miracles, and according to some scholars, faith in reincarnation.

Paralleling the growth of Christianity during the first centuries AD were a number of powerful movements whose views of God, humanity, and the universe were quite different from those of the mainstream Christian faith. One such group was the Gnostics, who took their name from *gnosis,* the Greek word for "knowledge." Generally, Gnostic thought blended Christianity with the ideas of Plato and other Hellenic philosophers who saw the universe in terms of real and ideal states of being. The corrupt, imperfect "real" world of earth and flesh could only be known through the senses; by contrast, the perfect "ideal" realm of God could be approached only through knowledge of the heart. Gnostics believed they were once spiritual beings who had been made to inhabit a body and live in a world of sin. But once they received gnosis, the knowledge revealed solely to them by Christ, complete redemption would be achieved. According to the writings of one group of Gnostics, this special knowledge unveils "who we were and what we have become; where we were or where we had been made to fall; whither we are hastening, whence we are being redeemed; what birth is and what rebirth is." For Gnostics there were two types of people—those bound to the earth and the flesh and those who could be enlightened. Initiates were chosen from the latter group to seek liberation from the body and all physical matter along various paths. Some teachers believed a state of ecstasy provided divine illumination, while others advocated fasting and meditation. The Gnostics were a closed society; they were said to carry stones inscribed with serpents and other symbols as talismans and proof of initiation, and to employ passwords and secret handshakes to identify themselves to other members of the sect.

A more extreme form of this dualistic religion was Manicheanism, named after its founder, the Persian sage Mani. Mani was born about AD 215 to a family whose religious beliefs were culled from a number of sources. Mani himself was initiated into the mysteries of Mithra, and he studied early Christian heretical sects before establishing his own religious philosophy in about AD 240, at the Persian court of King Shapur I. Mani and his followers regarded the world as

A Study in Contrasts

As a young Welsh doctor in the 1830s, William Price was a tangle of unorthodox beliefs. He thought if patients became ill, the doctor should pay. In a land known for lamb, Price espoused vegetarianism. Claiming matrimony enslaved women, he kept a mistress. A Christian clergyman's son, he claimed to be a reincarnated Druid.

On a trip to France in 1839, Price allegedly found "a precious stone, on which was inscribed the portrait of the primitive bard in the act of addressing the moon." The stone carried markings that Price claimed only he could decipher. He became obsessed with Druidism, believing that through him, and later his son, the ancient religion would be restored.

Dressed in a white tunic, green trousers, and fox-skin headdress, Price performed Druidic rituals. In 1884, he spoke at an art exhibition of his birth 3,700 years before, chanted a Welsh song, then stripped down to what resembled red long johns covered with green hieroglyphs.

The final act of Price's curious drama involved the 1884 death of his infant son. Hewing to Druidic rituals, Price cremated the boy. Villagers were horrified, and Price was jailed, since cremation was illegal. But his defense that "the land is for the living" swayed the judge, and within two years cremation became legal in Britain. In 1893, Price himself died, and his body was committed to the flames.

This portrait of William Price, in his symbol-covered scarlet suit, appeared in his 1871 work, The Will of My Father. There, Price proclaimed himself "son of the Welsh Primitive Bard."

Bahram I, to get rid of him. Mani was imprisoned, and in AD 276, he was crucified and his corpse flayed.

After his death, a trusted group of followers carried on the Manichean traditions, including its initiation rites and the use of its secret symbols and passwords; one annual ceremony commemorated the death of the prophet. Practitioners of Manicheanism were persecuted furiously by followers of other religions. Even so, branches of the sect soon began to appear throughout much of the known world. The religion sometimes took on a different name and new figurative language, and the farther it advanced into the West, the more Christianized it became. But some basic tenets remained the same, and say some historians, Manicheanism was later echoed in the doctrines of such organizations as the Cathars, the Knights Templars, and the Freemasons.

irreconcilably divided into the kingdoms of light and darkness, good and evil. They believed that Satan, born from the darkness, had robbed part of the light—or goodness—from primal man. Mani proclaimed himself the ''ambassador of the light'' and set out a system by which humans could rid themselves of the darkness. Manicheans practiced extreme asceticism in their struggle toward the light. They were forbidden, for example, to kill any animal or plant for food; in fact, they were even enjoined against the breaking of a single twig.

Mani traveled into what is now western China and as far south as India to spread his gospel. Although he had been held in high regard at the Persian court, by the time he returned home around AD 270, the royal milieu had changed. The priestly caste of the ancient Persian religion Zoroastrianism resented Mani's presence and succeeded in exerting considerable political pressure on the new king,

With its mingling of beliefs in duality, divine beings, and magic, the Mediterranean world of the second and third centuries AD created a fertile atmosphere in which mysticism could develop and flourish. It was during this period of time that the seeds of what would be an influential and complex body of esoteric doctrines—the Jewish Kabbalah—were sown. (The word ''Kabbalah'' has many variant spellings, the most common of which, ''Cabala,'' came into wide use after the ancient mystical system came under the influence of the Christians.)

The Cabala as it is known today emerged in southern France and Spain in about the twelfth century. But its original foundation may be traced back to the Jews of ancient Palestine and Egypt. For them, the Kabbalah's beliefs were based on a mystical view of God and of humanity's role in God's universe. The word *kabbalah* comes from the Hebrew word meaning "that which is received," and according to tradition, it was Moses on Mt. Sinai who first received the Kabbalah, along with the Ten Commandments. Deeming the divine knowledge of the Kabbalah too sacred to speak or write about directly, Moses, it was believed, hid clues to the divine truth in the Pentateuch, the first five books of the Bible. Those clues constituted in large part the study of the Kabbalah and were considered to be the "soul of the soul" of Jewish law.

The term *kabbalah* eventually became equated with any esoteric, occult, or mystical doctrine, but study of it originally emphasized prayer and the contemplation of esoteric writings on the Pentateuch and other scriptures. As the Kabbalah evolved, it came to share certain ideas with other ancient mystical systems, including those of the Gnostics and Pythagoreans. The Kabbalah did not restrict itself solely to instruction on the apprehension of God but included teachings on cosmology, angelology, and magic.

Only those determined to be worthy of the knowledge—possessing the purest motives and ideals—were chosen to study the Kabbalah. An important early text used in that study was the *Sefer Yezira* (Book of Creation), which appeared sometime between the third and sixth centuries AD. In its pages, initiates discovered an expanded theory of the creation of the universe. According to the *Sefer Yezira*, the spiritual world consisted of ten spheres, the *sefirot*. (*Sefirot* is a term related to the Hebrew word *sappir*, loosely translated as "sapphire" and interpreted as the radiance of God.) Each of the sefirot represented a different force or aspect of God, such as love, power, or understanding. These aspects were said to have emanated, or unfolded, from God, and as the sefirot embodied all aspects of creation, generation, and decay, they represented the universe itself unfolding.

Connecting the ten spheres are twenty-two paths, corresponding to the twenty-two letters in the Hebrew alphabet, and together they constitute the "tree of life," the visual representation of the creation. The *Sefer Yezira* also detailed the mystic meanings of each letter of the Hebrew alphabet and contrived a system of occult interpretations of various combinations of the letters.

Through meditation and prayer, devotees sought to scale the tree of life, experience the sefirot, and explore the relationship between humankind and the universe—in short, to gain divine illumination through ascension. A sort of guidebook detailing the landscape to be explored in this spiritual journey was written by a Spanish Jew, Moses de Leon, in the thirteenth century. This central teaching text for those studying the ancient mystical wisdom, the *Zohar* (Book of Splendor), was a mystical commentary on the Pentateuch. It contained a mixture of stories, poetry, commentaries, and visions based on Kabbalistic ideas and symbols.

 he esoteric and magical texts and teachings of the Palestine Jews had spread to Germany, France, and Spain, and the thirteenth through the fifteenth centuries there marked the golden age of Kabbalism. This epoch was shattered in 1492, however, by the expulsion of Jews from Spain. As the exiles moved to other lands, they took with them the Kabbalah, in forms transformed by suffering. But the Kabbalah also became public knowledge, and it was about this time that a Christianized version appeared.

The Christian Cabala, as it came to be known, combined Kabbalistic beliefs with those of another popular movement called Hermeticism. A fusion of Greek philosophy and the ancient religion of Egypt, the beliefs of Hermeticism were contained in a body of texts known as the *Corpus Hermeticum*. This work, whose author is unknown, was named after its principal character, Hermes Trismegistus (Hermes the Thrice-Great). Some occultists claimed that Trismegistus penned the works, that he was an Egyptian sage living in the times of the Pharaohs, and that he was a contemporary of Moses. Others associated him with the Greek god Hermes, whose Egyptian equivalent, Thoth, was the scribe of the gods and lord of the sacred books.

The *Corpus Hermeticum* takes the form of dialogues between Trismegistus, Thoth, and several other Egyptian deities, including Isis. Scholars point out that little in the text is truly original; in fact, much of the Hermetic world view is grounded in the philosophy of Plato. Hermetics saw the universe in terms of light and dark, good and evil, spirit and matter. Like their Gnostic contemporaries, practitioners preached a mind-body dualism and salvation through the possession of true and divine knowledge.

The strains of Kabbalistic, Hermetic, and Christian thought came together during the late fifteenth century as the Christian Cabala—Jewish arcana introduced to the Christian world mainly by a Florentine mystic named Pico della Mirandola. Florence proved receptive ground for Pico's Christian version of the ancient wisdom. The center of the Italian Renaissance, this bustling, cosmopolitan city was ruled for several centuries by the mighty Medici family and nurtured the genius of artists and writers such as Leonardo, Michelangelo, and Petrarch. As scholars rediscovered the classical world of Greece and Rome, Renaissance Florence was a time and place of great intellectual ferment. It was also the site of much religious turmoil, when widespread corruption in the Catholic church was spurring the Protestant Reformation. The revival of classical culture, along with a pervasive unease, spawned a nostalgia for an age when the world seemed simpler and more unified. In this climate, the Christian Cabala was especially appealing for its notion of an underlying unity among paganism, Judaism, Greek philosophy, and early Christianity.

The new movement also had the universal appeal of magic. Magic—especially belief in the power of certain numbers, letters, and words—enjoyed a long tradition among both Jews and Christians. The symbolic white, or good, magic contained in the Christian Cabala gathered its might in part from that tradition and from a variation on the popular ancient belief that the universe was constructed of concentric spheres. The Cabalists believed in three worlds. They aspired to rise from the elemental world, through the celestial world, and on to the supercelestial sphere, where the powerful Hebrew names of God were kept—the name of Jesus now being the mightiest of all. It was also believed that everything on earth had connections to a particular planet, whose power could be harnessed by cultivating the passions or emotions associated with it.

In a world as uncertain as that of the Middle Ages and Renaissance, with its constant wars and pestilence, people

were drawn to magic because it seemed to offer some measure of control over nature. White magic was even condoned by the Catholic church; black magic called forth devils, and so was damned as an abomination. The term *cabala* became synonymous with magic in both its positive and negative senses, and it later took on the additional meaning, in the word *cabal,* of a secret plot or intrigue.

The Christian Cabala drew a corps of enthusiasts dedicated to spreading its word. Pico della Mirandola was said to have been limited in his grasp of Kabbalistic lore, but his influence on his contemporaries and successors far exceeded the limits of his own writing. The most important of his converts was an older Renaissance con-

The seven-branched menorah, shown here in a fourteenth-century illustration from a Spanish Bible, represents the divine world of emanation—symbolism also found in the Kabbalists' tree of life.

practitioner of black magic, accused of conjuring demons and walking with the devil.

Many of the same factors contributing to the appeal of Hermeticism and the Christian Cabala were also responsible for the rise of Catharism, a heretical Christian doctrine that directly challenged the authority of the medieval Catholic church. The Cathars flourished in the twelfth century, a period of increased contact between East and West. The Crusades—the Christian effort to recapture Jerusalem and other parts of the Holy Land from the Muslims—were at their height, and Christian soldiers and the merchants who followed them to the Middle East were returning with ideas unknown to Europe since the end of the Roman

temporary, Johannes Reuchlin, an eminent German scholar. After meeting Pico and his friends, Reuchlin was so excited about their work that he went to live in Italy to learn Hebrew and study Hebrew literature. He defended Pico's doctrines and expanded them, making Cabalistic magic more accessible. Taking up the torch, in turn, from Reuchlin was German-born Heinrich Cornelius Agrippa, perhaps the greatest occult scholar of the sixteenth century. Agrippa wandered Europe's courts, attracting followers with a brand of Cabalistic thought that placed special emphasis on magic. During the Counter Reformation, the campaign by the Catholic church to suppress the swell of Protestantism and other alleged heresies, Agrippa was attacked unfairly as a

Empire. Among them was the heresy of Manicheanism. Although stamped out by the Church centuries before in the West, Manicheanism had survived at the very least as an influence in the remote eastern areas of Christendom and would strongly color Cathar doctrine.

Paradoxically, the twelfth century that saw the religious zeal expressed in the Crusades was also a time of growing disillusion with the Catholic church and the worldly ways of its clergy. From its humble beginnings as one of a number of religious sects in the Roman Empire, the Church had grown into an institution of wealth and privilege. Priests and bishops often led lives of luxury, while indulging in such corrupt practices as forgiving sins in exchange for

*This illustration from a fourteenth-century collection of his works depicts
Ramon Llull's 1292 crusade to Tunis, where the Spanish mystic and missionary attempted to
convert Muslims to Christianity. Llull's philosophy derived from the Kabbalah, and
his messages to the heathen included the use of symbolic Hebrew letters and geometric diagrams.*

Perched among the branches of the Egyptian tree of life, an epiphany of the Great Earth Mother—associated with Isis, among other goddesses—distributes the elixir of immortality to souls of the dead in this ancient Egyptian wall painting. Sacred trees, said to be sycamore figs, were thought to stand on the border between the living world and the next; deities in the trees allegedly eased the soul's journey with food and drink.

This fifteenth-century illustration from Ramon Llull's Opera Chemica depicts the Hermetic tree of life. The seven main branches and ten heads symbolize the seven planets, the ten spheres of Kabbalistic tradition, and the various aspects man sheds as he ascends the tree. The serpent wound about the trunk is variously interpreted as the wisdom necessary for enlightenment, and the primal energy of the soul. The figures surrounding the tree are making pronouncements about the serpent's power.

fashioned by the devil. A Cathar achieved salvation through knowing the true origin and destiny of the human race and by renouncing the satanic world of the flesh and living a life of abstinence and poverty.

Unlike the Catholics, the Cathars believed in reincarnation; if a person failed in one life, they maintained, the opportunity existed for success in another. They rejected baptism, the cross as a symbol, individual confession, and all religious ornamentation. Church services were simple and could be held anywhere. They consisted of a gospel reading, a brief sermon, a benediction, and the Lord's Prayer. The Cathars' back-to-basics approach to the liturgy anticipated the simplicity of some of the later Protestant sects.

money. It was largely in response to the Church's unseemly pomp and splendor that Catharism took root, first in northern Italy, then throughout southern France.

Fearing Church repression, the first Cathars kept their faith in secret. But the sect soon attracted such a following that it could operate openly under the protection of powerful feudal lords able to defy the pope. In southern France, Catharism and a vaguely similar movement known as Waldensianism virtually became the region's official religions.

Cathar and Catholic theology were starkly at odds. In the Catholic view, salvation came through the physical suffering of Jesus, a spiritual being who entered into the flesh in order to redeem humankind by dying on the cross. According to the Cathars, humanity's redemption came not from Christ's death, but from the example of the life he led on earth. Cathars also denied that the imperfect physical world could have been created by a perfect God; like the Gnostics and Manicheans before them, the Cathars rejected the Biblical view of creation and indeed all of the Old Testament. Instead, they believed earth and humanity were

Catharism had two classes, or degrees. Laity were known as credents, or believers. They were not required to follow the rigid rules of abstinence reserved for the elect *perfecti*, or *bonhommes* (good men), who formed the hierarchy of the Cathar church. Anyone, man or woman, aspiring to join the perfecti faced a probationary period lasting at least two years. During that time, he or she gave up all worldly goods, lived communally with other perfecti, and abstained from partaking of meat and wine. To avoid temptations of the flesh, an initiate was denied all contact with the opposite sex and vowed never to sleep naked. At the end of probation, the novice received the *consolamentum,* a rite combining the features of baptism, confirmation, and ordination that was held in public before a large congregation. There the initiate replied to a series of questions posed by a church elder, then promised to live a life of poverty, abstinence, and obedience to God and the gospel.

The Catholic church did what it could to combat the spreading Cathar heresy. At first, it tried to win Cathars

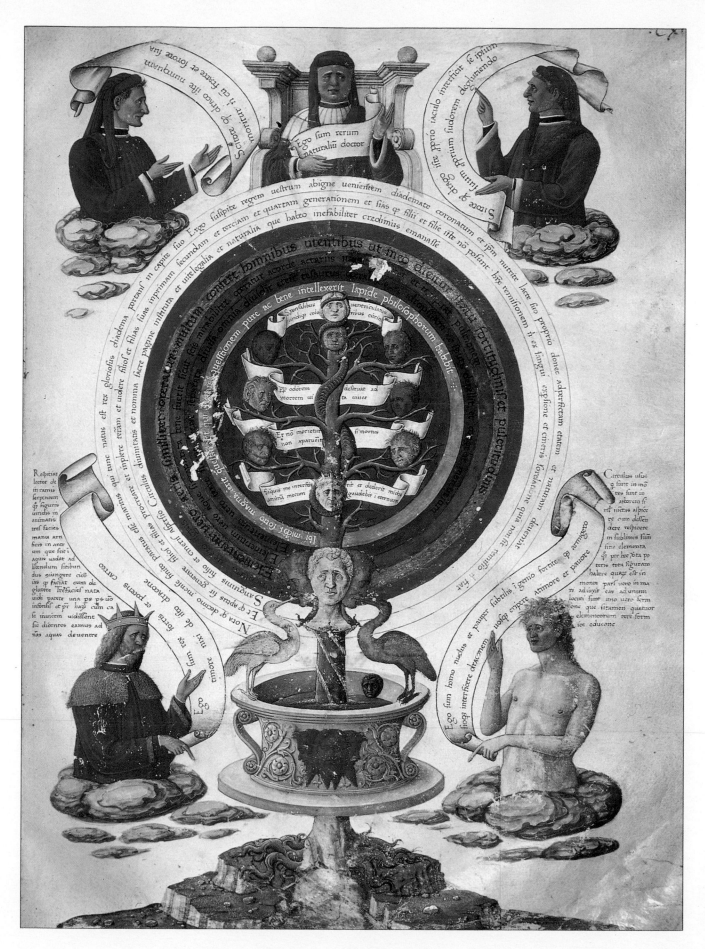

The fortress Montségur, located in the Pyrenees Mountains, was the Cathars' last stronghold. Thought to harbor treasure, including the Holy Grail, Montségur came under repeated attacks from Catholic crusaders. In March 1244, after a ten-month siege, the Cathars surrendered the fortress. More than two hundred men and women walked calmly, singing, down the mountain and into huge burning pyres where they died. No treasure was found.

back to the fold by dispatching teaching missions of Cistercian monks led by the head of the order, the future Saint Bernard of Clairvaux. The monks made few conversions, however, and the recalcitrance of the heretics dismayed Bernard, whose own efforts to reach them were met with boos and catcalls in the streets of Toulouse.

The Cathar regions of southern France lay under the political control of Count Raymond VI of Toulouse, himself a follower of the Cathar faith. Matters between Cathar and Catholic authorities came to a head when one of the count's squires murdered a special envoy sent to Toulouse by Pope Innocent III. The assassination so enraged the pope that he literally could not speak for two days. He then declared the Cathars ''worse than the very Saracen'' (a Christian term for Muslims) and called for a crusade to wipe out the heresy once and for all. His appeal was answered swiftly by many French knights, who were drawn to the effort for several reasons. This was the first crusade directed against an enemy within European borders, so it required neither the time nor expense of a crusade to the Holy Land. Also, in addition to the salvation promised anyone joining the crusade for at least forty days, recruits could look forward to gaining the material spoils of the conquered territory.

The crusade was launched in 1209, with 20,000 mounted knights at the head of a vast army. In their first major victory, the crusaders took the town of Beziers and massacred almost all the inhabitants, including many who regarded themselves as loyal Catholics. When the papal legate was asked how to distinguish between heretic and Catholic, he is said to have replied: ''Kill them all. God will look after his own.'' But the Cathar faith was strong, and the papal legions faced a long struggle. Almost forty years passed before the crusaders crushed the last armed resistance, and secret cells of the Cathar faithful survived for yet

In this fifteenth-century painting by the Florentine Fra Angelico, Saint Dominic presents the Cathars with a holy book, presumably the Old Testament, in an attempt to counter their heresy. Although the Cathars throw the book into the flames, it rises unscathed.

another half-century. A measure of the hold Catharism had on its followers was their willingness to be martyred. Thousands of perfecti, given a choice between death and converting to Catholicism, refused to renounce their faith. They died, sometimes starved to death chained to dungeon walls but usually burned at the stake in massive pyres. In the face of persecution and torture, some chose the Cathar rite of Endura, a sanctified form of suicide through fasting.

Not all sects were as benign as that of the Cathars. When Venetian explorer Marco Polo returned to Europe in the late thirteenth century after his now-famous travels to China, one story he set down was that of a sect he encountered in Persia, the Assassins. Polo described a beautiful garden, nestled between two mountains and known only to those who belonged to the cult. Guarded at its entrance by a well-fortified castle, the garden was allegedly patterned on the prophet Muhammad's vision of paradise. "In it could be found all the fruits and the most beautiful palaces in the world," Polo wrote. "There were channels—from one came water, from another honey and from another wine; there were the most beautiful ladies of the world, who sang and played instruments and danced better than any."

Only young men who wished to become Assassins could enter this Eden. When the leader of the cult deemed them ready for initiation, the men were fed hashish until they fell into a drugged sleep. Then, according to Polo, they were carried into the garden, where they awakened surrounded by untold splendors. No one who experienced this paradise, where every whim was indulged, ever wanted to leave. But in return for such delights, the Assassins were compelled to perform certain missions for their master or be expelled. Those missions were to kill, and the Assassins executed their assignments with blind obedience.

The Assassins—whose name is derived from the Arabic word *hashishin,* meaning "users of hashish"—first appeared in the eleventh century as a secret religious order. A sect derived from the Ismaili religion, the Assassins believed that there were seven links in the chain of creation and that divine wisdom would be revealed to man at each juncture as he moved toward God. Those who sought illumination underwent a special initiation prior to entering each stage of knowledge. According to some nineteenth-century accounts, the revelations at each new level negated all that had been taught before. At the highest stage, the ultimate secret of the Assassins was revealed: Heaven and

Hasan-i Sabbah, first grand master of the Assassins, offers drugged wine to young men seeking to join his cult in this fourteenth-century French painting. Initiation gained the neophytes access to Hasan's paradisiacal garden. In return for their pleasures, they killed as directed by the master.

hell were one and the same, all actions were meaningless, and there was no good or evil except the virtue of obeying the priest-king.

The founder and grand master of the Assassins, Hasan-i Sabbah, gradually became more powerful in the Arab world and set himself up as an independent prince. He alone changed the roles of the Ismaili initiates to those of assassins, warriors whose preferred weapon was a dagger and for whom death while performing an assassination was an honor. The Assassins usually stalked religious or political leaders and were held in awe and fear. According to Marco Polo, "No man who the Old Man [Hasan] has decided to kill can escape, and it is said that more than one king pays tribute to him in fear of his life."

Hasan-i Sabbah died in 1124, and with his death the power of the Assassins began to wane. The sect splintered, and by 1166, the Persian Assassins had returned to a more orthodox faith; their remnants were destroyed in the late thirteenth century by Mongol invaders who managed to out-terrorize even the infamous Assassins.

ut as with many of the secret sects of the ancient world, the influence of the Assassins' warrior cult was evident in yet another closed society, that of the Christian military order called the Knights Templars. Few medieval institutions enjoyed greater respect—albeit a respect tinged with fear and envy—than this militant order dedicated to protecting Christian pilgrims in the Holy Land.

The Order of the Knights Templars was founded in 1118 by French nobleman Hugues de Payns and eight other veteran soldiers. Concerned with assuring safe passage between the port of Jaffa (in what is now Israel) and the city of Jerusalem, the knights took their name, Poor Knights of the Temple, from the holy city's Temple of Solomon, the site on which they supposedly were first quartered. Jerusalem had been wrested from Muslim rule at the end of the First Crusade nineteen years earlier, but the Christian armies occupying the city and surrounding territories were constantly threatened by hostile Arabs. Since a more or less continual state of war existed between the two forces, it was with gratitude that the Catholic church welcomed the service of de Payns and his pious knights. In 1128, religious leaders holding a council at Troyes, France, decided to officially recognize the Knights Templars, as they came to be known, as a new religious order.

Though serving the needs of Christendom, a martial religious order was radically at odds with traditional church policy, which prohibited clergy from bearing arms. Knights were a warrior class, and the Church tended to view them as godless and licentious. In 1095, Bernard of Clairvaux de-

In the Night Journey, Muhammad's vision of cosmic mysteries, he saw himself ascend to God through seven celestial spheres.

Quest for the Divine

The ascetic Persian faith of Sufism, like other mystical religions, seeks union with God, or the Divine. The first Sufis were followers of the prophet Muhammad. They would sit outside the mosque on a platform, or *suffe,* and listen to him. Following his example, the Sufis sought to lose all sense of self and become united with God.

In the first step toward illumination, the devotee was cleansed. He was then introduced to a spiritual master, who served a special meal and assigned a *zekr,* or chant. The initiate was next taught the acts forming the path to the Divine—meditation, invocation of God's name, contemplation.

While Sufism was primarily descended from Islam, it also assimilated teachings of other religions and beliefs, borrowing from such groups as the Pythagoreans, Hermetics, and Buddhists. In turn, Sufism allegedly influenced teachings of the Templars. And some say Freemasonry began as a Sufi society, brought to Scotland masked as a craft guild in the fourteenth century.

Whirling Sufi dervishes show the spirit's spiraling journey to Divine union.

Denied ferry passage, a Sufi saint skims the water on his sacred prayer mat.

scribed them as "unbelieving scoundrels, sacrilegious plunderers, homicides, perjurers, adulterers." It was in part to channel the reckless energies of the knighted that the crusades were initially launched. The creation of the Knights Templars was seen as a way of redeeming a lawless class, and indeed, many of those recruited to the Templars had been previously excommunicated. Whatever his views on warriors in general, Bernard was a great admirer of the order and its unofficial patron. Calling them "Christ's legal executioners," he absolved Templars from the sin of killing as long as their victims were enemies of the Church.

Like other religious orders, the Templars took vows of poverty, chastity, and obedience, and except for bearing arms, they lived in every way like monks. The Rule of the Temple governing their daily lives was probably drafted by Bernard. It included strict silence at meals and the saying of prayers at set times. To ensure chastity, knights slept fully clothed in lighted dormitories and were forbidden to kiss even their mothers. Moreover, they could not attend any gathering that might make them long for family life. As soldiers of the Lord, the Templars vowed never to retreat in battle, even against overwhelming odds. A member faced severe punishment for breaking even the most seemingly trivial of rules. One knight, for instance, was expelled from the order for losing a borrowed horse he had used for running hares. (This was actually a double offense, since Templars were forbidden to hunt anything less noble than lions—which, for practical purposes, meant desert lynxes.)

The Templars' emblem was a horse carrying two knights, a symbol of poverty and brotherhood. Bernard clearly viewed his rough-hewed band more favorably than he did rich secular knights, noting that Templars were seen "rarely washed, their beards bushy, sweaty and dusty, stained by their harness and the heat." The Knights Templars wore white mantles emblazoned with a red cross and rode to battle behind a white-and-black banner called the Beauseant, after the piebald horses favored by the order's founders. The same word became their battle cry.

Like other medieval institutions, the Templars were organized according to a rigid hierarchy. The head of the order was the grand master. Below him, a great prior headed each of the many regional chapters found throughout Christendom. The white-robed knights were recruited from noble families and formed the order's officer corps; a secondary soldiering class of sergeants, or serving brothers, came from families without noble titles and wore black or brown mantles. Below these two fighting classes were lower ranks of esquires, or attendants, and other servants and laborers who cared for the Templar castles and estates.

Knights were initiated into the temple in a secret ceremony held at night in the guarded chapter house. The great prior would ask the assembled knights several times if they had any objections to admitting the novice to the order. Hearing none, he reviewed the rules of the order and asked whether the novice had a wife and family, debts or disease, and if he owed allegiance to any other master. Having answered in the negative, the novice knelt, asking to become a "servant and slave" of the temple and swearing obedience by God and the Virgin Mary. Finally the white mantle was placed on his shoulders, and the initiate was welcomed into the exalted ranks of Knights Templars.

The secrecy surrounding investiture and other Templar ceremonies lent mystery to the order and fed rumors about activities within its cloisters; adversaries whispered of sexual perversion and occultism. Ultimately, such accusations were leveled in public, and by the early fourteenth century, after more than two hundred years of service, the legend of the Knights Templars came to a sad and abrupt end.

The Templars' fall can be attributed to several factors. One was the winding down of the Crusades by the early thirteenth century, undercutting the order's original purpose. Another was the collective wealth of these "poor" knights. Maintaining a standing army in a series of fortifications a thousand miles from home required vast resources. Over time, the Templars accumulated large amounts of money, derived

The official seal of the Knights Templars, two knights astride one horse, symbolized brotherhood and the oath of poverty taken by members of the twelfth-century Christian military order.

Bernard of Clairvaux, a patron of the Knights Templars, preaches to his fellow Cistercian monks in the uppermost scene of this fifteenth-century painting. In the bottom scene, Bernard is summoned by a demon, perhaps representing Baphomet—a symbol of the prophet Muhammad, whom the Templars were accused of worshiping.

from gifts and the earnings of their estates, which as religious property were exempt from taxes. The Templars learned to manage their revenues with great skill and, in the process, became bankers for much of the Western world. Kings and princes entrusted their gold to the order, whose temples were the stoutest and most strongly defended structures in all Europe. It was perhaps inevitable that medieval monarchs—most of them perpetually strapped for gold with which to finance their incessant wars—should turn an envious eye toward the Templar coffers. The beginning of the end came on Friday, October 13, 1307, when Philip IV of France (himself a debtor to the order) commanded the arrest of every Templar in his kingdom. Philip accused the knights of heresy, but his motivation may have had less to do with piety than with the prospect of lining his pockets with Templar gold. A month later, at Philip's insistence, Pope Clement V gave all sovereigns carte

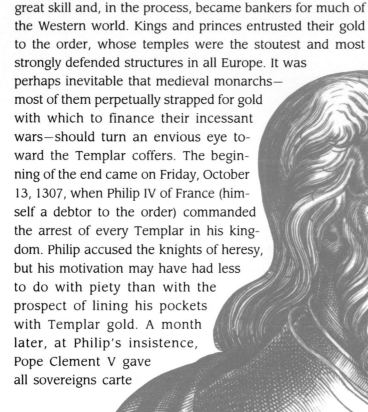

Bound with ropes and facing unspeakable tortures after his 1307 arrest in Paris, Jacques de Molay, Templar grand master, confessed to the charges leveled against his order.

blanche to arrest the Templars and take possession of their property.

A number of the charges leveled against the order pertained to the group's initiation ceremony, alleging that the novices vowed to engage in homosexual activities and blasphemous practices such as spitting or urinating on the cross. Their accusers claimed the knights worshiped the devil, sometimes in the form of a black cat that they kissed under the tail and other times as an icon known as Baphomet. The knights allegedly used oil rendered from the flesh of murdered infants to massage Baphomet, variously described as a stuffed human head or a jeweled skull mounted on a wooden phallus.

Baphomet was a corruption of the name of the Islamic prophet Muhammad, and the alleged worship of this grisly idol was part of a more general charge that the Templars were closet Muslims. Certainly, in the course of more than two centuries of living in the Middle East, the Templars had absorbed

much of the culture of their enemy. Many knights spoke Arabic, and in contrast to most other Europeans, they followed the Arab fashion of wearing beards. And they occasionally fought side by side with the Assassins against other Arab factions in the internecine warfare that, then as now, typified the Muslim world. Critics of the Templars pointed out similarities in the vestments and organization of the two groups and went so far as to accuse the knights of being a covert auxiliary of the Assassins. Most historians dismiss such charges. However, at least one Templar, the English knight Robert of St. Albans, is known to have converted to Islam and commanded a Muslim army. There is also a persistent legend that a "crusader tribe" descended from Templar deserters adopted Muslim ways and survived for centuries in northern Arabia.

On the basis of those allegations, King Philip's minions applied extreme measures to extract confessions from the Templars; within days of capture, thirty-six knights died from torture meted out in the monarch's dungeons. Three years later, in 1310, fifty-four Templars were burned at the stake. The persecution continued, despite Pope Clement V's admission in 1312 that the Church lacked the evidence to prove heresy. Once again bowing to pressure from the king, however, the pope decreed the order of the Poor Knights of the Temple dissolved.

Templars who had not perished under the king's torment were allowed to join another order or return to the

secular state. The knights' last grand master, however, Jacques de Molay, was sentenced to be imprisoned for life after making public his private confession. But de Molay embarrassed church and state officials by publicly declaring his order innocent. For this last act of impudence, de Molay was to be burned at the stake. As the flames engulfed him, he cursed both pope and king, summoning them to final judgment before God—Clement within forty days and Philip within a year. Both died according to de Molay's schedule.

Thus the secret sects of old flourished and faded, only to flourish again, to have their beliefs or teachings somehow reborn in new groups, springing up in different parts of the world. Sometimes the members enjoyed exalted status; at other times they navigated a long, tortuous route. However arduous the journey for members of those groups, the appeal of secret sects, of a tightly drawn circle of like-minded individuals embarked on a spiritual odyssey of their own design, was universal and strong, and not to be denied.

The Sacred Assassins

For centuries, travelers in India fell prey to the Thugs, a secret brotherhood that butchered innocents in the name of Kali, Hindu goddess of death and destruction. The sect, which dated back at least to the thirteenth century, included Muslims and Hindus, but all Thugs claimed a special relation to Kali, the Black Mother of Hindu lore. According to their myth, the goddess bisected a man-eating demon with her sword, only to find that each drop of his blood spawned another demon. Faced with a diabolic horde, Kali created two warriors from her sweat, giving each a cloth strip called a *rumal* for strangling her foes. Once the devils were dead, the goddess enjoined her two Thugs to keep their rumals and continue killing, generation to generation. They would help stamp out evil, she said—and earn a good living too, since Thugs also robbed their victims.

Most of the time, Thugs lived outwardly respectable lives, usually as craftsmen well-known in their home villages. But for a few weeks each year, they dedicated themselves to the slaughter that was their holy mission, their act of worship. Operating far from home to avoid being recognized, gangs of ten to fifty Thugs lured victims to their deaths through deception. In fact, the sect's name derived from the Sanskrit word for *deceiver*. They joined parties of traders or pilgrims and accompanied them until a chance for murder arose. When the time was right,

Clutching a severed head and a sword, bloody Kali, patron goddess of the Thugs, dances atop a corpse at an Indian cremation ground.

the assassins approached victims from behind, passed rumals around their necks, and jerked tight, all the while whispering to Kali to watch.

Before an expedition, the Thugs sacrificed a sheep to a blood-smeared, flower-bedecked image of Kali. Next to the effigy stood tools of the trade—noose, knife, and pickax. The knife was used in the ritual mangling of victims' corpses. Presumably, mutilation was pleasing to

Kali and practical: It made the victims difficult to identify.

Some travelers were immune from attack. Women, for instance, were usually spared in deference to Kali's gender, and holy men, certain craftsmen, musicians, and poets also enjoyed her protection. Lepers and cripples were exempt, since the Thugs feared contamination. Not wanting to risk reprisal from colonial rulers, the killers never molested Europeans either.

With dubious mercy, Thugs often adopted their victims' offspring, initiating the males into the sect, teaching them its secret language and signs. Thug initiation rites had a dignity befitting what the killers deemed their holy calling. Bathed and dressed in new clothes, the youthful initiate was handed his sacred pickax, which he held aloft under a white handkerchief that represented the rumal. Then he ate the holy food, a coarse sugar, while his fellows petitioned Kali for an omen of approval. The rite complete, the youth became a true Thug. With luck he would work his way up from apprentice duty—scouting for victims, helping to immobilize them, and digging their graves—to the rank of actual killer. Thug initiations were solemn but joyous; nothing gave a Thug father greater pride than having a son follow in his bloody footsteps.

It is estimated that more than a million victims died at Thug hands before India's British rulers stamped out the sect. The last known Thug was hanged in 1882.

Thugs waylay a lone traveler in this nineteenth-century painting. The assassins more often victimized whole groups, politely convincing merchants and pilgrims it was wise to travel in large bands for protection—from the very danger posed by the devious Thugs themselves.

Thug informants described the deadly sect's methods to an Indian artist commissioned by British officers trying to stamp out the brotherhood. In 1836, the artist painted these pictures depicting Thug predations. Below, a Thug encourages an unsuspecting victim to look skyward, exposing his neck to the strangler who is sneaking up behind him, rumal at the ready. At right, two Thugs immobilize a victim's hands and feet while a third killer ruthlessly strangles him.

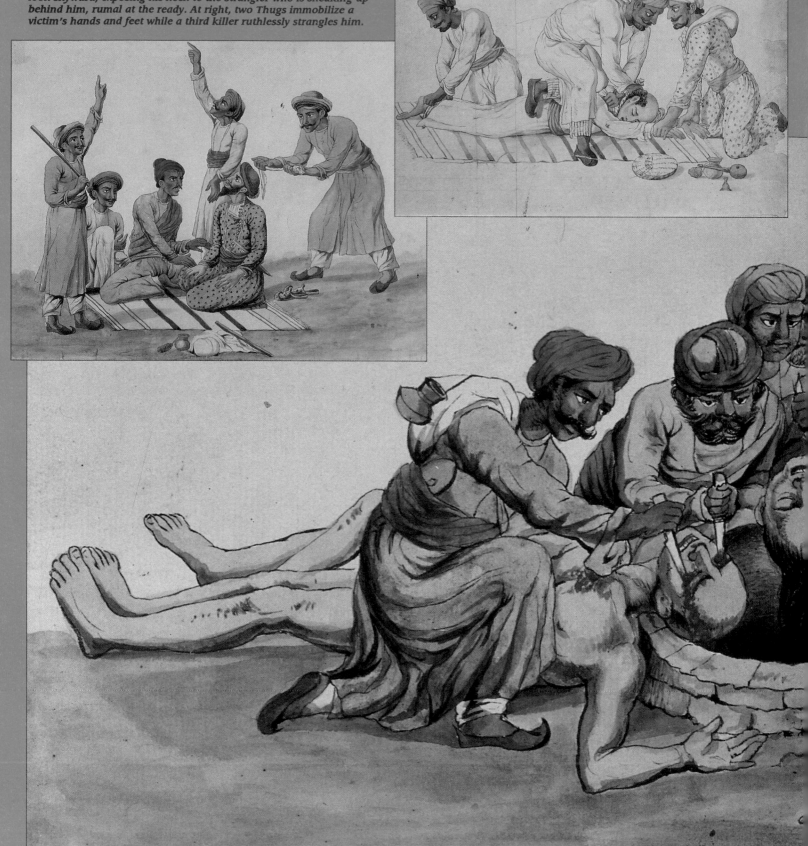

Thugs seldom left their victims at the murder site but carried them elsewhere to thwart detection. The sacred pickax, symbol of the Thug calling, was used to dig graves. Every pilgrimage season, thousands of travelers were killed by the Thugs, leaving relatives to wonder if wild beasts or disease had taken loved ones along distant roads.

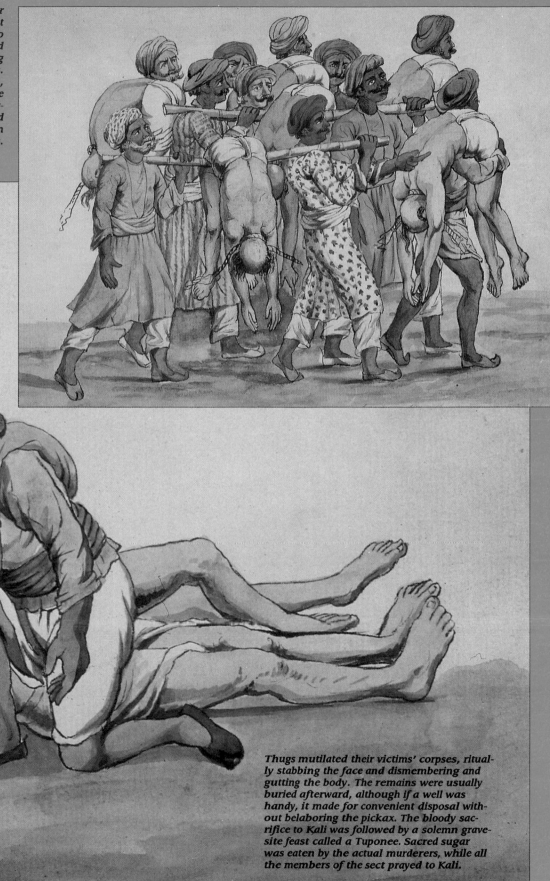

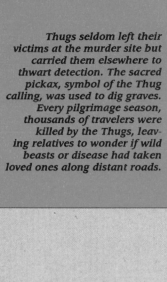

Thugs mutilated their victims' corpses, ritually stabbing the face and dismembering and gutting the body. The remains were usually buried afterward, although if a well was handy, it made for convenient disposal without belaboring the pickax. The bloody sacrifice to Kali was followed by a solemn grave-site feast called a Tuponee. Sacred sugar was eaten by the actual murderers, while all the members of the sect prayed to Kali.

The Death of the Deceivers

In 1826, Colonel William Sleeman, the civil administrator of the Jubbulpore district in Central India, set about suppressing the Thugs. He turned to captured Thugs to augment his information about the sect, breaking their code of silence with offers of clemency. Sleeman was then able to trace Thug networks and draw up maps of past murder sites and likely future ones. The colonel next began seizing Thugs with the help of his informants, British soldiers, native Indian troops, and armed irregulars.

Entire Thug gangs were rounded up and marched to cellblocks at the town of Saugor and to eventual trial. The trials, short on legal niceties, meted out swift, harsh punishment. Of the 3,689 Thugs tried before 1840, almost 500 died by hanging. The rest were jailed for life, except for 56 informants who were pardoned. Those sentenced to die on the gallows placed the nooses around their own necks and leaped to their deaths, displaying in one final act of contempt both their bravery and their smug superiority in the art of strangulation.

By 1848, another 651 Thugs had been tried, and except for isolated outbreaks, the reign of Thug terror came to an end.

If the British were harsh with unregenerate Thugs, they were charitable to informants and their sons, even establishing schools for their retraining. In time, stranglers and mutilators were transformed into skilled brickmakers, builders, or weavers. Their carpets became a sought-after specialty, so famous that Queen Victoria, whose agents had destroyed the brotherhood, commissioned one for Windsor Castle.

William Sleeman in an 1851 portrait

A British officer and his detachment of sepoys, Indian troops who served in the British army, ambush a Thug gang in this nineteenth-century engraving. Despite their boast of being perfect deceivers, the Thugs had no stratagems to protect them from their pursuers. They fell in droves to the British authorities.

Rehabilitated Thugs at Jubbulpore pose atop one of their carpets in this 1874 photograph. Their most famous rug, the one commissioned by Queen Victoria for the Waterloo Chamber at Windsor Castle, was an elaborately patterned giant that measured forty feet by eighty feet and weighed two tons.

CHAPTER 2

Rosicrucians: The Invisibles

Parisians of the seventeenth century were accustomed to seeing their walls and buildings plastered with notices. But the posters that greeted them one morning in August 1623 were extraordinary and stirred a considerable sensation. The broadsides informed Parisians that a certain secret and mysterious brotherhood had taken up residence in their midst and was prepared to bring true peace and wisdom to those who sought enlightenment.

One version of the notices declared, "We, deputies of the principal College of the Brethren of the Rosy Cross, are staying visibly and invisibly in this town by the Grace of the Most High, to whom the heart of the Just turns. We show and teach without books or masques how to speak the language of every country where we wish to be, to bring our fellow men out of the error of death." Another placard offered membership "to all those who wish to enter our Society and Congregation," and it again promised universal peace and wisdom. "We will teach them the most perfect knowledge of the Most High . . . and we will make them from visible, invisible, and from invisible, visible." Although the posters gave no further instruction as to how or where would-be members might apply to the Rosy Cross brotherhood, they suggested obliquely that those who were worthy would be recognized and contacted in due course.

Parisians were intrigued by the Rosy Cross posters, but the established Church of Rome reacted with fear and hostility. Having just emerged from half a century of strife with Protestant heretics, on matters ranging from Church ritual to medieval cosmology, the holy fathers were in no mood to tolerate a new group of nonconformists who promised to redefine the mystical relationship between God and Nature in terms that undermined existing authority. It was well known in France that this brotherhood, commonly called the Rosicrucians, had already attracted numerous adherents in Germany, the Netherlands, and England, those hotbeds of Protestant revolution.

In short order, spokesmen for the French church issued various manifestoes exposing the "Pretended Invisible Ones" and their "Horrible Pacts" with Satan. One tract reported that thirty-six "deputies" of the Rosy Cross had convened in the provincial city of Lyons on the very day of the posters' appearance in Paris; at the Lyons gathering, these disciples of the devil had divided up the globe and organized themselves into six parties of six members each; their mission was to carry their terrible messages and their foul practices to all of the major capitals of the world.

This tract went on to declare that two hours after the plots were hatched, the apostates celebrated a grand sabbath, at which a prince of the devil's infernal legions appeared before them, splendidly arrayed and glowing with the inner fires of Hades. The so-called brethren thereupon prostrated themselves before his awesome personage and swore they would renounce all the rites and sacraments of the Christian church. In return for their fealty, Satan's emissary bestowed marvelous powers, including the ability to transport themselves as by magic wheresoever they wished, to speak with such eloquence and apparent wisdom that people would always be drawn to listen, to disguise themselves so cunningly that they would always appear to be natives of whatever place they found themselves, and to keep their purses forever filled with gold—presumably through knowledge of alchemy. The manifesto con-

firmed that six missionaries had instantaneously been posted to Paris, where they went into hiding in the Marais, that noisome quarter of the city favored by Protestants and other supposed evildoers.

Another commentary, entitled the *Mercure de France,* attempted to ridicule the problem away. The author observed with tongue in cheek that the arrival of the Rosicrucians in the city had created widespread panic, in which otherwise reasonable people bid adieu to their senses. Some local hotelkeepers reported strange guests who vanished in a cloud when it came time to settle their accounts; others claimed that their customers had paid, but with gold coin that transformed itself into base slate immediately upon the person's departure. Several innocent citizens awoke in the night to discover apparitions looming over them, and when they cried out in alarm, the shadowy figures dematerialized. The *Mercure* concluded in amusement that it was not surprising to find prudent Parisians sleeping with loaded muskets by their bedsides and stoning strangers who ventured into their neighborhoods.

All of the anti-Rosicrucian pamphlets agreed that the task of identifying any of the Rosy Cross fraternity by outward signs would be well-nigh impossible. As one writer explained, members of this mysterious body "could not communicate with the people, or be communicated with, except by thought joined to the will, that is to say, in a manner imperceptible to the senses"—apparently a reference to mental telepathy. Under the circumstances, all Parisians who loved their king, their Church, and their God were asked to exercise extreme vigilance and to report any person who espoused ideas at variance with those of the Establishment. For its part, the Church promised to deal swiftly with anyone who was caught trafficking with the Rosicrucians, to punish them just as it would any common witch or devil worshiper.

Perhaps as a consequence, none of the "invisibles" was found, no more posters appeared, no applicants for membership made themselves known, and the Rosicrucians apparently vanished from Paris almost as suddenly as they had arrived. Or perhaps, as one skeptic suggested, the heretical and secret brotherhood had never come to Paris in the first place. Perhaps the posters were a Protestant hoax, intended to send the ever-vigilant church fathers rushing off on yet another wild conspiracy chase. Or possibly it was all just a cover for political intrigue, an English or German plot of some kind.

There was even a chance that the notices were simply a clever bookseller's ploy to promote interest in a new little pamphlet entitled *Fama Fraternitatis,* an allegorical work about a mysterious, Messiah-like figure named Christian Rosenkreutz and his small but doughty band of followers.

No one, it seemed, knew the truth of Rosicrucianism in Paris in 1623. And to judge from all the excited confusion about the brotherhood in England, Italy, the Netherlands, and Germany, there were few, if any, Europeans who could lay claim to the answers. All that can be said with certainty more than 350 years later is that the Rosicrucian promises of a universal peace and wisdom struck a deep chord of longing within many souls in strife-torn Europe. Try as the Church might to suppress the *Fama* and the other Rosicrucian manifestoes that soon followed, the concerns they addressed were not about to disappear.

But where had the Rosicrucians come from? Modern Rosicrucians have done their best to link the movement to the ancients of Egypt or India, on which account they claim to be "the oldest fraternal or secret order known to man." It is more likely, however, that the brotherhood was born during the Protestant Reformation and intellectual renaissance of the fifteenth and sixteenth centuries, with all the consequent tensions between new philosophies and entrenched theology.

What did the order's name mean, in the first place? Did Rosy Cross derive from Christian Rosenkreutz, the hero of the *Fama Fraternitatis?* Conveniently enough, Rosenkreutz does mean Rosy Cross in German, but it is just as likely that the name is a pseudonym borrowed from the brotherhood, not the other way around. The pairing of the rose and the cross is familiar symbolism, after all. In Christian allegory, the two symbols are often found to represent the Virgin Mary and Christ; a prayer inspired by the ancient *Litany of Loreto* speaks of the rose as "flower of the cross, pure womb that blossoms . . . Over all blooming and burning . . . Sacred Rose . . . Mary."

In modern secular interpretation, psychologist Carl Jung regarded the rose as a symbol deep in the human unconscious, as a maternal womb, and he linked the cross with humanity's inner desire to find fourfold patterns for most things. The cross appears in diverse mythologies all over the world, and for Christians it is equated with sacrifice and suffering.

A case also can be made that the founders of the brotherhood, being highly Protestant in their outlook, selected the rose and the cross because these symbols appeared on Martin Luther's coat of arms. On the other hand, there are those who maintain that the name is taken from alchemy, which the order was known to study—*ros* being Latin for "dew," which was considered an essential element in the transmutation of base metals into gold, and *crux* being the alchemical symbol for light as well as the sign denoting the four elements.

With so much conjecture and controversy about the order's very name, it is not surprising that over the centuries the Rosicrucians—or those who purport to be their spiritual descendants—have themselves had difficulty coming to a consensus on matters concerning the brotherhood's origin, ritual, and dogma. Indeed, it would appear that many among them have deliberately set about to fabricate new mythology and ancient history, either in the hope that wishing would make it so or as an attempt to discredit some competing group, of which the Rosicrucians have had their full share.

Any examination of this most intriguing of secret organizations must begin with the *Fama Fraternitatis,* the earliest document that clearly and unambiguously mentions the brotherhood by name and purports to tell the story of its foundation. Written anonymously in German, the pamphlet was part of a larger Protestant treatise entitled in its first English translation *The Universal and General Reformation of the Whole Wide World; Together with the Fama Fraternitatis of the Laudable Fraternity of the Rosy Cross, Written to All the Learned and the Rulers of Europe.* The German manuscript probably began circulating around 1610, and the work was subsequently published in several languages. The first printed edition appeared in 1614 in the town of Kassel in western Germany.

Readers who desired to join in reforming the world were invited to "leave the old course, esteeming Popery, Aristotle, and Galen, yea and that which hath but a mere show of learning." The author asserted that no one could apply for membership directly, but would-be applicants

Similarities between Reformation and Rosicrucian ideals are suggested by Martin Luther's coat of arms (above). Designed around 1524, it bears a five-petaled rose entwined with the cross, a motif later common in Rosicrucianism.

might "speak either by word of mouth, or else . . . in writing. And this we say for a truth, that whosoever shall earnestly, and from his heart, bear affection unto us" will come to the fraternity's notice. "And it shall be beneficial to him in goods, body, and soul."

Lest anyone think that the benefits might include lessons in practical alchemy, the author declared in the plainest language he could muster that "concerning the ungodly and accursed gold-making we do therefore by these presents publicly testify, that the true philosophers are far of another mind, esteeming little of the making of gold, which is but a subsidiary activity; for besides that, they have a thousand better things." Expressed another way, the Rosicrucians knew very well how to transform base metal into gold and how to make medicinal elixirs, and they could do either when it suited them, but their strongest alchemy was reserved for another, more laudable purpose: the transmutation of ordinary mortal intellect into spiritual and philosophical wisdom.

he *Fama* then went on to relate the life and death of one Christian Rosenkreutz, the purported founder and guiding light of the Rosy Cross brotherhood. According to the *Fama*, Rosenkreutz was born in 1378 somewhere in Germany, the child of a noble but impoverished family. Unable to care for their son, Christian's parents placed him in a monastery sometime before his fifth birthday. After learning "indifferently the Greek and Latin tongues," continued the *Fama*, young Christian set out with a monk on a pilgrimage to the Holy Land. The monk, unfortunately, died during a stopover in Cyprus. But the purposeful boy, related the *Fama*, "shipped himself over" to Damascus, where he stayed for a time.

Rosenkreutz apparently demonstrated great natural skills in medicine and healing, which brought him to the attention of the wisest men in the city. And he, in turn, found their knowledge of science, mathematics, and other arcane matters inspiring. The youth forthwith decided to put aside his original itinerary and to seek the wisdom of

Arabia at its fount. The sages of Damascus directed him to a city called Damcar—a place that has never been identified and is presumed by many to be mythical. In Damcar, the *Fama* recounts, the learned men "to whom Nature was discovered" received the precocious boy "not as a stranger, but as one whom they had long expected; they called him by his name, and showed him many other secrets"—among them mathematics, physics, alchemy, and a document the *Fama* refers to as the *Book M.* This last treasure, whose full name is thought by some to be *Book Mundi,* or Book of the World, is said to have held the secrets of the universe. Young Rosenkreutz decided that he would translate this prodigious work into Latin, so that he might share it with others upon his return to Europe.

After three years in Damcar, Rosenkreutz traveled to Egypt, where he studied natural history and, presumably, the metaphysical writings attributed to Hermes Trismegistus, the legendary ancient Egyptian sage. The youth then journeyed to Fez, in Morocco, where he was introduced to magic and to interpretations of the Scriptures based on the medieval Jewish system of mysticism known as the Cabala. Rosenkreutz marveled at the ease with which Arabs and Africans exchanged new ideas and amended old ones, their sole purpose being to advance the general state of knowledge for the good of mankind. And although he was troubled by the "impurity" of the magic practiced in Fez, said the *Fama,* he nonetheless could see ways to use it for the furtherance of his own Christian faith.

The *Fama* related that Rosenkreutz at last returned to Europe by way of Spain, eager to impart his new wisdom. In his innocence, he expected the learned ones of that land to rejoice at having their faulty knowledge, their obstructive procedures, and their misguided moral philosophy put right. Instead, said the *Fama,* the young scholar was greeted with derision and hostility: "It was to them a laughing matter; and being a new thing unto them, they feared that their great name should be lessened, if they should now again begin to learn and acknowledge their many years' errors." Rosenkreutz moved on, but he found the sages of other nations no more receptive to Arabian wisdom than the Spaniards had been—although some among them did demonstrate an avid interest in his alchemical skills, which he of course declined to share.

iscouraged, Christian Rosenkreutz returned to Germany to meditate on the folly of his fellow man. After several years of reflection, he concluded that the world was not yet ready for his great moral and intellectual reformation. But rather than let all the scientific and spiritual wisdom he had collected be lost forever, he determined to write it down in books that might be kept secret until the dawn of a more auspicious era. With so much work to be done, he invited three confreres from his boyhood monastery to become his helpers, and in this manner Christian Rosenkreutz and his colleagues formed a new quasi-monastic order, the Brothers of the Rosy Cross, or Rosicrucians, whose entire purpose, the author states, was to show the way to others.

Work proceeded slowly, for there were many other demands on the Rosicrucians' time. The medical skills that Father Christian, as he was now addressed, had taught the brothers became so well known throughout Germany that the sick clamored at the Rosicrucians' doors. There was also construction to be undertaken: Father Christian had determined to build a large temple, the Domus Sanctus Spiritus (or House of the Holy Spirit), as the order's spiritual home. Eventually, the brothers decided to initiate another four monks into their order, and together they completed Father Rosenkreutz's ambitious plan, producing a whole library on the arts and sciences.

When the work was done, there being no further reason for them to remain together, the Rosicrucians resolved to separate and to carry their medical wisdom to every corner of the earth. Before parting, they agreed upon six basic tenets, which would bind them forever: First, that none of them was to exercise any worldly profession but medicine and that their medical services would be provided to patients free of charge. Second, that they would never adopt a monk's habit, as did other orders, but rather would follow the custom of the country in which they traveled so as to remain inconspicuous. Third, that they would gather at the Sanctus Spiritus once each year on the "Day of C" (some historians speculate that this may be the Christian feast of Corpus Christi, which occurs on the Thursday following the eighth Sunday after Easter) to share information and renew their brotherhood. Fourth, that each brother would choose a worthy successor to whom he would transmit all his accumulated wisdom before death, so as to perpetuate the order's mission on earth. Fifth, that the initials RC—presumably standing for *Rosae Crucis,* in Latin—were to be taken as the brotherhood's seal, password, and most cherished concern. (They would also be used as a shorthand form of Rosenkreutz's name.) And sixth, that the existence of the Rosicrucian order and its special knowledge were to remain closely guarded secrets until the brothers should receive a sign to divulge them.

According to the *Fama Fraternitatis,* the brothers and their chosen successors carried out their mandate year after year, decade after decade, enjoying great acclaim as healers (one of them is said to have cured England's young duke of Norfolk of leprosy) while quietly preparing the ground for the moral reformation to come. Then in 1484, the story relates, Father Christian died, at the age of 106, "oppressed by no disease, which he had neither felt in his own body nor allowed to attack others, but summoned by the Spirit of God." He was buried by two of his trusted disciples, who were sworn to keep his final resting place a secret for the rest of their lives.

There followed a century or more of rest and renewal for the secret order. Then, in 1604, several of the brothers, including the author of the *Fama,* were engaged in a construction project at a hidden location, most likely in Germany, when they came upon a mysterious tomb. The tomb, which lay behind a concealed door, had inscribed upon it in Latin the words "after 120 years I will reappear." Upon entering the tomb, the brothers found an altar resting in the center of a seven-sided vault, each side of which was fur-

A seventeenth-century engraving of a mythical Temple of the Rosy Cross teems with Rosicrucian imagery.

ther divided into many compartments. Although the room could not possibly receive sunlight, there was a brilliant light shining within.

As the Rosicrucian brothers examined the compartments, they found not only copies of all the order's books, but a copy of the *Vocabularium* of Paracelsus, by the renowned Swiss physician and alchemist; Father Christian's life story; and mirrors "of divers virtues, as also little bells, burning lamps, and chiefly wonderful songs." The brothers concluded that they had uncovered the resting place of their order's founder.

The presence of a work by Paracelsus apparently provoked no particular comment among the discoverers. But it has greatly puzzled subsequent students of Rosicrucianism because Paracelsus, a picturesque figure whose real name was Theophrastus Bombast von Hohenheim, was not even born until 1493, nearly a decade after Christian Rosenkreutz is said to have been buried.

Everything, it seemed, had been providently laid out, so that if the order were to disappear for some reason, it could all be reconstituted from the treasures placed in the tomb. The brothers removed the altar and found beneath it, as recounted in the *Fama*, the "fair and worthy body, whole

and unconsumed," of Christian Rosenkreutz. Even in death, he grasped firmly in his hand a gold-lettered copy of *Book T*—which the *Fama* described as "our greatest treasure next to the Bible," although later scholars have branded this work a figment of the *Fama* author's imagination. Satisfied that they had done as Father Christian had wished 120 years before, the brothers closed the door of the vault and sealed it, knowing that it was now time to go forth with their message of worldwide moral renewal and to open the ranks to a new and larger membership.

 he *Fama* pamphlet had scarcely begun to circulate in learned Protestant circles when it was followed by two other slender but equally sensational works on Rosicrucian philosophy. The first of these, titled the *Confessio Fraternitatis Rosae Crucis,* appeared in 1615. Written in Latin, this work essentially repeated the message of the *Fama,* only more fervently and explicitly. It also offered a few additional details on membership—including the fact that the Rosicrucian order was open to worthies of all social classes. In addition, the treatise proclaimed the brotherhood's fundamental Christian belief, along with its condemnation of the pope, Muhammad, the "false Alchemists," as

The Lofty Visions of Jakob Boehme

Rosicrucianism's spread in seventeenth-century Germany may have gained impetus from a Görlitz cobbler named Jakob Boehme. Boehme reportedly had his first spiritual "illumination" in 1600 when, at the age of twenty-five, he sat gazing at the light reflected from a pewter dish. The revelation led the shoemaker to abandon his trade for mystical studies. In 1612, he published his first work, *Aurora,* seeking to explain such mysteries as evil, free will, and predestination. Boehme remained a devout Lutheran and apparently was not a Rosicrucian, yet he became a leading German mystic, producing some thirty books on the secrets of God, man, and nature.

Scholars see many echoes of German mysticism in Rosicrucian thought. *Aurora,* for example, promised "a new dawn of insight," as did the Rosicrucian manifestoes appearing in German at the time.

The all-seeing eye of God (left) appears on the title page of Jakob Boehme's Aurora. The former cobbler (above) was branded as a heretic when the book came out. But by his death in 1624, he had become a respected philosopher.

well as those who could not accept the new science.

Perhaps most significantly, the *Confessio* alluded to certain signs that had recently appeared from "the great book of nature." The alleged signs were new stars in the constellations Serpens and Cygnus. Czech astronomer Johannes Kepler had spotted the stars in 1604, the same year in which Christian Rosenkreutz's tomb had been revealed, and the *Confessio* saw them as heralds of the coming time "when the World shall awake out of her heavy and drowsy sleep, and with an open heart, bare-head, and bare-foot, merrily and joyfully meet the new arising Sun."

The third and last book in the Rosicrucian trilogy, *The Chemical Wedding of Christian Rosenkreutz,* appeared a year later in Strasbourg. Self-described as a "hermetic" or magical romance, this slim volume told a fantastical tale of adventure in which Rosenkreutz, now in considerably advanced years, had been invited to attend the wedding of mythical royalty. The nuptials seem to have actually been loosely based on the wedding in 1613 of the young man who was soon to be Frederick V, king of Bohemia, to Princess Elizabeth, eldest daughter of James I of England—an event of great political import throughout Protestant Europe. In any case, the story was replete with rich allegorical details, as well as cosmological, alchemical, astrological, magical, and chivalric symbols. These latter elements appear to have been the author's chief concern.

As the allegory began, Rosenkreutz was preparing for the celebration. All manner of trials, ordeals, and strange initiation rites were put before him, but he triumphed over them in what can be seen as a spiritual progression. Finally, he reached his destination and was greeted as the guest of honor. He was invested with the chivalric Order of the Gold-en Stone, an apparent reference to the legendary philosophers' stone, by means of which base substances could be turned into gold and silver. As in the earlier tracts, the author went to great lengths to indicate that the goal of Rosenkreutz as well as all the others who received the Golden Stone was a transmutation of the spirit and not the crasser sort of alchemy.

he *Chemical Wedding* appeared anonymously, like the other Rosicrucian works. Unlike the *Fama* and the *Confessio,* however, this tract was eventually claimed by an author, one Johann Valentin Andrea. This highly educated man had studied at the University of Tübingen, in Germany, in the first decade of the seventeenth century and was well acquainted with mathematics, optics, astronomy, and philosophy. He was also thoroughly versed in the great writings of Arabian and Hebrew scholars, in the humanist writers of the fourteenth and fifteenth centuries, in the newer writers of the Protestant Reformation, and in the works of John Dee, Elizabethan England's preeminent magician-scientist. Moreover, Andrea also knew the literature of the Egyptian Hermetics and of Christian mysticism and the Cabala, in large part because of his association with a small circle of visionaries who had gathered about Tübingen's brilliant professor of law, Christoph Besold.

Historians theorize that it was out of some enthralling sessions with Besold and his protégés that Andrea conceived the idea of writing *The Chemical Wedding*. But exactly what his intentions were, or what part he and the others may have had in writing the *Fama* and the *Confessio*, remains unclear. When Andrea finally admitted authorship of *The Chemical Wedding*, he was a respected and orthodox Lutheran clergyman, on record as being opposed to Rosicrucianism. He took great pains to distance himself from the work, calling it a satire that he had concocted in his foolish youth. At no time did he or his Tübingen friends ever lay any claim to the other manifestoes.

Even so, most historians believe that Andrea probably created all three of the Rosicrucian documents, with a strong assist from Besold and the others. Students of the Rosy Cross believe that the works were produced in the sincere utopian desire to promote precisely that general reformation of the world described therein. Moreover, the social and intellectual climate in Germany at the beginning of the seventeenth century was such that a group of young liberals might easily have devoted themselves to such a noble and heartfelt

German scholar Johann Valentin Andrea (above) admitted to writing The Chemical Wedding in his youth. He may have written other early Rosicrucian works as well.

cause. The preceding century, aflame with the conflicts of the Reformation and Counter Reformation and the ceaseless political maneuvers of petty princelings, had left Europe a far distance from unity, peace, or prosperity.

Whatever the truth, the appearance of the three pamphlets was the cause of great excitement and ardent debate. Armed with the visionary tracts, would-be Rosicrucians besieged the most learned men they knew, perhaps hoping to achieve a certain credibility merely by association. And, almost inevitably, charlatans began selling supposed Rosicrucian materials, such as alchemical secrets and pieces of the philosophers' stone, to the gullible for large sums of money.

One notably foolish victim, a Dutchman by the name of Ludovicus Orvius, reportedly paid a swindler an initiation fee equivalent to $1,000 in 1622, only to have the man disappear without divulging a single one of "nature's secrets." And a French nobleman, Henri, duke of Bouillon, opened his purse wide when a self-proclaimed Rosicrucian revealed what he said were the secrets of gold making. With the duke watching, the poseur mixed a few ounces of litharge (a yellowish lead oxide) with a small quantity of something he called his special Rosicrucian "transmutation powder"—in actuality an inert red powder that he had se-

cretly laced with real grains of gold. He then heated the concoction, performed a suitable amount of hocus-pocus, and held up a tiny nugget of precious yellow metal. Understandably dazzled by the possibilities, the duke insisted on buying every last ounce of miraculous powder in the adept's bag, and he put a large deposit on another shipment to be delivered later. No sooner had the imposter left with 20,000 crowns in his pocket than Duke Henri discovered that he had been duped: The expensive red stuff in his possession was worthless dust.

While some went to great lengths to give the appearance of membership in the supersecret order—especially if there was money to be made thereby—others were just as diligent in seeking to show that they had no connection with it, doubtless because of its heretical overtones and the shabby practices of some of its alleged practitioners. One prominent figure who worked hard to convince the world that he was not a Rosicrucian was René Descartes. The young French sage had first heard of the Rosicrucians when he was living in Germany during the winter of 1619-1620. Descartes was at the

An illustration from a 1598 manuscript titled **Splendor Solis** *depicts the rebirth of the soul through spiritual alchemy, a subject central to Rosicrucian thinking. Using the symbols of physical alchemy, which sought to turn base materials into gold, the artist shows a man emerging from mud as he enters the first stage of transformation. The queen in white represents the second stage, and the red head of the man, the final transmutation.*

time just beginning to formulate his theory that nature's laws were based upon determinate mechanical systems. Thus he was predictably intrigued by rumors of a society of men promising a new kind of wisdom and a "veritable science," as he put it, based upon the hospitable union of "theology, physics, and the mathematics."

Descartes evidently made efforts to contact the Rosy Cross brothers. But like everyone else, he failed. After several months of fruitless inquiry, he concluded that the whole business was an elaborate hoax. He was therefore astonished to find upon his return to Paris in 1623 that the city was in the midst of a Rosicrucian uproar—and that he himself was rumored to be an "invisible." Such was the clamor, in fact, that he began to fear for his safety, especially in light of the Church's dire injunctions against the sect. The naturally reclusive philosopher did the only thing he could think of to clear his name. As a contemporary biographer explained it, "He made himself visible to all the world, and particularly to his friends," and that apparently silenced suspicions.

The Chemical Wedding was the last seemingly direct communication from the Rosicrucian fraternity for a century or more. But over the next decades, numbers of prominent men who were not brothers of the Rosy Cross—or so they insisted—continued to offer persuasive arguments in the order's defense. Among the most influential were Michael Maier and Robert Fludd.

Maier was German, a native of the northern province of Holstein, had been trained as a physician, and was much taken with the work of Paracelsus. A brilliant if rather unstable iconoclast, Paracelsus had a decidedly metaphysical bent, and his interest in alchemy led him to practical dis-

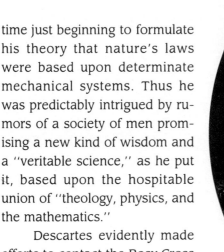

coveries that made him the foremost pharmacologist of his time. Maier was equally mystical of mind and had wide-ranging interests in philosophy and the natural sciences. He caught the attention of Emperor Rudolph II of Hungary, who brought him to Prague as his personal physician and private secretary. Rudolph had a passion for alchemy, and his court was the rendezvous of all the great adepts in Europe. At his death, his treasury was said to contain the equivalent of eighty-four bushels of gold and sixty bushels of silver, all allegedly produced by his court alchemists.

Maier seems to have caught the fever, for he no sooner arrived in Prague than he began to devote himself almost exclusively to finding the philosophers' stone—not, he said, for purposes of making gold, but for the chemical and philosophical possibilities that it offered. Shortly after Rudolph died in 1612, Maier secured an appointment to the court of Maurice, landgrave of Hesse, in Kassel, where the original Rosicrucian manifestoes were in the process of being published. Whether Maier, himself a Lutheran, first became interested in the Rosy Cross brothers while in Kassel is not known. Yet by 1615, when he traveled to England and met with Robert Fludd, another physician in the Paracelsian tradition, both Maier and Fludd were well aware of the Rosicrucians. The two doctors also seemed committed to the brotherhood's promotion, though apparently not as members themselves.

Upon Maier's return to Kassel he published *Silentium Post Clamores* (Silence after the Uproar), in which he argued that the *Fama* and the *Confessio* were sincere works that all men of goodwill should take to heart. He explained that the brothers' lofty stance in failing to answer their petitioners

was an indication of the rigorous standards the order set. Would-be Rosicrucians should expect to undergo five years of secret observation before hearing whether they were considered acceptable, a test that Maier noted was not unlike the waiting period imposed in ancient times by such groups as the Orphists, the Pythagoreans, and the disciples of Isis and Osiris.

Maier assumed that the majority of applicants would be judged unworthy and that those who did gain entrance would be sworn to secrecy. Thus, he reasoned, there was no way to assess the number of members—or their quality—except from within. As for the order's symbols, the rose and the cross, Maier thought they were meant as prescriptions for life: Those who desired to understand the rose (infinite wisdom) must first accept the disciplines of the cross (a series of ordeals). Maier added, somewhat apologetically, that he wished that the Rosicrucians' purposes could be expressed a little more directly, because he, too, thought they were somewhat obscure.

ne year later, Maier seems to have gained a better understanding of Rosicrucianism, for he wrote a series of expanded commentaries, titled *Themis Aurea,* on the six rules of the society as set forth in the *Fama.* He argued that persons wanting to form their own judgment of the Rosicrucians should be careful to distinguish between the multitude of impostors and the few true adepts of "incredible virtue" who alone held the secrets of "natural magic," of "perfection in all the arts," and of "the anatomy and idea of the whole universe." As though speaking from personal experience, Maier made several tantalizing allusions to people and places connected with the brotherhood that, he said, "will sufficiently instruct an intelligent reader, but more confound the ignorant." The intelligent reader familiar with Maier's milieu might well have construed his vague references to a riverside city with a Sanctus Spiritus church to be the city of Heidelberg, although there exists no concrete evidence that a Rosy Cross brotherhood was operating there at the time.

Gaining momentum, Maier published two books on behalf of the Rosicrucians in 1618. The first, *Viatorum,* was an allegorical work devoted to philosophical alchemy and spiritual transmutation, a development of themes introduced in Andrea's *Chemical Wedding.* The second, entitled *Atalanta Fugiens,* was a collection of intricate symbols accompanied by philosophical commentary on the correct paths to religious, alchemical, and moral truth.

Meanwhile, the Englishman Robert Fludd, a somewhat eccentric Oxford-trained physician and philosophical successor to John Dee, was laboring just as assiduously as Maier to promote the Rosicrucian brotherhood among his own countrymen. Fludd may have become acquainted with Rosicrucian ideas around the time that he met Maier in England or possibly even earlier, during his own six-year tour of Europe. That Fludd should also be attracted to the order's tenets is not surprising, for he had long been a devoted student of Hermetic philosophy, the Cabala, alchemy, and Paracelsian medical theories. In any case, he was sufficiently involved with the Rosicrucian cause—and incensed at its critics—to write in 1616 a rejoinder, triumphantly titled *A Compendious Apology for the Fraternity of the Rosy Cross, Pelted with the Mire of Suspicion and Infamy, but Now Cleansed and Purged as by the Waters of Truth.*

In the *Apology,* Fludd described the Rosy Cross brothers as true Christians and the spiritual descendants of Hermes Trismegistus. He declared himself to be a disciple without being a member, and he thought it possible that

The philosophers' stone, reputed to turn base metals to gold, appears everywhere in nature in this illustration from a 1618 Michael Maier treatise on spiritual alchemy. To Rosicrucians, the search for the mythic stone symbolized their quest for spiritual rebirth.

there was no formal Rosicrucian organization; a community of minds sharing the same spiritual and philosophic goals was quite enough to constitute a movement, in his opinion. "I affirm that every Theologus of the Church Mystical is a real Brother of the Rosy Cross."

Fludd followed this work a year later with another volume, in which he distinguished between bad magic and good magic. The Rosicrucians, he assured his readers, practiced only good magic, both mathematical and mechanical, along with the magic of the Cabala, which was directed at invoking the names of the angels. Fludd went on to review the current state of the arts and sciences and found them all wanting. In this Fludd echoed the earlier complaints of John Dee and the philosopher Francis Bacon, whose names have frequently, if circumstantially, been associated

with Rosicrucianism. Fludd singled out for broad reform the realm of mathematical sciences, including geometry, arithmetic, algebra, and optics, and he went on to express a kind of Rosicrucian dream that humankind's ethics, politics, law, theology, and economics might all be subjected to the scrutiny of virtuous people and ultimately made more harmonious.

By his own testimony, Fludd never received a direct communication from any of the Rosicrucian brothers, and when he died in 1637, it appeared that Rosicrucianism might die with him. Interest in the movement was flagging as newer, more fashionable intellectual and philosophical movements arose, both in England and on the Continent. However, it has been argued with some justice that the new societies—the Freemasons and the royal scientific brotherhoods among them—were

An Alchemist's View of Creation

Under attack from their critics, seventeenth-century Rosicrucians found a ready defender in Oxford-trained physician and alchemist Robert Fludd *(above)*. Apparently, Fludd had independently developed theories about man and nature similar to Rosicrucian doctrines. His massive work called *History of the Macrocosm and Microcosm* sought a unity between the macrocosmic universe and the micro-

cosmic world of the individual—a unity the brotherhood also espoused.

Fludd's theory of creation, depicted in five of the six engravings below and at right, is a central element of the *History*. As Fludd saw it, the raw material

of the cosmos was a dark, formless, and infinite abyss. In the initial act of creation, he said, there appeared a

Separation of the Waters

The First Appearance of Light

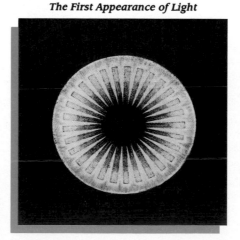

The Great Darkness

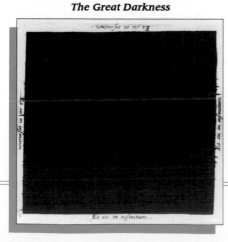

Rosicrucian in inspiration and that as such they were the first real fruits of fraternalism that Rosicrucianism ever bore. The nineteenth-century English writer Thomas De Quincey, who examined the connections between Freemasonry and the Rosy Cross brotherhood, concluded that Rosicrucianism had reached England as an idea only, without established rituals, members, or lodges. But in the benign climate of England, the order's utopian ideals had been readily absorbed and given concrete expression by the Freemasons, who were themselves an expanded and mystical outgrowth of the medieval masons' guilds of England *(pages 86-89).*

At any rate, very little was heard of the Rosy Cross itself for something like a hundred years after Fludd's death. Perhaps, as Rosicrucian tradition holds, the fraternity had entered one of its cycles of "outer silence," going still deeper underground while awaiting an auspicious day to emerge. As is the case with so much of the group's history, however, evidence to support this explanation is lacking, and it is equally plausible that the original movement simply died for lack of support.

Then, in the first decades of the eighteenth century, coincident with a periodic surge of public interest in the oc-

cult, Rosicrucianism reappeared. It took the form of several different organizations—each claiming to be the one true and ancient Order of the Rosy Cross. Each also claimed antecedents that reached much further into the mists of time than Christian Rosenkreutz's day. But the old emphasis on cosmic truths and spiritual enlightenment was lacking. The new Rosicrucians were by and large a materialistic breed, concerned primarily with such exercises of physical alchemy as medicinal chemistry and the manufacture of imitation gemstones. So it was that those who were most interested in becoming Rosicrucians were dilettantes and dabblers in pseudoscience.

To be sure, the newly incarnated Rosy Cross brothers were not necessarily frauds and quacks; they may very well have believed their own claims. Such was the state of scholarship and scientific inquiry in the early eighteenth century that all manner of historical "traditions" and "secret arts" were accepted without rigorous investigation and concern for evidence.

According to the famed essayist Sir Richard Steele, in one of his gossipy pieces for the widely read journal *Tatler,* England's Rosicrucians reappeared in 1709 as "a set of People who assume the Name of Pretty Fellows, get new

The Beginning of God's Creation

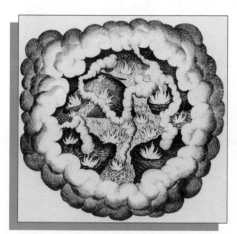

The Elements Locked in Chaos

Order Imposed by the Sun

spiritual form of light representing angelic intelligence, the "virtue of the heavens, the rational soul in man, and the life force of the lower realms."

Next, divine light separated matter into the upper and lower waters: The lower, seen in the third drawing as a dark cloud, remained passive, while the surrounding upper waters held the fire of love. At the fourth stage, the lower waters appeared as a chaotic mass, with the four elements battling

against each other. Restored to order in the next picture, the elements have aligned themselves into concentric circles of fire, air, water, and earth around the sun.

The sixth drawing linked Fludd's theory to the biblical Creation in Genesis. Crowned with God's primordial word *fiat,* or "let it be," the image depicts the angelic light that appeared on the first day at his command. In the *History,* the second and third days of Creation yielded the celestial firmament and the earth.

Names, have their Signs and Tokens like Freemasons but apparently distinct from Freemasons, and rail at Woman-kind"—this last possibly a wry allusion to the earlier Rosicrucian vows of chastity.

At the same time as the English group emerged, a band of German Rosicrucians apparently came together somewhere near Breslau, hard by the Polish border. Its chronicler was one Sigmund Richter, who wrote under the pen name of Sincerus Renatus. In 1710, he published a work entitled *A Perfect and True Perfection of the Philosophical Stone, According to the Secret Methods of the Brotherhoods of the Golden and Rosy Cross.*

Richter, who claimed membership in the mysterious fraternity, described it as consisting of separate Golden and Rosy branches, each with thirty-one members, or "adepti." Overseeing both groups was an "imperator." Whether there was any distinction between the two branches on the basis of their activities, religious affiliations, or national origins, Richter did not say. He did assert, however, that the old antipapist spirit had been replaced by an attitude of general religious tolerance, a sign that the partisan convulsions of the Reformation and Counter Reformation had finally diminished in force.

Richter's Rosicrucianism was notable for its new emphasis on rules and rituals. He listed fifty-two ordinances, some of them quite specific. Rule thirty-six, for example, ad-

An anonymous German manuscript dating from around 1800 shows the common Rosicrucian abbreviation, R.C., alongside such popular alchemical motifs as the union of the sun and moon and a serpent consuming itself.

monished that "no Brother on his travels shall carry the Treasure of Philosophy in the form of oil, but only in that of powder of the first projection, the same being contained in a metal box having a metal stopper." In addition, Rosicrucians were forbidden to "manufacture pearls or other precious gems larger than the natural size" or "to divulge the sacred and secret matter, or any manipulation, coagulation or solution thereof."

As of old, Richter's brothers of the Golden and Rosy Cross were expected to choose their own successors, but how this was to be accomplished was made much more explicit than before, as was a new brother's initiation and his subsequent career. When a new member had completed his training, he was to be received "in one of the Houses built at our expense," given a Sign of Peace together with a palm branch, kissed three times, and then formally enjoined to silence.

The initiate was then to kneel and recite the order's pledge, swearing "by the Living and Eternal God that I will never reveal the Mystery which has been unto me communicated to any human being whomsoever; but will preserve it in hiddenness, under the natural seal, all the days of my life. I will keep secret likewise all things belonging thereto, so far as they shall be made known to me. I will discover nothing concerning the position of our Order and the abode, name, or surname of our Imperator, nor will I show the Stone to anyone. All these things I promise to preserve eternally in holy silence, at the peril of my life, as God and His Word shall help me."

The master who had trained the initiate then cut seven locks of the new member's hair, wrapped each lock in a separate piece of paper on which was recorded the brother's birth name and sacramental name, and turned them over to the imperator for safekeeping. Thenceforth, the brother saluted other brothers with a ritual exchange of secret passwords, had minimal social contact with women—although he might marry if he very much desired to—and pursued the work of "the Stone and the Great Elixir," presumably meaning physical alchemy and medicine. According to one report, members of at least one lodge always carried on their persons a black silk cord. This was to be used to strangle themselves if they ever felt tempted to reveal one of the fraternity's secrets.

itualistic Rosicrucianism continued for the better part of the eighteenth century before gradually fading from the scene. One branch, known as the Asiatic Brethren of the Rosy Cross, sprang up in Amsterdam sometime before 1780. Evidently the brainchild of a Baron Hans Carl von Ecker und Eckhoffen, the Asiatic Brethren invited within their uncommonly hospitable circle Jews, Turks, Persians, and Armenians, in addition to orthodox Christians. The Rosicrucian group's teachings concerned such useful matters as how to make gold, how to prepare miraculous medicines, and how to tame invisible elemental spirits—of which there were four classes: sylphs of the air; undines of the water; gnomes of the earth; and salamanders, which inhabited fire.

Initiates of the Asiatic Brethren had to progress through five degrees of membership before obtaining sublime wisdom. First, as "seekers," they were required to dress entirely in black, including a round black hat with black feathers, a black sash with three rose buttons, and a sword with a black tassel. After fourteen months, the seeker was promoted to the rank of "sufferer," and for seven months he wore his cloaks, tassels, and feathers enlivened with bits of white. During this period, he participated in certain secret "researches."

The remaining degrees supposedly conferred progressively more important secrets. However, it would appear that the Order of the Asiatic Brethren was chiefly a money-making scheme that served to fill Baron von Ecker's pockets through membership fees as well as, perhaps, additional fees for more prestigious ranks. Like so many other rogue Rosicrucian groups, however, this upstart movement was able to survive only until it had exhausted the local population of easy marks.

Perhaps out of embarrassment, victims of these offshoot organizations seldom stepped forward to protest. One man who found the courage—and preserved his anonymity behind the pen name Magister Pianco—wrote an angry revelation in 1782 called *The Rosicrucian Unveiled.* The piece told of devoting years of patient study and a small fortune to climbing the Rosicrucian ladder, only to discover that the promised instruction in ''divine things'' was not forthcoming; indeed, it did not exist. Pianco said that his imperator was a terrifying bully, a sort of ''hybrid between man and beast. No honest Christian could cope with him without fear of being flayed alive. If doubts were suggested, he uttered blasphemies, of which the most violent miscreant would have been ashamed.''

The era did produce one figure who profited handsomely from his association with Rosicrucianism—or very possibly, from the appearance of such a connection, for he always allowed the matter of his membership in the organization to remain ambiguous. That man was the Comte de Saint-Germain, the celebrated savant and cavalier who seems to have led a dozen lives. Saint-Germain enjoyed enormous privilege in the royal courts of Europe over a period of thirty-five years.

The count first strode confidently onstage as a man in his early thirties in the London of 1743. Already, his astonishing talents had gained him access to the grandest salons, where he not only composed music and played the violin with exquisite grace, but also showed a prodigious memory for historical facts and spoke all the languages of Europe, as well as Chinese, Arabic, Sanskrit, and classical Greek and Latin. He was an inventor of note and demonstrated a high degree of skill in chemistry, particularly that of the dyestuffs then in great demand for clothing aristocrats in grand style. He was rumored to hold the secret for the transmutation of precious metals, gems, and pearls. In medicine, he was said to have compounded a formula to prolong life; in fact, he claimed to be 2,000 years old himself, and many marveled that the man never seemed to age.

The English author Horace Walpole said of the exotic count, ''He is called an Italian, a Spaniard, a Pole; and somebody that married a [woman] of great fortune in Mexico and ran away with her jewels to Constantinople; a priest, a fiddler, a nobleman.'' Walpole thought Saint-Germain a gifted musician but otherwise quite mad.

Years later, Saint-Germain would claim to be the son of a Hungarian prince and a German princess and to have been brought up in Italy by the Medicis. Some doubters scoffed that he was in reality a Portuguese Jew. Whatever his origins, he obviously looked the gentleman; when he arrived at the court of Louis XV shortly after his London sojourn, the ladies were most taken with him. The countess d'Adhémar wrote with something more than a strictly reportorial eye that ''his nether garments, which fitted very closely, suggested a rare perfection of form. His smile showed magnificent teeth, a pretty dimple marked his chin, his hair was black, and his glance soft and penetrating. And, oh, what eyes! Never have I seen their like.''

Men, too, were mightily impressed by the count. No less a personage than the renowned writer Voltaire described Saint-Germain simply as ''a man who never dies and knows everything.'' And the Italian alchemist, mesmerist, and necromancer Alessandro Cagliostro, who was in a better position than most to recognize fraud, had to acknowledge that his rival was a man of extraordinary and inexplicable talents.

hether Saint-Germain was ever inducted into the Rosicrucian order remains a mystery. Subsequent historians of the occult, including Helena Petrovna Blavatsky, the controversial founder of the philosophical and religious system known as Theosophy *(pages 126-145),* were only too glad to declare Saint-Germain the consummate Rosicrucian on the evidence of his supposed accomplishments. And Annie Besant, one of Blavatsky's most ardent disciples before following her own occult star to India,

The writings of French magician Éliphas Lévi (right) sparked a revival of Rosicrucianism in the nineteenth century—and lent it new emphasis on magic and the Cabala. The double-triangle Seal of Solomon is from an 1896 edition of Lévi's Transcendental Magic.

made an emotional case for Saint-Germain's being the re-incarnation of Sir Francis Bacon and Christian Rosenkreutz.

Certainly, Saint-Germain did come closer than any public figure ever has to fulfilling the external life that Rosy Cross brethren were thought to live, although he did so with considerably more panache and less spirituality than the founders may have envisioned. Besides calling himself Count Saint-Germain, he had at least a score of other names and noble titles, which he seems to have assumed for the sheer amusement of playing new roles. The count traveled so widely and often, conversing in so many languages, that the uninformed might well think he had some occult capacity for transporting himself by will alone, as the Rosicrucian manifestoes had said was possible. He did appear to be a man of tremendous goodwill, inspiring Prince Charles of Hesse to refer to him as "the friend of humanity" and "one of the greatest philosophers who ever lived." And he did in fact perform all sorts of Hermetic feats for his hosts, not the least of which was a likely sleight of hand in which he transformed flawed diamonds into perfect ones.

Perhaps one of the most intriguing oddities surrounding the count's life was the date of his death. He is said to have met his death in Schleswig in 1784, while a guest of Prince Charles of Hesse, from accidental contact with some poisonous substance that had been generated during one of his chemical experiments. Yet even in death, Saint-Germain seems to have lived on. He reportedly was seen and spoken with on numerous occasions for almost forty years, until the year 1820. Most often the occasions were grim:

65

the guillotining of Marie Antoinette in 1793, the death of the duc d'Enghien in 1804, the eve of the murder of the duc de Berri in 1820. It was as if the count wished to remind everybody that he was truly immortal, beyond the earthly death that carried off others.

By the time the count was last sighted, Rosicrucianism had entered another period of outer silence—perhaps to weather the profound political changes sweeping Europe and America. To be sure, pseudo-Rosicrucians were abroad as always, selling everything from pieces of the philosophers' stone to false memberships in the brotherhood. The fraternity's name remained alive, but most of the groups that had once gloried in ritual and rite under its aegis were either absorbed into the Masonic orders or had faded away entirely. But then, in the latter half of the nineteenth century, there was a resurgence of belief in the supernatural and occult, fields that nourished the eventual development of modern Rosicrucianism. Influenced by this heightened interest in the supernatural, the order would move even further away from the simple and quiet utopianism of the old brotherhoods.

The impetus came chiefly from the occult writings of Abbé Alphonse-Louis Constant, an apostate French cleric who had left the Church in order to pursue his interest in magic. Changing his name to Éliphas Lévi, the turnaway priest accepted the traditional notions on which much magic is based. These included the belief that man is a microcosm of the universe and that all things in the cosmos are bound together by an invisible network of inner correspondences, occasionally revealed to mortals through signs and talismans. But he was the first to connect the Cabala with fortunetelling Tarot cards.

In his *Transcendental Magic, Its Doctrine and Ritual*, first published in the mid-1850s, Lévi claimed to have discovered a clear link between the twenty-two letters of the Hebrew alphabet, the twenty-two trumps in the Tarot deck, and the twenty-two paths in the tree of life. In the unraveling of their meanings, Lévi said, would be found the keys to the mysteries of life.

Although Lévi claimed never to have been personally involved in Rosicrucianism, his theories of magic and correspondences primed a new generation of followers to revive the Rosicrucian movement, this time with magic and the

Eccentric Joséphin Péladan (right) became a notable figure in French Symbolist literature. The drawing above is from his 1884 book La Queste du Graal (Search for the Grail), one of a series of novels blending the occult and the erotic.

Cabala as the organizing principles. In 1866, for example, a group of English Freemasons formed the Societas Rosicruciana in Anglia "to afford mutual aid and encouragement in working out the great problems of life, and in discovering the secrets of nature." The SRIA, as the organization eventually became known, developed an ambitious new agenda that included the cultivation of "mental processes . . . believed to induce spiritual enlightenment and extended powers of the human senses."

Previous to this era, membership of Rosicrucian societies had been impossible to ascertain. But the SRIA seemed proud to report that in the early 1870s its English branch alone counted

144 members in the nine grades from zelator (a zealot in pursuing enlightenment) to magus (a wise man or magician). The English group had outposts in Germany, British India, the French colonies, and South America. Worldwide, the movement boasted approximately 500 followers. Eventually, however, some of the founding members decided to branch out, and in 1887, a number of them organized a new group called the Hermetic Order of the Golden Dawn, which seems to have been part Rosicrucian, part Theosophist, part pure magic *(pages 145-156)*.

At about the same time, in France, Éliphas Lévi's Cabalistic theories spawned additional Rosicrucian splinter groups. The first of these was the Ordre Kabbalistique de la Rose-Croix, an exotic organization founded in 1888 by the Marquis Stanislas de Guaita, a sometime poet with strong inclinations toward the Tarot and numerology. De Guaita's hierarchy consisted of a Supreme Council of Twelve, but there were scarcely any ordinary members. As one observer wrote, "Having nothing to govern, they remained in a state of expectant inertia," just barely keeping themselves afloat under successive imperators until 1918. One member of the Supreme Council who patently could not tolerate expectant inertia was Joséphin Péladan, who in 1890 organized his own schismatic Order of the Rose-Croix of the Temple and of the Grail.

If nothing else, Péladan was a magnificent eccentric. He went about Paris in monk's robes or medieval doublets, as the mood suited, and he liked to call himself Sar Merodack, which was a bastardized royal title concocted from ancient Assyrian and Chaldean. In his younger days, Péladan, a one-time bank clerk, had taken to writing occult-erotic novels and occult self-help treatises such as *How to Become a Fairy* and *How to Become a Magus.* His stated goal in starting a Rosicrucian brotherhood in competition with de Guaita's was that the Ordre Kabbalistique was too pagan in its practices and beliefs; he wanted to marry Rosicrucianism to a pure sort of Catholicism in what was to be a movement free of materialist taints.

Péladan's Rosicrucianism eventually stole the show

from de Guaita—not for reasons of religious orthodoxy, but because Péladan incorporated aesthetic and literary concerns in his version of the order. In Paris, bubbling at the time with creative ferment, such things had a wider draw than mere Tarot cards. Beginning in 1892, Péladan organized a succession of artistic salons, lectured on painting in the mystical manner, and produced several occult plays, including two that he insisted were the missing works of the great Greek dramatist Aeschylus.

or all the Rosicrucian activity in Europe, the order seems to have planted no durable roots in the United States until the first decade of the twentieth century. But when it finally did arrive in the New World, the brotherhood came in several interesting versions. Each had a different history that had been devised to endow the undertaking with tradition and authority.

The first to declare itself was the Rosicrucian Fellowship, established in 1907 by a German immigrant named Carl van Grasshof, who at the time of his conversion was an officer in the Los Angeles Theosophy movement. Van Grasshof claimed to have been initiated into the brotherhood by members he met during an extended trip through eastern Europe.

When he returned to his adopted California, he changed his name to Max Heindel and wrote a text called *Rosicrucian Cosmo-Conception,* setting forth the secrets he had learned. He then went out in search of followers, who were offered instruction at his headquarters in Oceanside, south of Los Angeles. Heindel's Rosicrucians were encouraged to believe in reincarnation, in the existence of spirit helpers, and in the deleterious effects of tobacco, alcohol, and meat, which they had to renounce before their initiation into the group.

Another sort of Rosicrucianism was offered by R. Swinburne Clymer, who around the same time declared himself chief magus of the Fraternitatis Rosae Crucis. Clymer's group, with headquarters in Quakertown, Pennsylvania, had a history supposedly going back to 1858. Its beliefs

An anonymous 1943 German manuscript that appeared amid the horrors of World War II contained this watercolor, which was a copy of an illumination from a 1785 German text called *Secret Symbols of the Rosicrucians*. The work depicts the struggle between good and evil, represented by the Garden of Eden's Tree of Knowledge.

closely paralleled those of Heindel's Rosicrucians, but there is little to indicate how many members it ever attracted. A third variety was the Societas Rosicruciana in America, which was founded in 1907 by Sylvester C. Gould and is currently based in Kingston, New York.

The last and most durable enterprise was the Ancient and Mystical Order Rosae Crucis (AMORC) of San Jose, California. This group claimed American lineage dating back to 1693, when a community of German mystics immigrated to Pennsylvania, seeking the "elixir of life" on the banks of the Wissahickon River near what is now the Germantown section of Philadelphia. The community apparently continued until 1801, when it seems to have broken up, the homes abandoned and the people

AMORC founder H. Spencer Lewis, photographed at the order's first headquarters around 1920, became involved in Rosicrucianism during a 1909 visit to France. The U.S. group he founded in 1915 is now the country's largest Rosicrucian society.

scattered—in accordance, say Rosicrucians, with an ancient 108-year cycle of rebirth, activity, rest, and waiting. Then, in 1909, the time of reorganization arrived.

The chosen imperator was H. Spencer Lewis, a practicing occultist, self-styled doctor of philosophy, and sometime advertising man. Lewis asserted that he had received from certain French adepts both his rank and his authorization to establish an order in the United States. As he told it, he spent six years at his arduous task, studying in Europe and working in cooperation with a founding committee to produce a first manifesto incorporating the ancient Rosicrucian teachings. When it was published in 1915, the document, according to AMORC's official manual, "was warmly greeted by a gathering of over 300 prominent students of the teachings who examined the official papers, seals and warrants possessed by Imperator Lewis, and formed the first American Council of the Order." Thus armed, and claiming to be the only true Rosicrucian order in America, Lewis and AMORC were off and running.

Whatever else he might have been, the imperator was a supreme showman and something of a genius at promotion. Although the transmutation of metals was abjured as an end in itself, on June 22, 1916, Lewis nonetheless put on an impressive display before a group of twenty-seven members of the order and a reporter from the *New York World*. Fifteen of the members had been issued cards instructing them to bring certain ingredients to the meeting, ingredients that were to remain secret, even from others among the chosen fifteen. At the appointed hour, after various prayers and a short discourse on alchemy, H. Spencer Lewis placed a piece of ordinary zinc on a porcelain plate, which was then set over the fire of a crucible. The various ingredients, including the petals of a rose, were then presented to Lewis, who placed them one by one on the plate with the zinc. According to one account of the meeting, "After the 16 minutes required, during which the

Imperator concentrated a little-known power of mind, the piece of zinc was transformed into gold—as was chemically established."

That was—or appeared to be—powerful magic, and on the strength of it, Lewis's group rapidly outdistanced all rivals. Lewis was not in the least selective or secretive in his membership drives, which were conducted chiefly through advertisements in popular magazines and newspapers. The imperator invited everyone, women as well as men, who were "sincere in wanting to better their own life and advance humanity" to enroll and begin mail-order instruction. In exchange for a $5.00 initiation fee and monthly dues of $3.50, the new Rosicrucian would receive a membership card, the secret password, a detailed diagram of the secret handshake, a magazine, and twice-monthly lessons teaching the mastery of life.

hose who pursued their "discourses" through twelve degrees could expect to develop will power, maintain health, improve memory, and overcome bad habits. Furthermore, they could understand the meaning of life, learn the truth about reincarnation, enhance personality, influence other people, improve intuition, and generally attain cosmic consciousness.

Members who completed their first degree at home and could not get to one of the lodges scattered around the country were told to initiate themselves into full membership. They were to stand before a mirror, tracing a cross on the glass while repeating "Hail, Rosy Cross," after which they were to meditate for three minutes and finally touch forefinger to forehead while chanting the word *peace*. In so doing, they would join a select group that, it was claimed, included Pharaoh Akhnaton, Plato, Aristotle, Jesus, Cicero, Saint Thomas Aquinas, Francis Bacon, Benjamin Franklin, and strangely enough, the French composer Claude Debussy. Those who chose not to become full members might also gain partial wisdom, the value of its contents not specified, as associate members—for only $1.50 monthly.

When H. Spencer Lewis died in 1939, his son Ralph carried on the work, assuming the title "Supreme Autocratic Authority, Imperator for North, Central and South America, the British Commonwealth and Empire, France, Switzerland, Sweden and Africa." Upon Ralph Lewis's death in 1987, the torch of leadership was taken up by a protégé, Gary Stewart, and the Lewis organization remains by far the largest sect bearing the Rosicrucian name today. By some accounts, AMORC boasts as many as 60,000 members in 100 American lodges and 26 affiliated foreign ones. The annual budget for advertising, printing, postage, and such may amount to $1,000,000, with a staff payroll exceeding $630,000 in one recent year.

The headquarters at Rosicrucian Park in San Jose sprawls across an entire city block and features splendid gardens and an impressive array of buildings with Egyptian motifs and statues of sphinxes. There is a large Egyptian Museum and Art Gallery, which is said to contain the finest collection of Egyptian and Babylonian antiquities in the western United States. In addition, members have the use of a science museum, a modern planetarium, an auditorium, and an instructional complex with classrooms, sound studios, and laboratories for the study of physics, chemistry, biology, parapsychology, and photography.

The ancient Rosicrucians, if indeed there really were any, would not recognize the place. But someone else might. In or about the year 1555, more than half a century before publication of the *Fama Fraternitatis* of Christian Rosenkreutz, Michel de Nostredame—the great French physician, astrologer, and prognosticator known as Nostradamus—penned one of the intriguing prophetic quatrains for which he remains famous. He wrote: "A new sect of Philosophers shall rise. / Despising, death, gold, honours and riches, / They shall be near the mountains of Germany, / They shall have abundance of others to support and follow them."

As was so frequently the case, particularly concerning matters of geography, Nostradamus was not entirely right. But chances are that he would not consider himself altogether wrong, either.

The Patriots of Freemasonry

The eighteenth century, the era known as the Enlightenment, saw the emergence of the modern world as we know it. It was a time of great political and cultural growth in Europe and, consequently, in America. Progressive thinkers espoused rationalism, the scientific method, the importance of the individual, the moral perfectibility of humankind. And if enlightenment was the message, Freemasonry was the universal language in which it was shared. The idealism of the day was a perfect match to the Freemasons' philosophy of tolerance, brotherhood, and humanism, and the sect became an important vehicle in disseminating those values.

Although the fraternity remained officially nonpolitical, its values naturally led members toward democratic beliefs; and in America, where many colonists chafed under repressive British rule, the Masons attracted dedicated, politically active men. As early as 1732, Daniel Coxe, the first colonial Masonic grand master, proposed a plan to confederate the American colonies, and by the 1760s, the brotherhood included such leaders as George Washington, Benjamin Franklin, John Hancock, and Paul Revere. These men envisioned a new society based on fraternity and equality. It was perhaps inevitable that they would play a key role in securing America's independence.

Paul Revere, talented gold- and silversmith as well as Freemason revolutionary, crafted a silver chaplain's jewel (above) for a lodge in Lexington, Massachusetts, in 1796.

Masons as Mohawks

Long before the American Revolution began in earnest, Bostonians angry at England's high-handed treatment of the American colonies began meeting regularly to air their frustrations and plot a response. These political freethinkers gathered at taverns and distilleries, including a pleasant pub called the Green Dragon Tavern in Boston's North End.

The Green Dragon was also the meeting place of St. Andrew's Masonic lodge. Not all lodge members supported the patriots' cause, but its leaders, including Paul Revere, John Hancock, and Dr. Joseph Warren, were committed to colonial rights. For them, a 1773 British move to exclude colonists from the tea trade was the last straw. Denouncing the Crown for discriminating against its colonial subjects through unfair taxation and restrictive trade, they resolved to help break the British stranglehold on American commerce.

Patriot zealot Samuel Adams

On the evening of December 16, 1773, three tea-laden ships from England were docked in Boston Harbor, posing an opportunity that did not go unnoticed by Revolutionary firebrand Samuel Adams--probably a Mason himself. At Adams's signal, dozens of men dressed as Mohawk Indians, their faces blackened with burned cork, swarmed Boston Harbor. They quickly commandeered the boats, and in less than three hours, they dumped 342 chests of tea overboard. Although the identities of these celebrants at the Boston Tea Party can never be known for certain, the band almost surely included Revere and other Freemasons.

Later, several Masons convened at the Green Dragon. The patriots had dealt the British a telling blow, and in the flush of victory the brethren sang: *Rally, Mohawks! Bring out your axes / And tell King George, we'll pay no taxes.*

John Hancock, Freemason and patriot

A 1789 engraving from a British history book depicts patriots, disguised as Mohawk Indians, dumping British tea into Boston Harbor. The print shows accurately that crowds gathered on the harbor shore to witness what would later be known as the Boston Tea Party.

GREEN DRAGON TAVERN

Where we met to Plan the Consignment of few Shiploads of Tea.
Dec 16 1773

John Johnson 7 Water Street
Boston Mass. 1773

The Green Dragon Tavern, shown here in a 1773 sketch by Freemason John Johnson, was short of patrons on the evening of December 16, 1773. Records show that a meeting of St. Andrew's Masonic lodge scheduled for the Dragon that night was adjourned "on account of the few Brethren present." There is little doubt where the absentees were: The inscription beneath Johnson's drawing reads, "Where we met to Plan the Consignment of a few Shiploads of Tea. Dec 16 1773."

Paul Revere: Master Craftsman

When twenty-five-year-old Paul Revere joined Boston's St. Andrew's Masonic lodge in 1760, his motives were probably fraternal and professional. The lodge gave him a chance to mix with men of backgrounds and interests similar to his own, and new friends meant new patrons for his gold and silver handiwork. Since Masonic ritual calls for a variety of medals, jewels, seals, and engravings, the artisan did a brisk business with a ready-made clientele.

But as political strife with Britain escalated, the young smith's interest in Freemasonry became less social and more centered on the patriotic fervor rife among his brethren. The 1770 Boston Massacre and the Boston Tea Party helped fuel his political passions, and he joined a group that met regularly at the Green Dragon Tavern to keep an eye on British troop movements.

Of course, Revere's best-remembered contribution to the cause was his famous 1775 midnight ride. Revere wrote of his adventure that his Masonic master, Joseph Warren, "sent in great haste for me, and beged that I would imediately Set off for Lexington." His mission was to warn fellow patriots that British soldiers were on the way.

After battles at Lexington and Concord, the British blockaded Boston, and the city's Masons suspended meeting for more than a year. Once they reconvened, Revere again became active in the sect. In time, he would serve as master of St. Andrew's lodge, then of another Boston lodge, and finally as grand master of the grand lodge of Massachusetts.

*Freemason
Paul Revere*

Revere's work for Massachusetts's King Hiram's lodge included this silver past master jewel, crafted around 1805.

Paul Revere's inflammatory engraving The Bloody Massacre showed British troops firing on a peaceful Boston crowd in 1770. Actually, the five people killed were part of a hostile mob. Still, revolutionaries cried massacre, and Revere's piece became potent propaganda for inciting anti-British sentiment.

This engraved invitation to a St. Andrew's lodge meeting was one of at least six such notices Paul Revere produced for various lodges between 1762 and 1784. The intricate designs, featuring Masonic symbols, were engraved on copperplates. Also available were the engraved certificates issued to Masons as they earned the three basic degrees.

This nineteenth-century engraving shows Revere's famous April 18, 1775, ride to Lexington. He and Freemason William Dawes sped off to warn patriots that the British were on the march. More specifically, they alerted John Hancock and Samuel Adams that British troops from Boston were coming to arrest them.

Freemasonry's Physician Patriot

The first major engagement of the American Revolution came on June 17, 1775, on a knoll outside Boston known as Bunker Hill. The British army outnumbered the American volunteers almost two to one, but the upstart colonists were tough, holding their ground against two vicious assaults. The English prevailed on their third try, however, forcing an American retreat. The grim British victory was costly to both sides: Each army lost about one-third of its men.

Fighting with the rebels was Dr. Joseph Warren, a passionate revolutionary and dedicated Mason. Grand master of the Massachusetts grand lodge, Warren was also a leading Boston radical. In 1774, he wrote the Suffolk Resolves, expounding the doctrine of forcible response to British injustices. Warren almost certainly helped plan the Boston Tea Party, and it was he who sent Paul Revere on his midnight mission to Lexington.

In the patriots' retreat from Bunker Hill, Warren was among the last to turn back. He was shot and killed. English general Gage, pleased to find himself rid of the outspoken rebel, reportedly remarked that Warren's death was worth that of five hundred men. The victorious British stripped Warren of his elegant clothes, wrapped him in a farmer's coat, and buried him in a common grave. But after the British evacuated Boston in 1776, Freemasons recovered Warren's remains and interred them according to the brotherhood's elaborate funerary customs.

Bunker Hill hero Joseph Warren

Joseph Warren's death was romanticized in John Trumbull's The Battle of Bunker Hill, a painting completed in 1820.

Freemasons escort Joseph Warren's disinterred body to the Massachusetts State House in this engraving from the 1800s. A former grand master, he was buried in 1776 with full Masonic honors.

A monument (left) honoring Joseph Warren and other heroes of Bunker Hill was erected on the battle site in 1794 by King Solomon's Masonic lodge of Boston. Thirty-one years later, France's marquis de Lafayette, a Freemason and a general of the Continental Army, laid the cornerstone for a large obelisk that would enclose the original memorial.

Freemasonry's French Connection

French progressives, like their American counterparts, embraced the philosophy of personal liberty. Many leading voices of the French Enlightenment were Freemasons, and the Nine Sisters Masonic lodge in Paris was a well-known gathering place.

Lodge members included the writer Voltaire and respected artist Jean-Antoine Houdon, who sculpted the busts shown here. And in 1778, a visiting American brother was admitted, statesman Benjamin Franklin.

Franklin, in Paris seeking French support for the American Revolution, was warmly received by the French. Through his Freemason contacts, Franklin met the marquis de Lafayette, a fiery young officer who immediately outfitted his own ship and sailed to America. In July 1777, Lafayette received his commission as major general in the Continental Army.

Around 1779, Franklin befriended yet another patriot at the Paris lodge, Continental Navy captain John Paul Jones. Jones was in France awaiting a new command; when he received his ship in August 1779, he christened it the *Bonhomme Richard* after Franklin's famous *Poor Richard's Almanack.* In the ship's first engagement against the British Navy, Jones was victorious—and joined the ranks of Freemasons who fostered American independence.

John Paul Jones

Benjamin Franklin

The marquis de Lafayette

On a visit to America in 1784, Lafayette presented this Masonic apron to his old friend, former commander in chief, and fellow craftsman, George Washington. The symbols adorning the cloth were embroidered by Lafayette's wife.

Captain John Paul Jones, aboard the French-built Bonhomme Richard, engages the British ship Serapis in a fierce battle depicted in this 1781 engraving. It was during this confrontation in 1779 that Jones declared, "I have not yet begun to fight!"

George Washington, Freemason

George Washington was only twenty in November 1752 when he joined the Freemasons. He rose quickly through the ranks, eventually becoming grand master of the grand lodge of Virginia.

Washington treasured his Masonic ties, perhaps never more so than during the years he led the Continental Army. The marquis de Lafayette, who served under him, once observed that the commander in chief rarely awarded independent commands to officers who were not Masons. Indeed, most of Washington's generals were brethren, among them Horatio Gates, Henry Knox, Israel Putnam, Baron von Steuben, and of course, Lafayette.

Washington used Freemasonry to forge unity among his soldiers—troops who largely identified not with a nascent nation, but with their individual colonies. The general welcomed the creation of at least eleven new military Masonic lodges, in which men from all the colonies intermixed. Thus a foot soldier could count himself a brother not only to his co-colonists, but to all Freemason soldiers and officers, even Washington himself.

Lodge meetings were much-needed morale builders for many of the war-weary men, and Washington personally visited as many lodges as he could. Even during the horrific winter at Valley Forge, regular meetings were held; Lafayette was said to have entered the brotherhood during a gathering there.

Washington valued the loyalty Freemasonry inspired. He once wrote that "the virtues that ennoble mankind are taught, nourished, and fostered in the halls of the Freemasons; they encourage domestic life and serve as a standard for the highest duties of State."

Dressed in the full Masonic regalia of a past master, President Washington sat for this portrait by William J. Williams, a fellow Mason, in 1794.

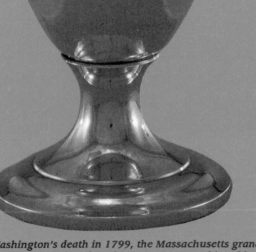

After Washington's death in 1799, the Massachusetts grand lodge of Masons commissioned Paul Revere to create this gold urn "as a deposit for a lock of hair . . . of the Hero and the Patriot."

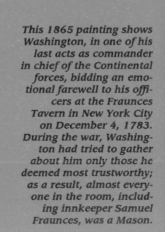

This 1865 painting shows Washington, in one of his last acts as commander in chief of the Continental forces, bidding an emotional farewell to his officers at the Fraunces Tavern in New York City on December 4, 1783. During the war, Washington had tried to gather about him only those he deemed most trustworthy; as a result, almost everyone in the room, including innkeeper Samuel Fraunces, was a Mason.

When General Benedict Arnold (right) betrayed his country to the British in 1780, his actions were doubly shameful: Not only had he committed treason, but he had also broken faith with his fellow Masons.

CHAPTER 3

Freemasons: Mortar and Mysticism

eep in the rich history of American politics, the name of William Wirt lies buried. Yet in 1832, the year Wirt ran for president of the United States, he commanded a considerable constituency. Of the twenty-four states then extant, he carried Vermont, and he drew eight percent of the nationwide total of 1,262,755 votes cast. He ran as the nominee of the Anti-Masonic Party.

Today, of course, the fraternal and service group known as the Free and Accepted Masons is a secure strand in the social fabric of the developed world. In the United States alone, some 16,000 lodges welcome several million member Masons, and the leading citizens of many a town consider it a privilege to belong. In some ways, however—in the observance of hidden rituals, the profusion of symbols and honorary titles and high-flown ceremonial language—the Masonic order remains the secret society it has been for centuries untold. And in the time of William Wirt, the Masons' ways made them the object of widespread suspicion and fear.

What electoral success Wirt enjoyed, he owed chiefly to a figure even more obscure than he: a man named William Morgan, who met his peculiar destiny in 1826 in the upstate New York town of Batavia. Morgan was fifty-two years old, married, a landless stonecutter who roamed from place to place. In his travels, he came to possess some of the jealously guarded secrets of the Masons, a coup that unnerved members of the local lodges. Warnings about Morgan quickly spread across the countryside. This notice appeared in a newspaper in nearby Canadaigua, New York, on August 9, 1826: "If a man, calling himself William Morgan, should intrude himself on the community, they should be on their guard, particularly the MASONIC FRATERNITY. Morgan was in this village in May last, and his conduct while here and elsewhere calls forth this notice . . . Morgan is considered a swindler and a dangerous man. There are people in this village who would be happy to see this Captain Morgan."

Morgan, whose self-proclaimed military title was as dubious as his intentions toward the Masons, had devised a plan to turn his special knowledge into profit. He contracted with the publisher of the Batavia *Advocate*, one Colonel David C. Miller, to write a book exposing the shrouded workings of Freemasonry. The optimistic Morgan figured the volume would earn him $2 million; a stupendous sum at the time.

There was little reason for the Masons of Batavia to be upset by Morgan's scheme; similar books, produced in Europe, had long been available in America. Nevertheless, the local lodge—which included five judges, the sheriff, six physicians, and the president of the village—were moved to action. A number of members arranged to have Morgan jailed over a trumped-up debt of $2.68. The next night, four Masons went to the jail, paid Morgan's phony entailment, hustled him into a closed carriage, and sped away. Morgan was never to be seen in Batavia again.

A sorry figure in the flesh, Morgan assumed heroic proportions in his absence. His partner, Miller, perhaps recognizing a way to make a sensation of Morgan's book, printed 50,000 handbills announcing in bold type the abduction and possible murder of Morgan and asking for information. On the circular, the word *mason* never appeared, but everyone knew whom Morgan had angered. It was common knowledge, too, that Masons threatened gruesome punishments to any who divulged their practices. So the backlash began. At the little town of Pavillion, twelve miles from Batavia, a prominent Baptist minister denounced Freemasonry as "dark, unfruitful, demoralizing, blasphemous, murderous, anti-Republican and anti-Christian—opposed to the Glory of God and the good of mankind." Rumors abounded: Morgan's throat had been cut; he had been pushed over Niagara Falls; his tongue had been torn out and his body buried in the sands of Lake Ontario. One fetchingly ingenious version had it that Masonic abductors had bent a large tree, put Morgan in the hole left by its roots, and then released the tree to snap back and crush him. That was only the beginning. After New York governor DeWitt Clinton, himself a Mason, convened a succession of special grand juries to determine the circumstances of Morgan's disappearance, the long-silent enemies of Freemasonry came forth from many quarters in high dudgeon. All across the Northeast and Midwest, where the Morgan case attracted publicity, Masons were ostracized. Ministers and teachers who were Masons were told to leave the order or lose their jobs. Masons were rejected for jury duty. They were insulted in the street. The Morgan affair had tapped a reservoir of popular hostility toward secret sects in general and

Foreshadowing a Masonic concept of God as the supreme geometer, a fourteenth-century painting shows the deity using a compass to define the limits of good and evil.

the Freemasons in particular. Political figures who had embraced Freemasonry, among them the towering senator Henry Clay of Kentucky, now found it prudent to sever their ties with the organization. A former president, John Quincy Adams, proclaimed that "Masonry ought forever to be abolished. It is wrong, essentially wrong—a seed of evil which can never produce any good. The existence of such an order is a foul blot upon the morals of a community."

othing beyond kidnapping was ever proved against those who spirited Morgan out of Batavia; it is thought likely that they simply relocated him in Canada and paid him a sum to keep him quiet. But the issue of Morgan's well-being was all but cast aside amid the popular uproar. Masonic membership plummeted, and dozens of lodges suspended activity. Still, there were the stubborn adherents, such as Daniel B. Taylor, a stalwart of the Stony Creek lodge in Michigan, who literally kept the light of Freemasonry burning in its darkest hour. "On lodge night," wrote James Fairbairn Smith, a chronicler of the state's Masons, "as soon as the stage arrived bringing the mail, he would get his newspaper and wend his way to the lodge room. On arriving there he would light a candle, place it in the window and then sit down to read. If no one else came, Brother Taylor waited the usual time 'to close the lodge.' Then he would blow out the candle, lock the door, and go home."

The controversy abated slowly through the 1840s and never returned with such virulence. But a shadow of hostility has trailed the sect in Britain since its earliest days, when it was thought to threaten the established hierarchy of church and crown. Over the centuries it has been blamed in part—by those who find sinister machinations behind every world event and trend—for the French Revolution, the rise of both fascism and communism, and even the brutal rampage of London's murderous Jack the Ripper. And, while the local Masonic lodge has generally become a familiar and comfortable feature of the civic landscape, the tremors of suspicion fade slowly. In the Soviet Union, of all places, a professor named Valery Nikolaevich Emelyanov sounded a dire warning before a Communist-party-sponsored conference in 1974. He told of a conspiracy by Zionists and Freemasons to take over the world by the year 2000. The "Judaic-Masonic pyramid," he said, cleverly alluding to a favored Masonic symbol, controlled "80 percent of the economy in the capitalist countries and 90 to 95 percent of the information media."

The object of all this wary attention originated in medieval England as nothing more than a kind of labor union for stoneworkers. The term *freemason* appears as early as 1375 in the records of the city of London. It referred to working masons who were permitted to travel the country at a time when the feudal system shackled most peasants closely to the land. Unlike the members of other crafts of the time—smiths or tanners, for example—the masons gathered in large groups to work on majestic, glorious projects, moving from one finished castle or cathedral to the planning and building of the next. For mutual protection, education, and training, the masons bound themselves together into a local lodge—the building, put up at a construction site, where workmen could eat and rest. Eventually, a *lodge* came to signify a group of masons based in a particular locality. In a 1983 book, American journalist and author George Johnson explained the popular allure of these crews. "The masons of the fourteenth and fifteenth centuries were as much architects as laborers," he wrote.

*Giorgione's painting The Three Philosophers makes the builder's art an allegory
for intellectual growth. The seated apprentice, square and compass in hand, symbolizes youth
building an edifice of knowledge. The middle figure is an overseer, representing
mature judgment; and the elderly man holding architectural plans possesses the wisdom of old age.*

A Free Mason
Form'd out of the Materials of his Lodge.

Behold a Master-Mason rare,
Whose mystic Portrait does declare
The Secrets of Free Masonry.
Fair for all to read and see,
But few there are to whom they're known,
Tho' they so plainly here are Shown.

A. Slade delin.

Published according to Act of Parliamt. August 1st. 1754. By W. Tringham in Castle Alley Royal Exchange. Price 6d. Colour'd 1s.

"To the uninitiated, their work seemed holy. Since ancient Egypt, large stone edifices have been monuments to power, celebrating the magic of priests or the divine right of kings. As outsiders watched, men—some armed with chisels and mallets, others with compasses, rulers, levels and squares—made temples grow from the ground."

To put it simply, the masons had exclusive, attractive jobs, and they were mindful of their special prestige and very protective of it. In a time without patents or copyrights, they jealously guarded the secrets and standards of their crafts. To protect their integrity as well as their status, it behooved them to ensure that all who claimed to know the building arts had, in fact, been properly trained. Their concern was legitimate, since wandering medieval stonemasons often found themselves among strangers, some of whom falsely claimed membership in the craft in an effort to ferret out secrets. To thwart these imposters, the masons invented an ever-growing body of code words and phrases, signs of recognition, and special handshakes. They asked certain questions in a particular way, and the right response verified that the newcomer was qualified to work.

By the seventeenth century, as the number and stature of masons grew, some lodges had begun to admit honorary members who were not stoneworkers. The London Masons' Company founded the Acception, a parallel organization for that purpose, in 1619. It took in as "accepted Masons" men who did not belong to the company but who were willing to pay double the initiation fee. Then, in 1717, four lodges in London created a supervisory body called a grand lodge, whose annual meetings attracted considerable attention and brought order to a swiftly growing movement. The historic transformation of masonry from a single craft guild to a powerful social organization had begun.

To be sure, the Masons did not throw open their lodge doors to just anyone. They found they were able to attract the cream of progressive London society: freethinking princes, philosophers, clergymen, members of the upper class. Just why aristocrats and intellectuals wanted to join a craft guild is not clear, but Masonic secrecy itself seems to have been a major attraction. Many would-be initiates hoped to learn the ancient mysteries and hidden wisdom that the Masons were thought to possess. Moreover, there was a growing interest in architecture and antiquity among wealthy amateurs. Whatever the allure, between 1737 and 1907 a total of sixteen princes underwent the elaborate initiation rituals as accepted Masons. Four of them became kings. Paradoxically, the Masonic message that so enticed the privileged ranks was one of universal brotherhood—the value of each man, regardless of his given social lot.

The first Masonic *Book of Constitutions* was drawn up by a minister of the Church of Scotland, Dr. James Anderson, and published in England in 1723. The *Constitutions* was first printed in America in 1734 by a grand master Mason, one Benjamin Franklin of Philadelphia. The landmark document declared boldly that those of different religions should, within the lodge's companionable atmosphere, be able to associate and discuss new ideas. "Though in ancient Times Masons were charged in every religion of that Country or Nation, whatever it was," explained the *Constitutions,* "yet 'tis now thought more expedient only to oblige them to that Religion in which all Men agree, leaving their particular Opinions to themselves; that is, to be good Men and true, or Men of Honour and Honesty, by whatever Denominations or Persuasions they may be distinguish'd."

 olerance and open-mindedness: These were potent notions in such a stratified era. "Perhaps in the last resort," wrote the British historian J. M. Roberts in 1975, "the greatest social importance of Freemasonry was simply the relief it provided from the triviality, narrowness and rigidity of so much 18th-century life." But conviviality was not the sole appeal to a wider public. Aristocrats were not alone in their thirst for life's esoteric meaning. People of lesser status also were lured by the belief that Masons, with their array of mystical costumes and secret codes, had somehow inherited the hidden wisdom of the ages.

Freemasons themselves created, embellished, and became captivated by the myth that special skills had been

Sir Christopher Wren, England's preeminent architect, holds a compass above the plan for Saint Paul's Cathedral in London in a portrait painted in 1711 to commemorate the masterpiece's completion. Masonic legend has it that for eighteen years during construction of the cathedral, Wren attended the nearby lodge of Saint Paul. He is revered as the last grand master of the so-called operative Masons, those who were real builders and craftsmen.

rade of esoteric medieval cults: the Gnostics, Cathars, Knights Templars, and Rosicrucians.

When the Masons explored these links, real or imagined, to occult groups of the distant past, it was as part of a larger search for truth. The late seventeenth and eighteenth centuries saw the flowering of the Enlightenment, that radiant epoch when unquestioning religious dogma was eclipsed by the belief in human reason and perfectability. Its triumphs were legion: the scientific discoveries of Isaac Newton and later, Benjamin Franklin, chemist Antoine Lavoisier, and astronomer William Herschel; the philosophy of John Locke and Immanuel Kant; the inspired irreverence of Voltaire; the sublime music of Mozart. (Franklin, Voltaire, and Mozart were all Masons. In fact, Mozart's last opera, *The Magic Flute,* is an allegory for the spiritual enlightenment initiates find in Masonry.) Freethinking and progressive Masonic lodges played an important role in disseminating new ideas in Europe and America.

In that unsettled time, when new knowledge sometimes seemed only to underscore how much was yet unknown, there were those who sought answers outside the usual rational disciplines. As always, mysticism had its adherents. Philosopher David Hume, in his 1757 book, *The Natural History of Religion,* explained the appeal of the occult to a society that, in some respects, had happily lost its age-old bearings. "We are placed in this world, as in a great theatre, where the sources and causes of every event are entirely concealed from us," Hume wrote. "Nor have we either sufficient wisdom to foresee, or power to prevent, those ills with which we are constantly threatened. We hang in perpetual suspense between life and death, health and sickness, plenty and want, which are distributed among the human species by secret and unknown causes, whose operation is oft unexpected, and always unaccountable. These unknown

delivered to them across the centuries. One romantic legend even had it that Adam was the first Mason and that the Masonic apron, a staple of the sect's traditional costume, represented his fig leaf. Only slightly less fanciful were other precursors proposed by diligent Masonic "researchers," who traced Freemason lineage to the builders of the Egyptian pyramids, then to ancient Greek cults such as the Pythagoreans and the Eleusinians, and finally through a pa-

causes, then, become the constant object of our hopes and fears; and while the passions are kept in perpetual alarm by an anxious expectation of the events, the imagination is equally employed in forming ideas of those powers, on which we have so entire a dependence.''

 ore than any of the other secret societies that flourished in Enlightenment Europe, the Masons were engaged in ''forming ideas of those powers.'' Throughout the Continent, the craft—as it came to be called—took root. Toward the end of the 1730s, there were lodges in Belgium, Russia, Italy, Germany, and Switzerland. But it seemed to have a special appeal in France, partly because of the rage then current there for all things British. In 1735, there were five Masonic lodges in Paris; by 1742, the number was twenty-two. Some forty-five years later, on the eve of the French Revolution, there were perhaps 100,000 Masons in France.

No sweeping revolt against the established order awaited England, where Freemasonry continued to prosper in an orderly and polite fashion. But the passions that swept France throughout the eighteenth century mutated the simple structure of the organization. In its original incarnation as a medieval craft guild, the masons required a seven-year course of instruction and apprenticeship for inductees before granting them full fellowship in the craft. Among full-fledged members, the most respected was the master mason, the man in charge of a building project. Three stages roughly corresponding to apprentice, member, and master persisted in the seventeenth-century English Masonry model, which enabled members to progress through three ''degrees'' of increasing prestige within the lodge. In France, however, degrees sprang up like wildflowers. Soon members were referring to one another as commander of the luminous triangle, doctor of the sacred fire, and sublime master of the luminous ring. No two lodges followed the same rituals. In some towns, against all Masonic precepts of classlessness, two lodges were established: one for noblemen and magistrates, the other for lesser bourgeois and artisans.

The proliferation of baroque degrees, combined with an increasingly feverish search for connections to ancient cults, proved worrisome to the rulers of lands like France and Bavaria, where the all-powerful Roman Catholic church wanted the sole allegiance of its subjects. The order's original English constitution cautioned that a member was "never to be concerned in Plots and Conspiracies against the Peace and Welfare of the Nation." But the basis of Freemasonry, wrote modern American historian James H. Billington, was "a moral meritocracy—implicitly subversive within any static society based on a traditional hierarchy."

It is not hard to imagine the alarm within the Church. Freemasonry was quickly developing its own ritual and history and legends, its own hierarchy, just as organized religion had. Only the grand master—the exalted leader of the nation's grand lodge—could grant the petition that would allow a new lodge. The proposed master and members of the new lodge would then be presented to the grand master, who would declare before the assembled petitioners that the lodge was duly constituted. Upon the installation of the new lodge master, he would be presented with the constitution, lodge book, and jewel of office. The master would then choose wardens, his two subordinate officers.

In the early eighteenth century, according to records, lodge meetings usually took place in a private room at an inn or tavern, with the members seated around a long trestle table. Much time was devoted to administrative busi-

Seated behind a table, Frederick the Great presides over initiation rites for his brother-in-law at the Potsdam lodge in 1740. Both wear the aprons and neck ribbons emblematic of the lodge. The Prussian monarch glowingly characterized the society as "bringing forth the fruit of every kind of virtue."

ness, but the highlight was—and remains—the initiation of new members or the conferring of higher degrees or orders upon existing members. This pageant, in which the elaborate and symbolic rituals of Masonry are played out, is now generally enacted in a specially furnished lodge room.

Before an initiation, an unvarying ceremonial dialogue occurs between the master and various officers of the lodge. Meanwhile, in an anteroom, a man called a tyler stands with his drawn sword, guarding against intrusions by strangers. His title probably derives from the archaic spelling of tiler, a roofer or tile maker and thus a likely member of the masons in their craft guild days. The tyler removes the candidate's jacket and tie and directs him to put aside all his money or any other metal objects. This is done, the candidate is told, so that if he ever meets a brother Mason in "distressed circumstances," he will remember that he was received into the order "poor and penniless" and will act with appropriate compassion. The left leg of the candidate's pants is rolled above the knee, his left breast is exposed, and his right shoe is removed and replaced by a slipper: In Masonic argot, he is "slipshod." Only initiates know for certain the exact meaning of these last three alterations in the candidate's attire. Some Masonic historians suggest, however, that they originated with the Catholic church's Society of Jesus and symbolize respectively the vow of poverty, proof that the inductee is not a woman, and a reminder of how Jesuit founder Ignatius de Loyola, who had a bad foot, began his pilgrimage to proselytize the heathen.

Once the candidate's garb is correctly disarrayed, the tyler blindfolds him—"hoodwinks" him, in Masonic terms—to demonstrate his "state of darkness." A rope shaped into

The Moorish Mason

Eighteenth-century Freemasons took great pride in their egalitarianism, sometimes demonstrating it by initiating members whose company they might otherwise have spurned. A celebrated example of Masonic broad-mindedness involved a one-time slave named Angelo Soliman. Born in North Africa in the early 1700s, Soliman was sold into slavery as a child. He was educated by a succession of wealthy European owners, wound up as a tutor in an aristocratic household in Vienna, and became a popular figure in court circles. Eventually he was freed, and he married a widowed baroness. In 1781, he was initiated into the prestigious True Harmony lodge, whose members included many of Vienna's social elite.

Soliman became grand master of the lodge and helped change its ritual to include the reading of serious academic and scientific papers—a practice that eventually spread to lodges throughout Europe and enhanced Freemasonry's reputation for intellectual rigor. Similarly, Soliman's membership in the brotherhood became a famous example of Masonic progressive thought.

Still, the former slave met with a most peculiar fate. When he died in 1796, his body was claimed by Holy Roman Emperor Francis II, who ordered it flayed and stuffed. (The monarch had the bizarre habit of collecting stuffed human corpses.) Francis then put the dreadful piece of taxidermy on display in his private museum, despite the pleas of Soliman's daughter and the outraged protests of his Masonic brothers. The grisly relic remained in the imperial collection until the Austrian revolution of 1848, when a grenade pitched into the palace library sent the remains of Angelo Soliman up in a merciful burst of flames.

An eighteenth-century painting purports to show Wolfgang Amadeus Mozart (far right) in the splendor of his Viennese lodge.

The composer, who wrote music for many Masonic ceremonies, was once kept afloat financially by a wealthy fellow Mason.

a running noose, or cabletow, is placed around his neck. The candidate, by now rather humbled, is led to the door of the main chamber, where he is confronted by the inner guard—an officer who bars his passage by holding the point of a dagger to his breast. After a tense moment or two, the candidate—still blindfolded—is brought into the chamber to confront the lodge master and other members in attendance. The novice must answer precisely a series of ritual questions that are put to him by the master. Kneeling before him, the candidate swears not to "reveal, write, indite, mark, engrave or otherwise delineate any part of the secrets in Masonry." If he fails in his word, the candidate agrees to have "my throat cut across, my tongue torn out by the root, and buried in the sand of the sea at low water mark."

 fter the oath is sworn, the master orders the blindfold and noose removed and explains the significance of the trials the candidate has just undergone. Then the master discloses to the initiate the secret step, sign, and handshake of an entered apprentice mason. As revealed in various exposures of Masonic ritual, these are, respectively: a short pace with the left foot, bringing the right heel into its hollow; a hand drawn rapidly across the throat; pressure of the thumb on the joint of a fellow Mason's index finger while shaking hands. Finally there is the password: "Boaz," which means "in strength."

Each new entered apprentice is provided with a set of tools, which evoke the society's origins as a collection of laborers but which are said to also represent certain virtues or significant ideas. He receives a gavel, which symbolizes the force of conscience; a chisel, which represents the advantages of education; and a twenty-four-inch ruler, which stands for the twenty-four hours of the day. After a period of study, an entered apprentice may become a second-degree, or fellow craft, Mason. At this point, he is given a square (representing morality), a level (representing equality), and a plumb (representing rectitude). Third-degree Masons, called master masons, receive a trowel bespeaking brotherly love; the trowel is used to cement together the individual

blocks that in Masonic symbology represent individual human beings. In the lore of the craft, a Mason's progress in reaching a more exalted status is likened to his progress in constructing a temple. The metaphor is simple—higher personal attributes equal greater skills as a builder.

To the eighteenth-century Roman Catholic church, all this sounded suspiciously like a rival religion, and the response was a swift strike. In 1738, Pope Clement XII issued the first in a series of papal denunciations of Freemasonry, ordering the excommunication of all Catholics who had been initiated into the craft. The Vatican denounced Masonry's oath of secrecy as a threat to the sanctity of the confessional and the authority of the Church. It opposed close association with men of different faiths and cited "other just and reasonable motives" for its stance. Throughout Europe, secular officials enforced the Church sanctions, penalizing and even torturing Masons. The craft's fortunes ebbed and flowed depending on who was in power, but Masonry had reached the point where it could not be obliterated. Its adherents were too many and too influential.

Besides, the Masons were certainly no strangers to persecution. Even before the first papal bull, English Masons were often accused of being in league with the Antichrist. "For how should they meet in secret places and with secret Signs taking care that none observe them to do the work of God," one pamphleteer wanted to know, "are these not the ways of evil-dom?" Similar attacks suggested that lodge meetings were merely a cover for alchemical experiments, known by all to be the work of the devil. After the official launching of London's grand lodge in 1717, regular exposés of Freemasonry were published. Many charged that lodge meetings featured homosexual debauchery, including sodomy and flagellation. The exclusion of women from the craft made this an enduring theme. Politics, as well as moral outrage, sometimes fueled anti-Masonic feeling. In 1735, the meetings of Dutch lodges were banned because of fears that the brethren were secretly involved in nefarious political doings. Similar bans followed in Sweden in 1738 and Switzerland in 1745. The empress of Austria closed lodges in her country, including the one in which her husband was grand master. Thus the pressures against Freemasonry did not originate with Pope Clement XII, nor were they the exclusive province of the Church. Nevertheless, the pontiff's displeasure raised the stakes: It put the most powerful religious body in the world officially at odds with the sect.

Freemasons responded by retreating ever more deeply into the glorious history of the order's supposed forebears. Masonic scholars were continually "discovering" links that may or may not have existed with individuals and groups that, themselves, may or may not have existed. One such bloodline that gained wide acceptance among Masons stretched back to Hiram Abiff, a minor biblical figure.

According to the Masonic legend, when King Solomon ascended to the throne of David, he dedicated his life to building a temple to God and a palace for the kings of Israel. Solomon contracted with King Hiram of Tyre, just north of

ancient Israel, for an army of masons and carpenters to help the Jews build the temple. Hiram of Tyre sent the workers, led by the grand master of the Dionysiac architects, Hiram Abiff. Described as the most cunning, skillful, and inquisitive workman who ever lived, Abiff commanded 183,600 craftsmen, overseers, and laborers. He used a system of signals and passwords by which any foreman could quickly assess a worker's level of skill.

Three daring craftsmen of a lower rank decided to force Abiff to tell them the password of the master's degree. Knowing that he always went to the unfinished sanctum to pray, they lay in wait for him, one at each of the main gates to the temple. Hiram started to leave by the south gate and was confronted by a man brandishing a twenty-four-inch gauge. The master builder refused to reveal the secret word and for this was struck in the throat. He turned to the west gate and was struck in the breast with a square. Finally, he

The skull of martyred Knight Templar Jacques de Molay lies before his funeral pyre between the remains of his enemies Pope Clement V and King Philip IV in this 1812 French watercolor. The Templars' red and white banner figures in the regalia of certain modern Masons who claim spiritual descent from the medieval knights.

The title page of The Secrets of Free Masonry gives a grisly, diabolic—and fictional—picture of Masonic rites. Fabricated by an unscrupulous French journalist, the 1886 book was widely accepted as evidence of Masonic Satanism and debauchery.

staggered to the east gate and was struck dead by the third worker, who was armed with a maul. The murderers buried Abiff in a hastily dug grave, and those who later found the body placed a sprig of acacia on the spot. In Masonic lore, Abiff is the sect's great martyr, his dire fate a reminder of the seriousness of Masonic vows of secrecy.

Among the many Masons who have paid homage to Hiram was Rudyard Kipling, who also offered a variant spelling of the builder's name, in his poem, "Banquet Night": "Carry this message to Hiram Abif / Excellent Master of forge and mine: / I and the Brethren would like it if / He and the Brethren will come to dine."

The Masons developed a similar fondness for—and kinship with—Pythagoras, the Greek philosopher and mathematician of the sixth century BC who taught that numbers reflected the harmony of the universe. His students lived together, developing a society based on the study of geometry, astronomy, arithmetic, and music. After five years of learning, the members of the so-called outer circle were initiated into the inner circle, where they discovered mystical doctrines based on the relationships between numbers.

Pythagoras did more than search for a numerical basis to the universe. He and his disciples also gained positions of power in several Greek city-states and tried to apply their idealistic beliefs to government. Finally, though, a group of citizens rebelled and massacred the philosopher-kings.

In time, it began to seem that any historical figure or movement that could lay claim to virtue was somehow connected to Masonry. In Paris in 1738—just as the papal threat against the Masons was being proclaimed—the man designated as orator of the grand lodge of France, Andrew Michael Ramsay, delivered a remarkable speech. It was immediately translated into English as the "Apology for the Free and Accepted Masons." To be sure, Ramsay began rather defensively by noting that the purpose of the order was "to make men lovable men, good citizens, good subjects, inviolable in their promises, faithful adorers of the God of Love, lovers of virtue rather than reward."

With that disclaimer, Ramsay went on to say that Masons were nothing less than the spiritual descendants of the Knights Templars, the band of medieval French knights who protected pilgrims traveling to and from the Holy Land during the Crusades (pages 33-39). It was Ramsay's conceit that the Crusaders were Masons as well as Templars and that the secret words of Freemasonry originated as the watchwords of military camps. He said that by the end of the Crusades, several Masonic lodges had already been built on the European continent. Prince Edward, son of the English king Henry III, allegedly took pity on the vanquished Christian armies in Palestine after the last Crusade and brought them back to Britain in the thirteenth century. In his homeland, according to Ramsay, the prince—who later reigned as Edward I—established a colony of brothers renaming themselves Freemasons.

Such a genealogy was bound to appeal to Frenchmen and, to a lesser extent, Englishmen. But some found it a trifle outlandish and devised a slightly different scenario.

Unmasking an "Occult Force"

In 1939, on the eve of World War II, Rudolf Hess advanced the latest in a long list of anti-Masonic theories that had been invoked for centuries as a pretext for persecuting Masons. The Nazi deputy führer wrote that the Third Reich was threatened by a sinister Judeo-Masonic conspiracy, which among its other crimes was fomenting the imminent conflict.

Hess and his fellow Nazis found a champion for this theory in Bernard Faÿ, a prominent French historian. A scholar of American civilization, Faÿ believed that a cabal of Freemasons plotted both the American and French revolutions, and he saw a similar conspiracy at work in twentieth-century Europe. The 1940 German occupation of France gave him a forum for his views, and he became an enthusiastic instrument of Nazi persecution.

In 1943, Faÿ helped concoct a lurid film called *Forces Occultes*, the story of a young Frenchman who infiltrates the brotherhood to expose its role in starting the war. The movie relied heavily on sensational imagery—a giant spider creeping across the screen, maps displaying vast zones of alleged Jewish and Masonic influence, and a gloating Mason stretching his arms over a flaming globe.

While Faÿ displayed a flair for propaganda, he had far greater impact as the Nazi-appointed administrator of the Bibliothèque Nationale. As chief of the national library, he directed research into the archives of France's secret societies, coming up with the names of some 170,000 "suspects." The information led to the deportation of 520 French Freemasons and the death of 117.

After the war, Faÿ was sentenced by a war crimes tribunal to life in prison. In 1953, after serving seven years, he was pardoned by presidential decree.

French anti-Mason Bernard Faÿ

A poster for Forces Occultes shows the initiation of its hero, who as a cinematic object lesson is corrupted by evil Masons.

They proposed that, yes, the Freemasons did exist in some fashion during the Crusades but that they became acquainted with the Knights Templars by building their strongholds, hospitals, monasteries, and churches. In this way, the Templars' charitable and gallant qualities were conveyed to the Freemasons.

Other Masonic offshoots and variations grew luxuriantly in the fertile soil of the Enlightenment. One of the

This one-inch-square medal was worn by early members of Phi Beta Kappa, founded in 1776 and modeled on Freemasonry. The fraternity ceased its secret rites in the 1800s, becoming strictly an academic honor society.

most fascinating deviations from the mainstream was the Egyptian Rite, founded by one Count Cagliostro. Regarded by many historians as a charlatan—Thomas Carlyle derided him as the ''Prince of Quacks''—the count is rated by others as an important figure in the history of hypnotism, telepathy, psychic healing, precognition, spiritualism, and alchemy. In 1776, he appeared in London, a twenty-eight-year-old of mysterious background but living the lavish existence of a nobleman. His wife, the beautiful Lorenza Feliciani, was invariably arrayed in the best clothing and jewelry; Cagliostro himself, while rather stout and pug-nosed, was tremendously charismatic. He installed himself and Lorenza in an elegant apartment, declared himself an accomplished alchemist, and at once collected a circle of admirers.

One year after arriving in London, Cagliostro was initiated into the Masonic order. Soon afterward, having absorbed much Masonic lore and having glimpsed its potential, he went to the Continent and began promoting an Egyptian lodge with himself on the throne as grand Cophta. Detractors liked to parody the name as grand coffer, reflecting Cagliostro's reputation in some circles as a con man. Still, the count's particularly magical brand of Masonry had great appeal. He opened lodges in Holland, Germany, and even in distant St. Petersburg. In Warsaw, he displayed his alchemical skills before the king of Poland. In Strasbourg, the claim was heard that the great Cagliostro had cured 15,000 people in three years.

The count's personal history was a matter of some dispute. Some thought him a Spaniard, others an Italian, a Pole, or an Arab. A cynical few said he was a small-time Sicilian swindler named Giuseppe Balsamo. When asked where he hailed from, Cagliostro would merely laugh and say he was born in the Red Sea and raised in the shadow of the pyramids. The source of his wealth was no clearer. He had married into a Mexican fortune, some said; others argued he had murdered an Asian prince for the money. His own answer, given before the French Parliament, was this: ''What difference does it make whether I am the son of a monarch or a beggar, or by what means I procure the money I want, as long as I regard religion and the laws and pay everyone his due? I have always taken a pleasure in refusing to gratify the public curiosity on this score. Nevertheless I will condescend to tell you that which I have never revealed to anyone before. The principal resource I have to boast of is that as soon as I set foot in any country I find there a banker who supplies me with everything I want.'' Cagliostro had answered fully and explained nothing.

he Egyptian Rite, such as it was, bore the strong influence of the Hebrew Cabalists, who believed Moses taught a special wisdom to an ancient elite even as the Old Testament was being written for the masses. The Cabalists held that God's Word generated the cosmos and that the ten numerals and twenty-two letters of the Hebrew alphabet were the elements of which the world was made. Indeed, certain words—such as Jehovah—were so awesomely powerful that they were never to be uttered. Cagliostro, promoting the idea that certain words had hidden meaning and strength, told his followers that the Egyptian Rite could regenerate them physically and morally, ultimately guiding them to perfection.

Both men and women were admitted to the count's lodges, a practice highly unusual in Masonry. Certain cere-

Brothers at War

Masonic lore abounds with examples of the strong bonds Masons feel for one another. One such story tells of Colonel John McKinstry, an American officer captured by Indian allies of the British during the Revolutionary War. As this nineteenth-century French engraving shows, McKinstry was bound to a tree and

about to be burned alive when he made the secret sign of appeal for help from a brother Mason. To his astonishment one of his captors stepped forward and halted the execution. His savior was Joseph Brant, a Mohawk chief educated in Europe and initiated into the craft in London. Brant had returned to his tribe, but his Masonic loyalties remained. He delivered McKinstry to British Masons, who in turn escorted him to an American outpost—their own allegiance to the brotherhood transcending loyalty to their country.

monies were slightly different for each sex. In receiving the women, for example, the grand Cophta breathed into the initiate's face, saying, "I breathe upon you this breath to cause to germinate in you and grow in your heart the truth we possess." Reports of other Cagliostro ceremonies describe how he thrust a sword skyward and beseeched archangels to intercede for him with God. It was also said that after certain rites of purification, he would hypnotize a child who would then see visions and speak prophecies. Cagliostro often told those assembled that he possessed a healing philosophers' stone and that he would agree to sell grains of it. The demise of the count poses yet another riddle, but many historians believe he died in an Italian prison, where he had been sent for trying to open an Egyptian Rite lodge in Rome.

In the same year that Cagliostro was establishing himself in London, a Bavarian law professor named Adam Weishaupt was founding a philosophical organization of unparalleled ambitiousness. Called the Order of the Illuminati, this aggregation existed for only about a decade before it was banned and eradicated by the government. But its influence and notoriety are still felt today, partly because of the profound association it formed with Freemasons. The stated purpose of the Order of the Illuminati was "to encourage a humane and sociable outlook; to inhibit all vicious impulses; to support Virtue, wherever she is threatened or oppressed by Vice; to further the advance of deserving persons and to spread useful knowledge among the broad mass of people who are at present deprived of all education." The sentiments in this manifesto may seem as unassailable as those in the 1723 Masonic constitutions. But what Weishaupt left unsaid was just as important: He believed that the Jesuits who held sway over

Sisters of the Brotherhood

On January 6, 1770, a curious advertisement appeared in England's *Newcastle Weekly Chronicle.* It related the adventure of a Mrs. Bell, landlady of the Crown, a tavern where the local Masonic lodge met each month. It seems that Mrs. Bell broke into a chamber next to the lodge room, punched two holes in a connecting wall, "and by that stratagem discovered the secrets of Masonry." The notice claimed that Mrs. Bell was the first woman ever to obtain Freemasonry's secrets and was now prepared, for a modest fee, to make them "known to all her sex."

History does not record how many women took advantage of Mrs. Bell's offer, nor whether the enterprising landlady had indeed learned any thing of interest. But it appears that she was on to a good thing. By the 1700s, as Freemasonry's prestige grew, so did its allure for women—whom it strictly excluded.

Loftily invoking their descent from all-male medieval craft guilds—and asserting that women could not keep secrets—Freemasons had guarded their male-only status through the centuries. Even women monarchs were denied membership. England's Queen Elizabeth I, wrote one Masonic historian, "was not graciously disposed towards Freemasonry; merely because she, as a woman, could not become a Mason." In 1764, Archduchess Maria Theresa of Austria banned Freemasonry in her realm—after unsuccessfully importuning three masters for the secrets of their lodges.

Despite the strictures, Masonic lore is peppered with references to "Lady Freemasons."

Elizabeth St. Leger wore her Masonic apron proudly, even though her girlhood initiation, prompted by her accidentally overhearing lodge secrets, was apparently her first and only Masonic rite.

The lavish trappings typical of French Adoptive Masonry are demonstrated in this 1830 engraving.

Most allegedly were initiated to ensure their silence after they overheard its rituals. Only one of the tales, that of Elizabeth St. Leger, daughter of an Irish peer, seems credible.

In 1710, when Elizabeth was seventeen, she fell asleep in her father's library and awoke to overhear a lodge meeting in progress in the next room. She tried to creep away undetected but was caught by the lodge guard. The penalty for eavesdropping on Masonic ritual was death, and Elizabeth's irate brothers urged that she be executed forthwith. But cooler heads prevailed, and the frightened girl was taken into the lodge to guarantee her silence.

The only other certain case of a woman's admittance to a regular Masonic lodge was that of the Hungarian countess Barkoczy. When her father died without a son, she was declared by her country's courts to be his heir. As this gave her legal status as a male, she was initiated into a local lodge—all of whose members were then promptly booted out of the order by the grand orient of Hungary, the nation's top Masonic governing body. Barkoczy's membership was nullified.

In France, where Freemasonry was all the rage in the late 1700s, female aspirations to join the fun reached a fever pitch among aristocrats. The grand orient of France responded with Gallic gallantry by recognizing a quasi-Masonic women's movement known as Adoptive Masonry—so-called because each lodge was sponsored, or "adopted," by a male lodge. Launched in an opulent *fête d'adoption* on March 25, 1775, when the duchess of Bourbon was installed as the first grand mistress, the adoptive lodges appear to have been little more than playthings for ladies of the court. The women wore dainty aprons, and meetings were giddy coed gatherings that generally wound up with festive fancy balls. "Everybody participates," wrote Queen Marie Antoinette happily in 1781.

Eight years later, the French Revolution brought Adoptive Masonry to an abrupt halt; but the movement was revived in 1805, with Napolean's empress Josephine installed as France's grand mistress. In the U.S., Adoptive Masonry spawned an imitator in the Order of the Eastern Star, founded in 1867 for women relatives of Freemasons. It still flourishes. But Freemasonry itself remains as resolutely male today as it was in 1785, when a German Mason wrote: "The hearts of Freemasons are certainly open to women, but the Lodges are closed to them."

Bavaria were oppressors, responsible for the benighted condition of the country and its people, and that the entrenched power of the Church must be challenged and eventually replaced. What Weishaupt sought, George Johnson has written, was "a world where the divisions of class, religion, and nation were overcome and all people were united in a universal brotherhood. Like the French philosopher Rousseau, Weishaupt envisioned a day when mankind would regain a natural sense of equality and happiness, uncorrupted by organized religion and class distinctions." His ultimate goal, although he was careful not to say so, was a bloodless revolution that would establish the millennium on earth.

As naive as Weishaupt's aims may have been, his tactics were shrewd. His disciples were assigned a rigorous program of study, working their way through increasingly complex ideas until they earned the title of Areopagite (after the members of the ancient high court of Athens). Mindful that his ideas would provoke the powerful, Weishaupt erected an all but impenetrable wall of secrecy around the order: Indeed, only Areopagites were to know that he was the leader. Written communications between members had to be encoded. Illuminati leaders and the sites of lodge meetings were given secret names borrowed from ancient times. Members were encouraged to spy on one another and file intelligence reports to superiors.

Freemasonry, to Weishaupt, offered a ready-made recruiting ground. He knew enough about the Masons to be sure that such freethinkers would be receptive to his message, and he added to the Illuminati organizational chart several ranks that would allow Masons to come aboard. From Bavaria, the Illuminati spread steadily through Aus-

Usually excluded from white lodges, many American blacks such as this unidentified nineteenth-century Mason joined the Prince Hall order, founded by a black Boston clergyman.

tria, Switzerland, Bohemia, Italy, and Hungary, attracting several thousand members—many of them Masons. Then, in 1794, Weishaupt's grand adventure went sour.

A new, much more conservative ruler, Duke Carl Theodore, took power in Bavaria, and at once he issued an edict banning all unauthorized societies. A second edict the following year explicitly singled out Freemasons and the Illuminati, and that was enough for Weishaupt, who fled the capital city of Munich and sought refuge in Regensburg. The final collapse occurred when Carl Theodore's men raided the house of a former Illuminati member and found a trove of incriminating documents, including letters written in the mysterious code. Among the confiscated writings were some that, for their time, tipped the balance of free thought dangerously toward lawlessness and immorality: treatises defending suicide, descriptions of experiments with chemicals, a disclosure that Weishaupt had sought an abortion for a woman he had impregnated. The papers were published by a government commission, and a dark legend was born.

he Illuminati became the talk of Europe. By 1790, more than fifty works about the group had been published, detailing the order's diabolical schemes and pagan practices and frequently implicating the Freemasons for good measure. A number of writers speculated that the Illuminati had not disbanded but had merely gone into hiding. When the great uprising of 1789 dethroned the French monarchy and church, many people, frightened at a world seemingly spinning out of control, searched for a culprit. The Freemasons and the Order of the Illuminati were convenient, even logical, candidates. It had not escaped notice that Masonic triangle symbols had appeared in the emblems of French revolutionary groups, nor that such leaders of the revolt as Lafayette and the duke of Orléans were in fact Masons. What was overlooked was that while some Masons stormed the Bastille, others supported the political establishment. For some, the final proof of Masonic complicity came from the always persuasive Count Cagliostro. From his jail cell in Italy, he suddenly announced his knowledge of a worldwide Illuminati-Freemason conspiracy. This apparently was the count's desperate attempt—an unsuccessful one—to gain leniency.

What is today called the conspiracy theory was born in the flood tide of books, pamphlets, and articles denouncing the Illuminati and linking them to an ever-lengthening list of other supposed plotters. The scope of the accusations is reflected in the title of one anti-Illuminati book, published in 1797: *Proofs of a Conspiracy against All the Religions and Governments of Europe, Carried On in the Secret Meetings of Free Masons, Illuminati, and Reading Societies, Collected from Good Authorities.* The book was an international bestseller, and thirty years later, when Masons were implicated in the disappearance of William Morgan from Batavia, New York, many an American thought to take a dusty copy of *Proofs of a Conspiracy* from the shelf and thumb through it again.

The anti-Illuminati scare reached its height at the turn of the nineteenth century, and a number of leading American political figures who also happened to be Freemasons found themselves on the spot. When a Lutheran minister wrote to George Washington about his fears, Washington replied that he knew of "the nefarious and dangerous plan and doctrines of the Illuminati" but that he was sure American Freemasonry was not involved. Thomas Jefferson read *Proofs of a Conspiracy* and other anti-Illuminati tracts and

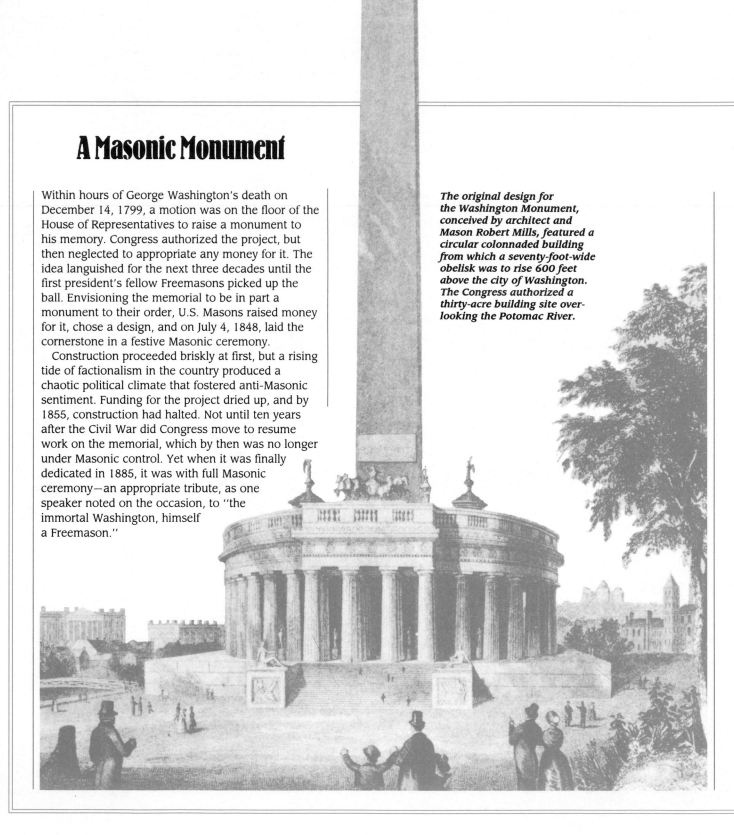

A Masonic Monument

Within hours of George Washington's death on December 14, 1799, a motion was on the floor of the House of Representatives to raise a monument to his memory. Congress authorized the project, but then neglected to appropriate any money for it. The idea languished for the next three decades until the first president's fellow Freemasons picked up the ball. Envisioning the memorial to be in part a monument to their order, U.S. Masons raised money for it, chose a design, and on July 4, 1848, laid the cornerstone in a festive Masonic ceremony.

Construction proceeded briskly at first, but a rising tide of factionalism in the country produced a chaotic political climate that fostered anti-Masonic sentiment. Funding for the project dried up, and by 1855, construction had halted. Not until ten years after the Civil War did Congress move to resume work on the memorial, which by then was no longer under Masonic control. Yet when it was finally dedicated in 1885, it was with full Masonic ceremony—an appropriate tribute, as one speaker noted on the occasion, to "the immortal Washington, himself a Freemason."

The original design for the Washington Monument, conceived by architect and Mason Robert Mills, featured a circular colonnaded building from which a seventy-foot-wide obelisk was to rise 600 feet above the city of Washington. The Congress authorized a thirty-acre building site overlooking the Potomac River.

For more than twenty years, the unfinished Washington Monument (below), stood forlornly on a swampy site called Murderer's Row because of the criminals and Civil War deserters who congregated there. When construction resumed in 1879, the land was filled in and the elaborate original design scrapped in favor of a simple obelisk. The 100-ounce aluminum capstone was set in place on a perilously windy day in December 1884, in a Masonic dedication ceremony (right) conducted on a special platform 572 feet above the ground.

dismissed them. "As Weishaupt lived under the tyranny of a despot and priests, he knew that caution was necessary even in spreading information, and the principles of pure morality," Jefferson wrote. "This has given an air of mystery to his views, was the foundation of his banishment . . . and is the color for the ravings against him. . . . If Weishaupt had written here, where no secrecy is necessary in our endeavours to render men wise and virtuous, he would not have thought of any secret machinery for that purpose."

 ost Americans seemed to follow the same reasoning as Jefferson, and the specter of the Illuminati-Masonic alliance never loomed so large in the United States as elsewhere. And yet, from that time to this, the name Illuminati has surfaced in the works of conspiracy theorists on the American political fringe. Just as some Freemasons wanted to believe that they were the spiritual heirs of knights of the Crusades, some Americans want to believe that the work begun by the Illuminati is being finished today by the Trilateral Commission, the Federal Reserve Board, or secular humanists. George Johnson points out that the 170-year-old *Proofs of a Conspiracy* was reissued in 1967 by the John Birch Society, which apparently considered the Illuminati a clear and present danger. According to one fringe group, Johnson reports, "the symbol for the Illuminati conspiracy appears on the back of the one-dollar bill: an all-seeing eye atop a pyramid, taunting us with its hidden message each time we pay another dollar into a network engineered to keep us in darkness."

All but vanished is the kind of anti-Masonic fervor that infected the American republic in its early years. Recently, membership has slackened somewhat, and Masonic officials have voiced concern that the organization may wither if it cannot meet the needs of the young, who seem generally less interested in joining fraternal organizations. Yet the craft's most perilous times seem far behind. Masonry today retains its tantalizing aura of the exotic, while having long ago shed the baggage of blasphemy and subversion that its members had to carry. Evil, power-hungry Masons continue to exist only in the remotest reaches of the conspiracy theorists' imaginations. In the minds of most people, the Masonic order is as benign—as staid, really—as the Kiwanis, the Lions Club, or any number of similar upstanding civic and service groups.

The Masons, of course, being true to their venerable heritage of linkage with the occult, are more inclined toward arcane panoply and high-flown titles than most run-of-the-mill civic or social groups. The old English Masonic model involving three degrees of membership still exists, and many Masons stop at the third degree, that of master mason. Others, however, go through a ceremony called the royal arch, which admits them to a spectrum of higher degrees. The Ancient and Accepted Rite of Masonry is a system of thirty-three degrees that offer such titles as perfect master, prince of Jerusalem, grand pontiff, chief of the tabernacle, commander of the temple, grand elected knight kadosh, grand inspector inquisitor commander, and sublime prince of the royal secret. And the Ancient and Accepted Rite is but one of a staggering array of rites and orders.

There are also a number of social organizations that draw their membership from Masonry without actually being connected with it. In the United States, the most visible of these is the Ancient Arabic Order of the Nobles of the Mystic Shrine—better known as the Shriners—which admits only those who are at least thirty-second-degree Masons. Memorable to many for parading in exotic regalia at their various conventions, the Shriners also have a serious purpose: Over the years, they have raised millions of dollars for charity. Similar Mason-related groups that engage in good works include the Mystic Order of Veiled Prophets of the Enchanted Realm and the Tall Cedars of Lebanon. Female relatives of master masons may join the Order of the Eastern Star; boys, the Order of DeMolay and the Order of Builders; and girls, the Order of Job's Daughters and the Order of Rainbow. For the most part, however, such clubs enjoy Masonic favor only in America. English Masons, apparently dubious of the social

clubs' frivolity, can suspend their members for joining such societies.

Whether merely for social contacts or for soul-satisfying enlightenment, Freemasonry for centuries has attracted legendary men of history, heroes and villains alike. Indeed, a 1967 work called *10,000 Famous Freemasons* takes up four volumes of thumbnail biographies. Along with Mozart, the great composers Franz Liszt and Franz Joseph Haydn were Masons. Masons of literary note include Johann Wolfgang Goethe, Alexander Pope, Sir Walter Scott, Robert Burns, Rudyard Kipling, Oscar Wilde, and Mark Twain. A host of American presidents and British kings and princes have belonged to the brotherhood. English prime minister Winston Churchill was a member. So, it is reputed, was the mastermind of the Russian Revolution, Lenin, and Mohammad Reza Pahlavi, shah of Iran. Benedict Arnold was a Mason, but the quality of the craft's American military men improved thereafter: Sam Houston, John J. Pershing, and Douglas MacArthur were among them. Masons in aviation range from Charles Lindbergh to numer-

ous American astronauts. Entrepreneurs of the brotherhood include John Jacob Astor and Henry Ford. Joseph Smith, founder of the Mormons, was a Mason; and it is said that certain secret rituals of Mormonism show the influence of Masonic rites. Doubtless, Masonry's stellar membership over the years was something of a buffer against intolerance directed at it.

A kind of milestone in the acceptance of Freemasonry was reached in 1965, when the Vatican quietly disclosed that Roman Catholics would no longer be excommunicated for joining the organization in the United States or Britain. Thus was put aside a prohibition that began 230 years earlier and had been affirmed by seven popes in sixteen pronouncements. It was at the historic meeting of the Second Vatican Council in the mid-1960s—the same conclave that decided to permit the celebration of Mass in languages other than Latin—that a move to reappraise the Church's position on Freemasonry began. The Vatican continued to ban Masonic membership in Italy, France, and other countries that adhere to the so-called European grand orient lodge form. That system, it said, remains anti-Catholic or atheistic. But the significance of the Church's shift was clear—indeed, it was front-page news. The oldest, fiercest, most

Famed polar explorers Robert Peary (left, en route to the North Pole in 1908), his companion Matthew Henson (right), and Admiral Richard Byrd (center), were welcomed into the brotherhood as exemplars of Masonic virtue.

Astronaut Edwin E. "Buzz" Aldrin carried a banner bearing a Masonic emblem in his pocket when he walked on the moon on July 21, 1969, during the first lunar landing, the Apollo 11 mission.

implacable opponent of Freemasonry had finally relented.

Still, a tattered legacy of ill will lingers here and there and may never entirely disappear. In modern-day Spain, for example, there are those who well recall the persecution of Masons after the dictator Francisco Franco's rise to power in the late 1930s. Franco turned his wrath against the many prominent legislators, intellectuals, and military officers who had been initiated into the lodges under the previous, liberal Republic. A Law for the Repression of Masonry and Communism was quickly enacted and a tribunal was formed specially to judge Masons. "There were hundreds of executions of Masons, and those who could fled abroad and had their property here seized," a Madrid lawyer, Francisco Epinar Lafuente, later recalled. "Franco really believed in the Masonic conspiracy, and the Francoists to this day are attacking us just like in the old days." Not until the late 1970s did Spain drop its prohibition against Masonic membership, and even then the grand master of the order, Jaime Fernandez Gil de Terradillos, felt constrained to insist: "We are not a secret society, but a discreet one."

In Italy, the discovery in 1981 of a spurious Masonic lodge called P-2 brought about the collapse of the government—albeit a not uncommon occurrence in postwar Italy. Headed by a mysterious financier named Licio Gelli, P-2 was found by magistrates and a special parliamentary com-

mission to be the covert headquarters for a cadre of influential politicians, businessmen, and military officers who plotted everything from financial chicanery to a political coup. Within the lodge, Gelli carried the title of Il Venerabile, the venerable one.

The scandal forced a reorganization of the Italian secret services and ruined the careers of dozens of civil servants and politicians. Gelli fled the country but was apprehended and extradited to Rome from Switzerland in February 1988. Among the many urgent questions Italian authorities had for the one-time Mason was what had happened to $1 billion looted from an Italian bank in 1982? "The P-2 was more than a subversive political organization," said Pino Arlacchi, a sociologist at the University of Florence. "The documents collected by the parliamentary commission show it was a kind of full-service international organization influencing everything from arms sales to purchases of crude oil."

Occasional episodes like the P-2 affair provide just enough fuel to keep the fires of anti-Masonry simmering, particularly in predominantly Catholic lands and among those who espouse reactionary politics. During the French presidential election of 1988, the candidate of the far-right National Front, Jean-Marie Le Pen, had no trouble filling a 1,200-seat convention center in Amiens. One of his listeners, a sixty-nine-year-old man in a natty tweed suit, told a reporter he was attending the rally to protest that France was being "run by the Freemasons."

But such mutterings are part of the price Masons must ever pay for the privilege of exclusivity. In the statutes of the Bavarian Illuminati, drafted in 1781, the architects of that super-secret society pledged "to remain clandestine as much as possible, for whatever is hidden and secret has a special attraction for men; it attracts the interest of outsiders and enhances the loyalty of insiders." So it remains with the Freemasons, although much of the interest of outsiders may always take the form of angry suspicion, a surly curiosity about just what is going on within the silent walls of the mysterious lodge.

A Man of  Many Sects

The Wickedest Man in the World was but one of the labels attached to Aleister Crowley; he said that his own mother first called him the Beast, after the Bible's Great Beast of Revelation. He embraced both names; for him, evil was a religious pursuit. The notorious Englishman belonged to several secret sects, was influenced by others, and founded his own. His quest throughout was mind-altering "magick" (Crowley added the "k" to distinguish his magic from mere conjuring), and his ultimate methodology was sex, performed with scores of partners, men as well as women (for whom he held an ineluctable fascination).

In a sense, Crowley was born into a sect, in 1875, and spent his life rejecting it. His father, a Warwickshire brewer, was a member of the Plymouth Brethren, austere Christians whose theology Edward Alexander Crowley hated. He renamed himself, replaced his parents' saints with biblical villains, and avidly sampled carnal pleasures—and perverse delights. For example, to test the adage that a cat has nine lives, he dosed one with arsenic, chloroformed it, hanged it above a gas jet, stabbed it, cut its throat, smashed its skull, burned it, submerged it, and threw it out a window.

Crowley died of heart and lung problems in 1947. He was a heroin addict by then, wheezing out his final days in a boarding-house. But before his decline, few experiences of spirit or flesh eluded him. He climbed mountains, wrote poetry, painted, dipped into Eastern religions—and, more deeply, into drugs. He lived the words that he had made his incantation: Do What Thou Wilt.

A Struggle for Supremacy

The first sect Crowley joined was the Hermetic Order of the Golden Dawn, a secret society founded in England in 1888 to study the occult. It attracted some of the leading intellectuals of the time, including the Irish poet William Butler Yeats. To practice its magic, Crowley rented Boleskine House on Loch Ness in Scotland, named himself the Laird of Boleskine, and set about trying to summon up his guardian angel. Legend has it that Crowley attracted a host of evil spirits instead.

It was Crowley's own personal demons, however, that undid him with the Golden Dawn. He persuaded the order's chief, Samuel Mathers, who was living in Paris, to initiate him into a higher grade of the multitiered sect. The Golden Dawn's London lodge was outraged at this presumption, and fury intensified when Crowley, ostensibly on Mathers's behalf, tried to seize the London headquarters. The order wanted nothing to do with Crowley, Yeats later declared, "because we did not think a mystical society was intended to be a reformatory." In 1900, both Crowley and Mathers were ousted.

In 1911, Crowley joined another cult: the Ordo Templi Orientis, or Order of the Templars of the East, founded in Germany in 1902. The basis of OTO was a belief that sex was the key to man's nature and that orgasm, properly ritualized, could be a supernatural experience. This central secret of the order conformed, coincidentally, to ideas espoused by Crowley in his own writings. Delighted to find like-minded souls, Crowley agreed, in 1912, to be head of the order for Great Britain.

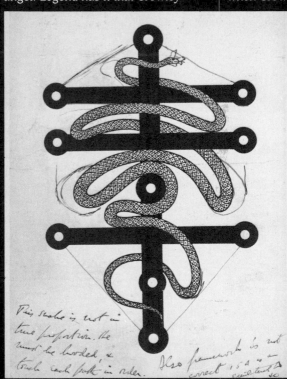

This snake is not in true proportion. He must be hooded & touch each pak in order. Also framework is not correct 15 4 + a equilateral so

The Serpent of Wisdom coils around the Cabalistic Tree of Life in this Crowley drawing. The tree represents the universe, and the serpent's path symbolizes the route to supreme power.

Crowley wears the robe of a Golden Dawn initiate at his 1898 induction. But Frater Perdurabo (Brother I Will Endure, as he was called in the order) was ill-suited to submit to any asceticism, let alone the Golden Dawn's six months of fasting, prayer, meditation, and abstinence from sex. Soon he was at odds with other members.

In a ceremony staged in 1899, Crowley—called Osiris Risen for this affair—folds his arms to formulate the Pentagram, the Golden Dawn's ritual for banishing evil spirits. Doubtless, the Golden Dawn's pomp and pageantry appealed to Crowley's penchant for drama. But the stringent asceticism practiced by some of the order's members was anathema to the world's wickedest man.

Under the new name of Baphomet, Crowley (below) wears the masonic garb of the Ordo Templi Orientis, or OTO, in 1916. Baphomet was alleged to be the androgynous and lusty idol, akin to Pan, of the medieval Knights Templars. Crowley's OTO title was "supreme and holy king of Ireland, Iona, and all the Britains that are in the sanctuary of the gnosis"—the Greek word for knowledge.

Sex and Sacrifices

Banished from the Golden Dawn, Crowley borrowed its rituals and in 1907 set up a splinter group, the Silver Star, or Argentinum Astrum (AA). It was on his travels two years later with an early AA acolyte, a worshipful youth by the name of Victor Neuburg, that Crowley had the revelation that sex could be a means to magic. The event occurred on a mountaintop in Morocco.

In 1920, Crowley took up residence in a rundown farmhouse in Cefalu, Sicily, bringing along with him two mistresses and their three children, one of whom was Crowley's daughter. Crowley called this AA sanctuary the Abbey of Thelema.

Outwardly, a day at the abbey was almost monastic, featuring much ritual chanting and ceremony. But sex, enhanced by a cornucopia of drugs, dominated the scene.

New disciples soon joined the party. They included an American actress, Jane Wolfe, about whom Crowley had fantasized wildly. But when she proved to be a tough-looking woman about his own age, he exiled her for a month to a tent located near the farmhouse. (Perhaps she was not too put off by the move; she found the farmhouse squalid and referred to one of Crowley's mistresses as "filth personified.")

In late 1922, Crowley received two more visitors, Raoul Loveday and his wife, Betty May, an artist's model. Betty May, who had seen a bit of the world, was appalled by the Crowley ménage. But the ingenuous Loveday became the Beast's devoted disciple. Already in fragile health, possibly from dysentery and hepatitis, Loveday collapsed and died shortly after a ceremony in which a cat had been sacrificed and its blood drunk. In the ensuing scandal, amid rumors that human infants as well as animals had been killed, the Italian government moved to expell Crowley from Sicily.

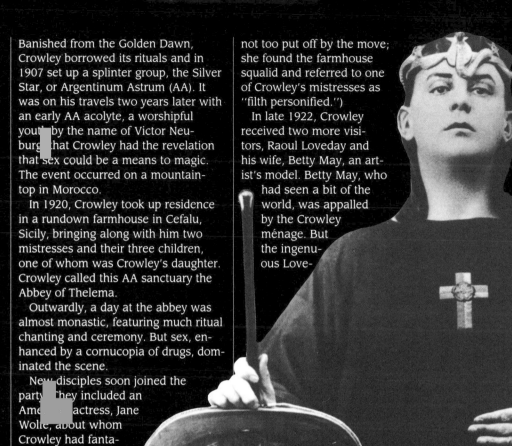

Wearing the Egyptian serpent crown, Aleister Crowley poses with several ritualistic artifacts— bell, sword, cup, holy oil, his Book of the Law, and a tablet that is known as the Stele of Revealing.

The death of Raoul Loveday (right) at the abbey caused a furor in Britain after his widow, Betty May (above), provided a London tabloid with details of "drugs, magic, and vile practices."

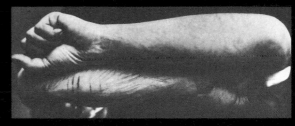

The razor-slashed arms of acolyte Victor Neuburg attest to the punishment that Crowley forced followers to inflict on themselves for using the pronoun I. The grammatical prohibition, designed to destroy all sense of self, was imposed on all members of the AA.

Crowley (standing, right) conducts the ceremony of Saturn, a segment of the Rites of Eleusis, in London's Caxton Hall in 1910. No relation to ancient Greece's Eleusinian mysteries, the Rites of Eleusis were like medieval morality plays, but inverted; they exalted the Antichrist. Promising ecstasy for the price of a ticket, Crowley scheduled the rites for seven consecutive Wednesdays, one rite for each of the seven known planets. While Victor Neuburg danced and Leila Waddell, one of Crowley's mistresses, played the violin, Crowley read his poetry. The show received mixed reviews.

Loves of the Beast

Crowley had an insatiable need for women, and women—to their misfortune—seemed to need him. His contempt for them was total: He said they ought to be a convenience brought " 'round to the back door, like milk." But he had two wives, scores of mistresses, and countless encounters with prostitutes.

Crowley called each of his female partners a Scarlet Woman, after the Biblical consort who coupled with the Great Beast. The first was Rose Kelly, the sister of a distinguished English artist. Crowley married her in 1903. When they met, Rose was a flirtatious young widow, engaged to two men and loath to marry either. Crowley offered to rescue her with a marriage of convenience. Within a few days, however, the pair were in love.

For Rose the magic soon faded. Their first child died of typhus in 1906 during a trip through Asia. A second child was born in 1907. By then, according to Crowley, Rose was drinking at least a bottle of whiskey a day. The couple divorced in 1909—the year Crowley had his mountaintop revelation linking sex and magic— and two years later Rose entered an asylum.

The same fate was met by his second wife, a flamboyant Nicaraguan named Maria de Miramar. At least one more mistress was institutionalized, and others committed suicide or drank themselves to death after parting company with Crowley.

The most resilient of Crowley's women was Leah Hirsig, a school-teacher the Beast met in New York in 1918. She followed him to Paris and then to the Abbey of Thelema, where they set up housekeeping with Ninette Shumway, an acquaintance of Leah's. Shumway was a nanny for their daughter, Poupée, and was named by her employer as his Second Concubine. The threesome did not work out well. Ninette fought Leah for Crowley's favor, Poupée died, and Leah miscarried. Even so, Leah kept a grip on both her sanity and her lover, matching Crowley drug for drug, deed for perverse deed. Ejected with him from Thelema, Leah shared Crowley's exile, tolerating his new mistresses. In 1925, however, Crowley finally ran off with another woman. He and Leah still corresponded for a time, but in 1930, Leah renounced her role as Scarlet Woman and returned to America and schoolteaching. She died in 1951, surviving Crowley by four years.

Even in middle age, bald and bloated, the Beast continued to attract Scarlet Women. On a London street in 1934, a nineteen-year-old girl rushed up to him and declared that she wanted to have his baby. Crowley took her to bed. She, too, later entered an asylum.

Sister Cybele, Crowley's mistress and otherwise known as Leila Waddell, was an early member of the Argentinum Astrum. Here she displays the mark of the Beast between her breasts. Crowley's female disciples were painted or branded with the mark.

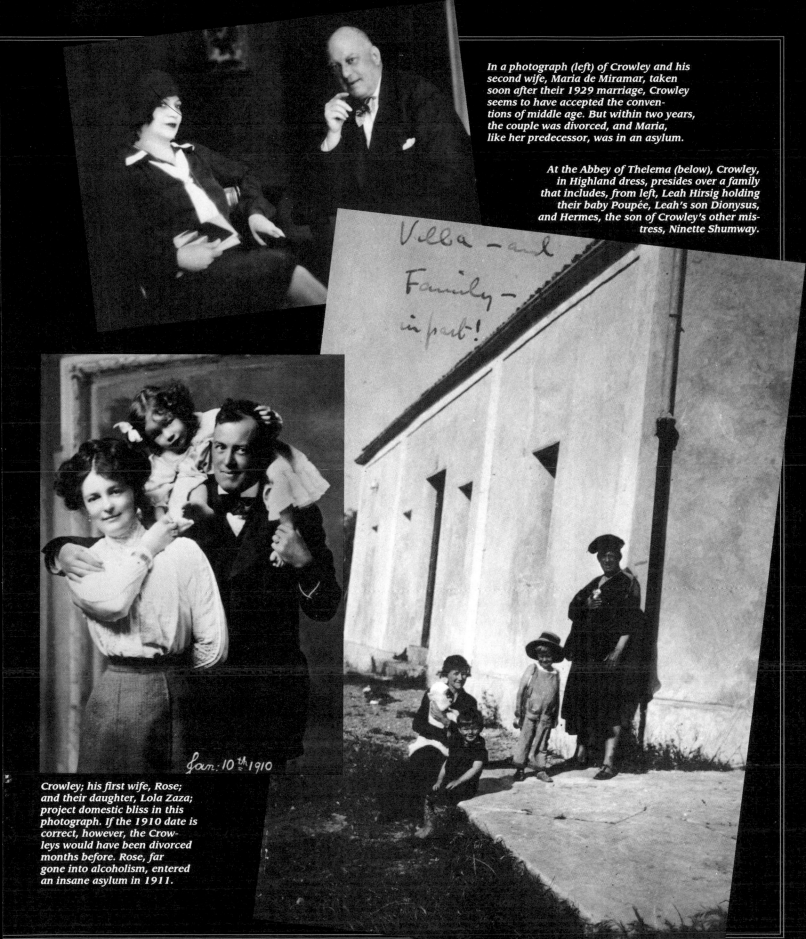

In a photograph (left) of Crowley and his second wife, Maria de Miramar, taken soon after their 1929 marriage, Crowley seems to have accepted the conventions of middle age. But within two years, the couple was divorced, and Maria, like her predecessor, was in an asylum.

At the Abbey of Thelema (below), Crowley, in Highland dress, presides over a family that includes, from left, Leah Hirsig holding their baby Poupée, Leah's son Dionysus, and Hermes, the son of Crowley's other mistress, Ninette Shumway.

Villa – and Family – in part!

Jan: 10th 1910

Crowley; his first wife, Rose; and their daughter, Lola Zaza; project domestic bliss in this photograph. If the 1910 date is correct, however, the Crowleys would have been divorced months before. Rose, far gone into alcoholism, entered an insane asylum in 1911.

A Case of Wanderlust

Crowley was an inveterate seeker who wandered far from post-Victorian England. Egypt and the Orient were especially important in his quest for the magical merger of body and spirit.

Honeymooning in Cairo in 1904, Crowley and his bride were walking outside the National Museum when Rose suddenly began mumbling confusedly about the ancient Egyptian god Horus. She led her husband into the museum to an antique tablet that bore the god's image. As it happened, the tablet's exhibit number was 666, the number the Bible ascribes to the Beast. Crowley took this happenstance to be prophetic of his special fate, a notion bolstered over the next month by the purported first appearance of Aiwas, his guardian angel. By

Crowley's account, it was then that Aiwas began dictating the Book of the Law, containing the sacred injunction, Do What Thou Wilt. The angel also enjoined his mortal charge to "take wine and strange drugs"—advice the Beast chose to follow enthusiastically to a bad end.

Crowley returned to England, but not for long. The next year, he went east again, to the Himalayas to climb the world's third-highest mountain, Kangchenjunga. It was a disastrous expedition. A fellow mountaineer later said that Crowley, who insisted on leading the trek, took impossible approaches and treated the porters brutally. For instance, he expected them to walk barefoot over ice. They deserted in droves, and several disenchanted climbers took some of the remaining porters and headed back to camp. When six of the party fell down a slope in an accident, Crowley refused to go to their rescue. Four died. Crowley then deserted the expedition himself and absconded with the money that had been earmarked to pay its bills.

For Crowley, who outraged every standard of civilized behavior, it was the start of complete social ostracism at home. No matter. Home was never where he wanted to be.

Costumed as the Beast of Revelation, Crowley hails a sunrise, possibly in Tunisia, where he fled after eviction from Thelema.

Chameleon-like, Crowley assumes the form of Fo-hi, the Chinese god of joy and laughter. Crowley believed that there was something Oriental about his appearance and wrote that he felt an instant affinity for certain philosophies and occult systems of ancient China.

Crowley sits astride a horse on the Deosai Plateau in the Himalayas in 1905, the year he led the ill-fated expedition to Kangchenjunga. There were allegations afterward that he had not only misused the porters, but had even eaten one or two. Cannibalism was a charge not even Crowley's sworn enemies believed, but the rumor persisted for years.

Allan Bennett (above), one of the few members of the Golden Dawn to befriend Crowley, shared his London apartment for a time and instructed him in magic. Although the abstemious Bennett was Crowley's opposite in temperament, their friendship continued across years and continents. When Bennett went to the East to become a Buddhist monk, Crowley followed and learned yoga from him. Crowley, shown at right in yoga positions, believed that the discipline could "produce genius at will."

The Magician's Art

Never a victim of self-doubt, Crowley believed that he was a genius in the arts as well as in sexual magick. As a painter, he compared himself with the great French artist Paul Gauguin. As for his poetry, he noted in his autobiographical *Confessions* the remarkable coincidence that his native county in England produced the nation's "two greatest poets—for one must not forget Shakespeare."

Yeats, who abhorred Crowley, thought he may have written no more than one or two lines of real poetry. More neutral critics characterized his work as second-rate. In any event, Crowley was prolific, producing a torrent of poetry about magic, sex, and the devil, as well as several hardcore pornographic works with such names as *White Stains* and *Snowdrops from a Curate's Garden.*

In 1922, he published a thinly veiled semiautobiographical novel, *The Diary of a Drug Fiend,* in which an ex-airman named Sir Peter Pendragon is rescued from heroin addiction by a Mr. King Lamus, who lives in an Abbey of Thelema. Crowley borrowed the name King Lamus from a Homeric character, the ruler of a tribe of cannibal giants.

In later years, Crowley turned from poetry to painting, covering the abbey's walls with demonic and pornographic drawings. Crowley himself was one of his favorite subjects. He admitted that he lacked "mechanical precision," but his paintings had a primitive power and a strong sense of color. "His pictures are interesting solely through their revelations of a complex soul haunted by a multitude of fantastic visions," said a critic at a show of Crowley's work in Berlin in 1930. The show may have received extra attention because of Crowley's disappearance months before. Earlier that year, to annoy a quarrelsome mistress, Crowley had faked suicide, leaving a note under a cigarette case at the edge of a steep cliff. He resurfaced at the art gallery.

In fact, Crowley's greatest contribution to the arts was second-hand. He was the model for the title character in *The Magician* by W. Somerset Maugham, a contemporary. More recently, some rock musicians have embraced Crowley, perhaps for his Do What Thou Wilt message or his use of drugs. Among the faces on the jacket of the Beatles' "Sergeant Pepper's Lonely Hearts Club Band" album is the Beast's.

A self-portrait of Crowley as the Great Beast depicts the forelock that he styled as a phallus. Crowley also filed his teeth to points, vampire fashion, and sometimes sank them into the wrists of women when he met them.

Guardian of the Waste Land, a pen-and-ink sketch of what Crowley called an "astral" landscape, reflects his fascination with the East. Among the many titles that Crowley chose to bestow on himself was Wanderer of the Waste.

The Island of Magicians, a watercolor painted by Crowley in 1921 at Thelema, demonstrates his strong sense of color as well as his mediocre technique. The symbolism was meant to be intuitively appreciated, but one emblem is obvious: The blue sun has Crowley's own features.

CHAPTER 4

Sacred Masters and Secret Chiefs

uring the stifling summer of 1874, a forty-two-year-old New York lawyer and freelance journalist named Henry Steel Olcott wangled a newspaper assignment on a subject of abiding interest to him—Spiritualism. He traveled to Chittenden, Vermont, to cover a lengthy series of séances that were luring believers and the curious to the farm of a surly bumpkin, William Eddy. As matters turned out, Eddy's nightly performances produced only a shopworn batch of spirits—American Indians, drowned sailors, Civil War soldiers, small children, and other séance staples of the day.

Life on the farm was, therefore, considerably enlivened one warm October day by the arrival of a woman whose unusual appearance prompted Olcott to whisper to a companion: "Good gracious! Look at that specimen, will you." Arrayed in a costume that featured a scarlet shirt in the fashion of Giuseppe Garibaldi's Italian revolutionaries, the new guest was an outsize female (she weighed 224 pounds) with, as Olcott wrote later, a massive Mongol-like face and short, crinkly blonde hair "like the fleece of a Cotswold ewe." After lunch, Olcott followed the woman outside and watched as she rolled her own cigarette. Thereupon the lawyer-journalist, who fancied himself a man of the world, whipped out a light and said in his most gallant French, "Permettez-moi." So, in a conjunction fraught with significance for the future of occult science and philosophy, Henry Steel Olcott met the astounding Helena Petrovna Blavatsky, a Ukrainian-born eccentric who would change the direction of his life and the lives of many others—not only in that era but in ours as well.

To use Olcott's word for it, he and Madame Blavatsky quickly became "chums." Each of them, he explained, "felt as if we were of the same social world, cosmopolitans, free-thinkers." The bond was strengthened after they returned to New York, when Olcott received a letter in gold ink on green paper, signed by the grand master of something called the Brotherhood of Luxor. "Sister Helen," the grand master told him, "will lead thee to the Golden Gate of truth." Olcott apparently needed little convincing. Estranged from his wife, he took to paying Blavatsky's rent, and within a year, he had set up housekeeping with HPB, as she liked to be called, in a modest Manhattan apartment. There she presided over a Sunday evening salon of earnest Spiritualists, Cabalists, Masons, Rosicrucians, and other occult-minded guests. During one of these sessions, on the night of September 7, 1875, Olcott conceived an idea that would forever link his name to that of Helena Petrovna Blavatsky.

After hearing a lecture on "The Lost Canon of Proportion of the Egyptians," he scribbled onto a scrap of paper the fateful question, "Would it not be a good thing to form a Society for this kind of study?" The note was passed to HPB, who signified her agreement. Next evening, with sixteen people present, a resolution to that effect was adopted. After a few subsequent meetings, Olcott was named president of the new society, and Blavatsky was elected secretary. Despite her modest title, HPB was, then and for the rest of her life, the charismatic leader of the organization.

Next began the quest for a suitable name. Olcott later recalled that several were suggested; among them were the Egyptological Society, the Hermetic Society, and the Rosicrucian Society, but "none seemed just the thing." Finally, someone decided to turn to a

dictionary and came up with the word *theosophy,* meaning "divine wisdom" or "knowledge of God" and suggesting both an esoteric aura and a scientific system of probing occult truths. That was it. The Theosophical Society it would be, and its avowed purposes were to "form the nucleus of a Universal Brotherhood of Humanity," to study ancient and modern religions, philosophies, and sciences, and to investigate "the unexplained laws of Nature and the psychical powers latent in man."

It can fairly be argued that these events, although they occurred more than a century ago, marked the dawn of what nowadays is called the New Age—and are testimony to the fact that the New Age is not actually as new as is sometimes supposed. For the Theosophical Society was to become in effect a great cultural funnel through which much of the occult wisdom of the ancients and of the East was collected and passed on to twentieth-century Western civilization. More than any other single entity, the society was responsible for discovering and reviving interest in the mystic arts and beliefs that later were taken up by adherents of the New Age, ranging from astral travel to Zen and encompassing astrology, reincarnation, karma, gurus and swamies, transcendental meditation, vegetarianism, and a general attitude of acceptance of the supernatural.

Although the Theosophical Society was the major agent in this movement, its franchise was not exclusive. Other like-minded groups and individuals, many of them inspired by the Theosophists, took up the same work in the late nineteenth century. Most memorable among these was a secret sect known as the Order of the Golden Dawn, a small band of occultists who sought more than a theoretical familiarity with the ancient arts: They were dedicated to the actual practice of applied magic. Considered together, the histories of the Theosophical Society and the Golden Dawn represent a remarkable development in Western life, the rise of a significant subculture that embraced old mysteries and rejected the strictures of rationality just when the Age of Reason was reaching its apogee.

For almost two centuries, rationalism had dominated the intellectual culture of Europe and America. The industrial and scientific revolutions had brought about the victory

Russian-born Helena Petrovna Blavatsky (left)—or HPB, as she liked to be called, was a charismatic, madcap mystic who found new directions for her lifelong occult enthusiasms when she met Colonel Henry S. Olcott (above) in 1874. Olcott, a Civil War veteran, lawyer, journalist, and psychic investigator, became Blavatsky's devoted disciple. Together they set out to explore the ancient mysteries of the world and to that end founded, in 1875, the Theosophical Society.

of the material over the spiritual, of reason over superstition. With the 1859 publication of Charles Darwin's *Origin of Species,* science seemed to seize preeminence over conventional religion. Truth was to be found in a test tube; humankind's descent from lower mammals was held to be more rational than creation in the divine image; and spiritual speculation gave way to what one early Theosophist called "dense materialism, which cannot conceive of consciousness as anything but a function of flesh and blood." Worst to contemplate, scientific materialism carried to its logical conclusion seemed to allow no escape from the irrevocable finality of the grave. Such gloomy spiritual pessimism provoked a widespread reaction, described by the Irish poet William Butler Yeats—who was himself a member of both the Theosophical Society and the Golden Dawn—as "the revolt of the soul against the intellect."

Theosophists and the magicians of the Golden Dawn played leading roles in this cultural rebellion, which in both its style and substance can be recognized as the antecedent of the upheaval in America and Europe during the 1960s. Participants became fascinated by the religions and mysticism of the East, for instance.

And, as in the 1960s, many artists were caught up in the movement. In fact, theosophy has been credited as a factor in the late nineteenth-century renaissance of Irish literature because Irish writers such as Yeats, George Russell (better known as AE), Charles Johnston, Charles Weekes, and John Eglinton found inspiration in its teachings. An entire group of painters based its work on occult images *(see pages 157-169).* French composer Erik Satie, whose measured, haunting melodies are still loved today, drew inspiration from study of the Cabala. Oscar Wilde's *The Picture of Dorian Gray* demonstrated his preoccupation with magic, and his wife was an initiate of the Golden Dawn.

Some occult-minded bohe-

This pencil sketch of the supposed path to enlightenment was made by Madame Blavatsky in 1874. She purportedly completed it in a darkened room in less than thirty minutes. The picture shows a pilgrim beginning the spiritual journey in the boat of life, guided by a figure representing the higher self. Trials, symbolized by the lion, stag, and peacocks, are met and overcome. The trek ends with the illuminated self, bearing the torch of enlightenment and the lute of peace, driving the chariot of service out into the world.

mians—like their hippie heirs seventy or eighty years later—believed drugs helped them to probe the esoteric depths. They smoked opium and hashish (the resin of the marijuana plant) and sometimes ate the latter mixed with a portion of jam. Hashish, noted one writer-magician, "always encourages, and sometimes provokes spontaneously, the projection of the astral body." Madame Blavatsky smoked the drug throughout her adult life.

 nd occultists frequently widened the arena of their rebellious interests to include politics. The so-called Celtic Revival, which led eventually to formation of the independent Republic of Ireland and the rise of Scottish nationalism, depended in the early days on writers, Yeats among them, who gave shape and credence to the idea of an Irish nation or a Scottish nation. These spinners of national myth reached deep into Celtic folklore and came up with occult elements—witchcraft and fairies and secret Druidic wisdom—that distinguished their peoples and gave political leaders traditions to build on. Some students of the occult took up other nations' political causes: Annie Besant, a leader of the Theosophical Society, became a key figure in India's drive for freedom from British rule.

Occultists were also thoroughly involved in a welter of quasi-political and idealistic movements of the era. They were active in the socialist Fabian Society, in organizations of ardent vegetarians, and in various humane associations dedicated to preventing cruelty to animals. One noted Theosophist and antivivisectionist, Anna Kingsford, fervently believed that she had successfully employed magic—learned from a leader of the Golden Dawn—to kill by remote control, so to speak, two scientists who experimented on animals. She tried to use the same techniques to kill Louis Pasteur, whose animal experiments figured in the invention of vaccination, but said she only made him ill.

Perhaps her claims did not sound as outrageous then as now. It was, after all, a time when a respected industrial chemist (a man named George Cecil Jones) could also be known as one of London's foremost alchemists. Such was

the milieu that Henry Olcott and Helena Blavatsky's Theosophical Society helped to create, and in which it flourished.

Madame Blavatsky was a wildly contradictory character. A quasi-religious leader, she swore like a sea cook in three languages. She was a volatile adventurer who extolled the virtues of a tranquil, contemplative life. Most of all, she was a tireless—and perhaps sincere—pursuer of ultimate truth, although she sometimes utterly disregarded ordinary truths, especially when they pertained to her. Although the actual facts of her life were far stranger than most fiction, she felt obliged to embroider them with fantastical threads that became inextricably mixed up with Theosophical thought—to the considerable confusion of followers and critics alike.

She was born in the Ukraine on July 31, 1831, to an army officer and his wife, a popular novelist. Little Helena was precocious in peculiar ways. She later claimed that from the time she was four years old, she "could make furniture move and objects fly apparently, and my astral arms that supported them remained invisible." She also had a distressing habit of gazing fixedly into the faces of visitors, then gravely predicting when and where they would die. And she enraptured other children with wonderfully fanciful stories. As a sister recalled, Helena could spin the "most incredible" tales with the "cool assurance and conviction of an eye-witness."

Shortly before her seventeenth birthday, Helena was married off to a forty-year-old czarist general and provincial vice-governor, Nikifor Blavatsky. He would contribute to HPB only the name she retained for the rest of her life, for she soon found him tiresome and, after three months of marriage, left him and made her way to Constantinople.

At this point, the facts grow somewhat fuzzy. By Blavatsky's own account, which was frequently amended, her wanderings carried her to the Orient, central Asia, and India, to Africa and throughout Europe, to the United States and Canada, to Central and South America. During those journeys, she said, she was initiated into the Druzes, a Middle Eastern Muslim sect; studied dervish rituals; attended secret Voodoo rites; probed the magic of Japan's mountain-worshiping Yamabushi sect; rummaged through ancient Mayan ruins on the Yucatán Peninsula; spent three nights in the Great Pyramid of Cheops; acquired a fortune by trading in Sudanese ostrich feathers; and trekked in a covered wagon across the American Rockies.

Yet of all Madame Blavatsky's recounted travels and travails, none could match in its profound meaning, both for her and for the Theosphical movement, the seven years she said she spent in a hidden Himalayan valley in Tibet, where resided a community of avatars, supersages who had selflessly delayed their own entry into nirvana in order to remain on earth and assist humankind. These Mahatmas, or Masters, were to play a crucial part in the development of Theosophy, instructing Helena Blavatsky in the ancient wisdom that unmasked the mysteries of the universe.

It seems possible, however, that virtually none of those tales of travel and adventure was true. In particular, there is no proof whatever that she ever set foot in Tibet and a good deal of evidence that she did not. Not only did its terrain and climate place it among the most inaccessible of the world's lands, but Tibet's borders had been legally closed to all foreigners since 1792. Beyond that, even Blavatsky's most ardent admirers have had a difficult time in trying to fit the seven-year period of her Tibetan sojourn into her busy itinerary.

Yet Blavatsky's real life was hardly less venturesome than the one she invented (although it is still difficult to make out fact from fiction). From Constantinople she made her way to Egypt, where she was introduced to the mind-altering effects of hashish, took a course in snake charming, and consulted with a Coptic magician (who disappointed her by saying, "I have no doubt you are here in search of knowledge—of occult and magical lore; I look for coin").

HPB next moved to London and from there traveled the international opera circuit with a middle-aged Hungarian singer, who claimed to have married her. By some accounts she was married three, or possibly four, times, without ever having divorced her first husband, and gave birth to at least one child, an unfortunate hunchback named Yuri, who died in childhood. Madame Blavatsky insisted that Yuri had been adopted, and at age fifty-four, she would declare with a straight face that she was still a virgin.

Like a genie that refuses to stay bottled, she kept popping up from place to place—in Tiflis as the manager of an artificial-flower factory, elsewhere in Russia as a spiritualist medium who caused a brief stir, and in England as an assistant to the celebrated medium Daniel Dunglas Home.

By 1871, Blavatsky was back in Cairo, where, she said, she received advanced training in occultism from the Brotherhood of Luxor, an Egyptian order so ancient and so mysterious that nobody else ever heard of it. She also founded a Société Spirite, which failed to attract a following, and set herself up as a medium—an enterprise that foundered when clients discovered on the premises a long glove that had been stuffed with cotton, apparently for use as a disembodied hand. In the fuss that followed, HPB left in some haste for Europe. There, in Paris on a July day in 1873, she received word from her mystic Masters, as she told the story later, that she should immediately set sail for the United States. The next day, she took steerage passage for New York and her Theosophical destiny with Olcott.

hroughout their years together, Olcott insisted that the relationship was one "of soul to soul, not that of sex to sex." Whatever the degree of intimacy, life in the Olcott-Blavatsky household was seldom dull. The two were a study in opposites—the rambunctious HPB, with all her bohemian ways, and the gentle Henry, product of a pious Presbyterian upbringing, a former colonel (he still liked to be called by his rank) who had served respectably, if not gloriously, as a Civil War staff officer. Helena hectored him constantly, embarrassing guests by berating him as an "idiot," a "blockhead," and a "psychologized baby." But Henry took it all in quiet stride. As a frequent visitor recalled, Olcott "was crazy as a loon on anything relating to Blavatskyism, though perfectly sane on every other subject." Since Helena was obviously hopeless as a cook

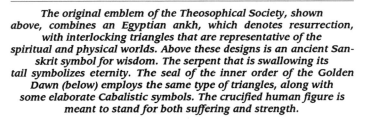

(as Henry quickly realized after seeing her attempt to boil an egg by placing it on live coals), Olcott took over all of their culinary chores.

Still, there were compensations. Whenever she felt in a congenial humor, Helena could delight Henry with "an imperious gesture" of her hand—whereupon "*ping! ping!* would come, in the air whither she pointed, the silvery tone of a bell." And then there was the memorable night when Olcott expressed a yearning for some juicy grapes. Well then, replied Helena, "let us have some." At her request, the gaslight was briefly extinguished, then relighted. "To my amazement," Olcott later wrote, "there hung . . . two large bunches of ripe black Hamburgh grapes, which we proceeded to eat."

Whatever Olcott's competence in the kitchen, or HPB's legerdemain in other arenas, the real cement of their relationship was their shared interest in the Theosophical Society. Sadly, the society had its problems getting off the ground. It had begun in a burst of occult enthusiasm, but it soon seemed to languish, and Madame Blavatsky's mood did not help. She seemed sullen and preoccupied, declining to attend society meetings, distressing her followers by her refusal "to do the slightest phenomenon." Clearly, something was preoccupying her, but not even Olcott, who at this point

had not yet moved in with her, could figure out what was troubling her. Then one day Blavatsky showed him some sheets of manuscript, accompanied by the perplexed comment "I wrote this last night 'by order,' but what the deuce it is to be I don't know." In that strange fashion began the writing of Helena Blavatsky's *Isis Unveiled,* which in time would become a classic of occult literature.

The "order" that had put HPB's pen to paper was of mysterious origin. As its title indicated, *Isis Unveiled* at first looked to Egypt as the chief source of ancient enlightenment; and Isis, the Egyptian fertility goddess, was apparently the book's guiding spirit, often appearing before the author's very eyes—or so HPB alleged. As the work progressed, however, the focus shifted sharply to India; Isis receded into the dimness of time, and to the fore as the book's presiding genius came the Mahatmas who dwelled in their Himalayan retreat.

The typical method of transmission was by a powerful force that Blavatsky called astral light. Although Henry Olcott could not himself see the astral light, he would long remember how HPB used it: "Her pen would be flying over the page, when she would suddenly stop, look out into space . . . and begin copying on her paper what she saw." Sometimes, however, a Ma-

The original emblem of the Theosophical Society, shown above, combines an Egyptian ankh, which denotes resurrection, with interlocking triangles that are representative of the spiritual and physical worlds. Above these designs is an ancient Sanskrit symbol for wisdom. The serpent that is swallowing its tail symbolizes eternity. The seal of the inner order of the Golden Dawn (below) employs the same type of triangles, along with some elaborate Cabalistic symbols. The crucified human figure is meant to stand for both suffering and strength.

hatma would take over the actual writing chores. Olcott distinctly recalled a night when Madame Blavatsky had worked so late that she fell sound asleep in her chair. Next morning, "she showed me a pile of at least thirty or forty pages of beautifully written HPB manuscript, which, she said, had been written for her by—well, a Master." Olcott also noticed that the styles of handwriting in the manuscript varied a great deal, apparently according to which Master was in charge at the time.

Published in 1877 in two sprawling volumes that totaled almost 1,300 pages and were priced at a stiff $7.50, the 1,000-copy first edition of *Isis Unveiled* sold out in a mere ten days. Within the next year, two more printings were gobbled up by an audience clearly yearning for a cosmic vision that looked beyond the religious and scientific orthodoxy of the day. Inevitably, *Isis* attracted some criticism: One newspaper denounced it as "a large dish of hash," another dismissed it as "discarded rubbish," and the *New York Times* dealt it an even unkinder cut by refusing to review it at all.

More worrisome than critical displeasure were the charges of plagiarism that would plague Madame Blavatsky for the rest of her life and would continue after her death. Foremost among the accusers was William Emmette Coleman, a Spiritualist-minded scholar who spent three years in his study of *Isis Unveiled* and came up with about 2,000 instances in which HPB had neglected to credit passages that had been lifted verbatim from other writers attached to Cabalistic, Hermetic, Masonic, and especially Rosicrucian societies. Eventually, even Colonel Olcott would admit that his friend had perhaps sinned against accepted literary practices, but he hastened to note that she had merely copied down what she had seen in the astral light.

Even so, the critical carpings and the ethical condemnations were somehow wide of the mark. Clownish though the author of *Isis Unveiled* may sometimes have seemed, her book was seriously intended to be seriously read by truth seekers of serious mind. In its essence, *Isis* postulated that all of humanity's multifarious faiths and divergent philosophies had originated in a single source, an ancient, secret doctrine that was "the alpha and omega of universal science." Only through knowledge of that occult wisdom could science and religion be reconciled, and only through understanding could there come a world in which there would be "no sectarian beliefs . . . Brahmanism and Buddhism, Christianity and Mohametanism will all disappear before the mighty rush of *facts.*"

 he secret doctrine was in the hands of the adepts of the Tibetan brotherhood. The Masters were not divine, but as living men they had supposedly achieved such an advanced state of being that they were no longer encumbered by normal human processes: When traveling—and they were by no means recluses—their astral selves could leave their physical bodies, then materialize when and where they wished. Similarly, although they frequently used the regular mails or employed Madame Blavatsky as a courier, they could also communicate by astral light.

Aside from its strong thrust toward the East, *Isis Unveiled* displayed a definite antipathy toward the Christian church and its clergy. In the preface to the second volume, HPB informed her readers that the book "contains not one word against the pure teachings of Jesus, but unsparingly denounces their debasement into pernicious ecclesiastical systems." Yet she consistently downgraded Christ, both in and out of *Isis,* by placing him at a lower level than Buddha in the hierarchy of the Mahatmas. And once, when asked about her views as to Jesus' nature, HPB airily replied, "I have not the honor of the gentleman's acquaintance." By such irreverent attitudes, she needlessly acquired an institutional enemy that would one day do her harm.

Despite such distractions, *Isis* was largely an argument for the existence of the secret doctrine. As such, it offered little of what would later become the sum and substance of Theosophist thought. Theosophy as a creed was as yet unformed. The clay was still in the hands of the sculptress, who would tirelessly mold it until it emerged a decade later in the pages of another monumental book as an intricate, integrated doctrine of religious, philosophical, and scientific belief.

While writing *Isis*, HPB became obsessed with India, and now she was afire to transfer her Theosophical operations to the subcontinent. The sagging fortunes of the Theosophical Society were looking up. Presumably thanks to the success of *Isis Unveiled*, such luminaries as Thomas Alva Edison and General Abner Doubleday, the Civil War veteran who earned more renown for his supposed invention of baseball than for his military prowess, had recently signed up for membership. Lodges had been established in London and Bombay, and plans were under way for a chapter in Japan. Still, there were certain inducements aside from India's siren song that may have prompted HPB to decamp at this point. There was increasingly nasty talk of her being a bigamist, for one thing. Moreover, her occult acumen suffered unfavorable reviews at the hands of D. D. Home, who was far and away the most influential medium of his time. Personally and professionally, strategic retreat seemed in order; and, temporarily leaving the affairs of the New York group in the hands of Abner Doubleday, Olcott and Blavatsky set off for India on December 18, 1878.

They fared well in their newly adopted homeland. Unlike most Westerners, and especially unlike the subcontinent's British overseers, the two Theosophists seemed genuinely interested in Indians and Indian culture. They established themselves in Bombay's native quarter and mixed freely with Indians of low caste and high.

Perhaps because of the relative proximity of the Mahatmas' Himalayan stronghold, Blavatsky's concept of them underwent a transmigratory change. In *Isis Unveiled*, HPB had sniffed at the idea of reincarnation as "the teratological phenomenon of a two-headed infant." In India, however, where reincarnation was widely accepted, it made sense to explain the Masters' extraordinary powers as resulting from their countless incarnations—and reincarnation became a basic Theosophical tenet.

Beyond that, the Mahatmas who dealt most closely with Madame Blavatsky began to acquire their own distinct personalities. Master Morya was an old friend; HPB said she had first met him in England back in the early 1850s, when he was already 125 years old. An imperious member of India's warrior caste, Morya was a stern, forbidding fellow whose letters sometimes got downright rude (the occasions for such missives generally coincided with HPB's moments of pique). Of much more felicitous disposition was Master Koot Hoomi, scion of a family of Kashmiri Brahmans. Koot Hoomi had spent enough of his youth in Europe to have acquired fond recollections of Munich's famous beer halls.

Many of HPB's new Indian disciples accepted the corporeal existence of the Mahatmas without quibble. One especially ardent student named Ramaswamier was determined to see with his own eyes a Master in the flesh and therefore followed Blavatsky one day when he thought she was setting out for the Himalayas. He soon lost her trail but proceeded alone and on foot into the wilds of Sikkim, bound for Tibet. Ramaswamier encountered a leopard and then a wild cat. Fortunately, since he was armed with nothing but an umbrella, neither took an interest in him. On the second day of his trek, Ramaswamier was approached by a horseman he at first thought to be a Sikkimese official. "But . . . I looked up at and recognised him instantly . . . I was in the awful presence of him, of the same Mahatma, my own, revered *guru* whom I had seen before in his astral body on the balcony of the Theosophical headquarters . . . I knew not what to say: joy and reverence tied my tongue." Ramaswamier's account was given wide circulation by a Theosophical journal.

Meanwhile, Henry Olcott was gradually immersing himself in India's native ways. In time, he grew a beard that would have graced any Sikh, took to wearing sandals and Indian-style robes, and became a Buddhist—a conversion that was in no way incompatible with Theosophy, which recognized the validity of all religions. He also labored mightily for the Theosophical Society: In a single year, he calculated, he journeyed some 7,000 miles, set up forty-three new Theosophical lodges, and gained thousands of recruits. He and HPB began to drift apart, both physically, because of his travels, and philosophically, because Olcott wished to subordinate Theosophy's occult aspects to social reform and the idea of universal brotherhood.

HPB was having none of that: Occultism was her nectar and ambrosia, and she relentlessly wooed influential disciples to her cause. Chief among them was Alfred Percy Sinnett, editor of the *Pioneer,* a daily newspaper that was the powerful voice of the British

Empire in India. As it happened, Sinnett had a raging thirst for occult phenomena, and no sooner had HPB met him than she started trotting out her tricks. At first they amounted to nothing more miraculous than some sleight of hand with handkerchiefs, traditional table rappings, and a revival of the unseen bells that went *ping, ping.*

Sinnett was unsatisfied but intrigued. He had heard of HPB's famed Mahatmas, and he wanted positive proof of their existence. Thus he invited her for a lengthy stay at his home in the town of Allahabad. During her stay, HPB tried

Described by Madame Blavatsky as benign immortals living in the Himalayas, these two Mahatmas, or Masters, supposedly guided her mystic quests. Morya (right), whom HPB described as the older and more authoritative one, allegedly showed himself to her in London in 1851. And she claimed that Koot Hoomi (left) came to her in a dream in 1870. So that her fellow Theosophists might also view her mentors, HPB commissioned Hermann Schmiechen in 1884 to paint them from her descriptions.

to give Sinnett the evidence he wanted. She showered him with letters—in some cases, literally—from Koot Hoomi and, to a lesser extent, Master Morya. Sometimes the letters were found on Sinnett's pillow, sometimes they appeared on his breakfast table, and sometimes, during his visits to Theosophical Society headquarters, they fluttered down from the ceiling itself.

 innett was convinced—so completely convinced, in fact, that in 1881 he wrote a book extolling the doctrine, one that stirred English interest in Theosophy. Sinnett's enthusiastic labors in his occult cause embarrassed the *Pioneer*'s conservative British owners, who sacked him. In 1883, Alfred Percy Sinnett returned to London, where, by now, Theosophy was all the rage; and in 1884, Helena Blavatsky and Henry Olcott determined to ride the crest of the wave by visiting England. Little did they reckon that they were leaving behind them serpents in their Indian paradise.

Needing someone to look after affairs at the Theosophical Society headquarters, which had recently been moved from Bombay to Adyar, overlooking the Bay of Bengal near Madras, Blavatsky placed her trust in an unpleasant couple named Emma and Alexis Coulomb. HPB had hired Alexis Coulomb as a carpenter and handyman, while Emma had become a sort of glorified housekeeper—and, as it turned out, a magician's assistant.

Hardly had HPB departed for England than the Coulombs got into a succession of spats with leading members of the Theosophical Society, who eventually told them to pack up and get out. In retaliation, the aggrieved Emma Coulomb went to the *Christian College Magazine,* a journal run by Protestant missionaries who had long been yearning to put the anti-Christian Helena Blavatsky in her place. The result was a series of disclosures, published in the magazine under the gleeful title ''The Collapse of Koothoomi.'' They offered extracts from as many as forty highly imprudent letters, allegedly written by HPB to Mrs. Coulomb, as proof of Madame Blavatsky's shenanigans.

Among many other things, Emma claimed that Helena

had ordered her to construct a turban-wearing dummy that, when carried about outside on moonlit nights, would appear as a manifestation of Koot Hoomi. Moreover, said Emma, the letters that fluttered down from the ceiling, far from being delivered by astral mail, had in fact been dropped through a crack. As evidence, one of the incriminating letters, referring to a particular visitor to Theosophical Society headquarters, required that a message from one of the Masters ''must fall on his head.''

Upon the publication of Mrs. Coulomb's charges, HPB raced back to India, denying everything and threatening to sue for libel. But lawyer Olcott was adamant against any such action. Vowing to resign as president of the society if HPB filed suit, he explained that litigation would inevitably lead to a trial of ''the truth of Esoteric Philosophy'' and ''the existence of the Mahatmas.'' Thoroughly frustrated, HPB sailed for Europe. She would never again set foot on the soil of her beloved India.

But the worst was still to come. Soon after their triumphal arrival in England, Blavatsky and Olcott had been approached by representatives of the recently founded Society for Psychical Research. The group's intentions seemed positive: The SPR had been formed at least as much in the hope of authenticating as of debunking the sort of occult occurrences in which HPB specialized; its membership included several stalwarts of the Theosophical Society, and it requested an opportunity to examine HPB's ''marvelous phenomena.'' Blavatsky cheerfully agreed to cooperate.

As part of its inquiries, the SPR had dispatched to India a young Australian, Richard Hodgson, for an on-the-spot look. His initial feelings had been favorable toward the society. ''Whatever prepossessions I may have had,'' he wrote later, ''were distinctly in favour of Occultism and Madame Blavatsky.'' That attitude, of course, was significantly altered by the Coulomb revelations. Moreover, Hodgson had a reliable report of an instance in which a loyal disciple of Blavatsky showed a visitor the shrine, a wood box in which letters from the Masters miraculously materialized. To demonstrate that the shrine was solid and contained no hidden chambers, the Theosophist slapped the box sharply—causing a secret trap door to open. The Australian investigator was satisfied that a trick slot had been made to house the Mahatmas' mail—a slot that Blavatsky or her accomplices could fill or empty at will. In his 200-page report, Hodgson not only confirmed most of Emma Coulomb's accusations but added some of his own.

Among his charges was one that inspired a sad, touching footnote to the history of Theosophy. The investigator alleged that the devoted acolyte Ramaswamier, who believed he had met a Mahatma on the road in Sikkim, had actually been duped by a costumed man whom Blavatsky sent to play the role of the Master. Another local Theosophist was so greatly disturbed by the allegation that he set off to see for himself whether the Mahatmas really existed. This man, Damodar K. Mavalankar, informed no one of his plan to visit the mountains of Tibet—where a frozen corpse thought to be his turned up some time later. Theosophical lore denies the apparent futility of Mavalankar's death, however, holding that he did find the home of the Mahatmas before dying.

The international scandal that followed Hodgson's report should have been enough to silence anyone—anyone, that is, but HPB, whose finest hour was yet to come. Old beyond her years, deep in disgrace, and already suffering from Bright's disease, a kidney disorder that would eventually kill her, Madame Blavatsky traveled in Italy, Germany, and Switzerland before finally settling in England—where, incredibly, she produced her masterpiece, a massive, 1,500-page tome she called *The Secret Doctrine.*

The Secret Doctrine became the true unveiling of Theosophical thought when it was published in 1888. Supposedly based on the oldest book in the world, *The Stanzas of Dzyan,* which other scholars have yet to unearth, *The Secret Doctrine* presents Theosophy in a broad range of complexities. As expounded in the book and later refined by Blavatsky's Theosophical successors, life exists within a cosmos whose nature is spelled out in bewildering detail. It contains countless universes, each the home of numerous

solar systems. Presiding over each solar system is a logos, or solar deity, whose chief ministers are seven planetary spirits. Beneath them in the pecking order are huge arrays of *devas,* or angels. Evolution on each planet is governed by a chief celestial being.

The evolution of life takes place at progressive levels, moving from mineral to vegetable to animal to human to superhuman, or spiritual. Thus, even the smallest pebble or the humblest blob of clay contains a seed of life that may be carried by the stream of evolution into the composition of an Einstein, a Saint Augustine, an Attila the Hun, or for that matter, a Koot Hoomi.

Human history, according to *The Secret Doctrine,* is recounted in terms of seven succeeding "root-races." The first, descended from residents of the moon, dwelt on a continent named the Imperishable Sacred Land. The second, variously known as the Hyperborean race, the Sweat-born, and the Boneless, inhabited a vast territory in the vicinity of the North Pole. Since neither of those races had bodies, they reproduced by spiritual means.

The third root-race allegedly lived and died in Lemuria, an enormous land mass that reached southward from the Gobi Desert and subsequently sank to the floor of what is now the Indian Ocean. The Lemurians were the first people to possess bodies, an asset that enabled them to engage in sexual intercourse. The fourth race occupied Atlantis, which rose and fell in the present eastern Atlantic Ocean.

 he root-race that currently peoples planet Earth is the fifth, or Aryan, which sprang up in northern Asia and expanded to the south and west, and which includes Anglo-Saxons as a subrace. The last two root-races have yet to appear, Blavatsky opined, but when they do, humanity will have run its course on earth and will move to another planet to begin the cycle again.

The human constitution consists of several bodies—physical, astral, mental, and ethereal—some of which are shed as an individual climbs the rungs of countless incarnations toward the spiritual state that exists at the top of the evolutionary ladder. The ascent toward purity is long and hard, says *The Secret Doctrine,* and progress in each incarnation is dictated by karma, the "unseen and unknown law which adjusts wisely, intelligently and equitably each effect to its cause." Karma represents the results of earthly behavior, carrying over from one incarnation to another as a measure of ethical and moral existence. To Madame Blavatsky, karma was "an unfailing redresser of human injustice, and of all the failures of nature; a stern adjuster of wrongs; a retributive law which rewards and punishes with equal impartiality."

Those whose karma has enabled them to achieve the summit of earthly perfection are of course the Mahatmas, superhumans who have voluntarily delayed the bliss of merging into the universal oneness and opted instead to remain on earth to serve as custodians of the accumulated wisdom of the ages. They are the propagators of the logos's will, and they are the guides and teachers of humankind.

Thus, in her eccentric genius, Madame Blavatsky

Annie Besant (left) became Theosophy's driving intellectual force following the death of Blavatsky in 1891. In occult matters, however, she deferred to Charles Leadbeater (above), a self-proclaimed psychic whom Besant described as "a man on the threshold of divinity."

had pieced together a mosaic of immense intricacy, benevolent in its dedication to moral justice and free of the dogmas that constrict many established religions, offering to distressed humanity a scheme of life and a vision of the future that was not hobbled by the clinical rules of Darwinian science. The popularity of this optimistic form of evolution enabled Blavatsky and Theosophy to rise above the fraud scandal and gain yet more converts for the society.

Theosophy was not without rivals, however. In the year *The Secret Doctrine* was published, the society known as the Order of the Golden Dawn was founded in London, attracting some Theosophists to its ranks with the whispered allure of elaborate secret rituals and the study of magic. As a countermeasure to this competition, Blavatsky founded a similar organization within

In 1882, this estate in Adyar, India became the Theosophical Society's headquarters.

the Theosophical Society. Called the Esoteric Section, it limited membership to a select few advanced students, who would probe the mysteries of the occult much more deeply than did ordinary Theosophists. This elite cadre soon became the ruling force of the Theosophical Society. Even then, HPB's work was not finished. During the waning years of her life, Blavatsky established the magazine *Lucifer* and wrote *The Voice of Silence*, a collection of precepts that is still revered by Theosophists.

On May 8, 1891, while she was seated in her favorite armchair, Helena Petrovna Blavatsky died. The event made front pages in many parts of the world. Although much of the press took the opportunity to repeat the fraud story, some newspapers were ready to acknowledge her many accomplishments. London's *Pall Mall Gazette* called her "one of the most remarkable women of our generation." The New York *Tribune*, in an evaluation that time would validate, observed that no one else "has done more toward opening the long sealed treasures of Eastern thought, wisdom and philosophy."

In *The Secret Doctrine*, Blavatsky had promised two more volumes that would complete the trail she was blazing "into the well-nigh impenetrable jungle . . . of the land of the Occult." Considering her remarkable reputation for transcending both adversity and the physical laws of nature, it is not unlikely that some of her devoted followers half-expected the promised books to appear from beyond the grave—or even that some may still expect them today.

William Q. Judge (left), a founder of the Theosophical Society and head of its American branch, struggled with Annie Besant for overall control of the organization. As a result, the American group seceded from the society. Judge lived only a year after the break, and Katherine Tingley (right) followed him as the American leader.

Thus peace finally came to Madame Blavatsky—but not to the Theosophical movement, which during the following decades would be sundered from within and challenged from without. The damage to the society would doubtless have been far greater than it was, perhaps even fatal, had not HPB designated as her successor an Englishwoman who was as strong as she but was of a completely different character.

Annie Wood Besant was driven by enthusiasms.

The Subtle Body

An Indian thought system that impinged slightly on Theosophy was a Hindu and Buddhist sect known as Tantra. The cult, which still exists today, aims at stimulating the body's energies and funneling them into a great force that carries the seeker toward spiritual fulfillment.

Although most Indian cults posit asceticism as a path toward enlightenment, Tantra espouses ecstasy—the sexual quest to mystically reunite two deities who were sundered at the time of cosmic creation. Tantra teaches that before creation, the male and female gods Shiva and Shakti were fused in cosmic oneness. But at the birth of the universe they were separated, and their parting symbolized the subsequent duality of all things on earth. Tantra strives to rediscover the divine unity and know thereby the enlightenment and ecstasy of the gods.

The sect's methodology involves performing certain rites, including some consisting of prolonged sexual intercouse between a man and woman seeking the same spiritual goals.

Nevertheless, Tantra is less orgiastic, in the usual sense, than highly disciplined. For example, great emphasis is placed on breathing exercises called *pranayama* and on gaining control of such physiological processes as body temperature, heart rate, and the reflexes that trigger ejaculation. Other disciplines include meditation and the use of mantras, short syllables such as "om," which are used to concentrate the body's energies.

Like other Hindus, Tantrikas believe that body awareness and control put one in touch with the "subtle body," an entity composed of channels for vital energy. The subtle

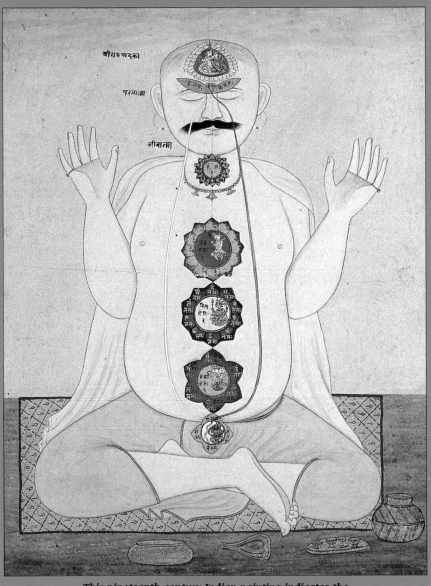

This nineteenth-century Indian painting indicates the positions of the seven chakras, or energy centers. Each chakra is believed to relate to a body organ and to a particular deity.

body is also believed to house seven energy centers called *chakras*, which lie along a continuum from the base of the spine to the crown of the head. Also at the spine's base, it is said, lies the coiled, sleeping snake called Kundalini, a symbol for the goddess Shakti. Tantrika practice supposedly

awakens the serpent, who begins ascending toward the crown chakra. As it rises, Kundalini vitalizes each chakra until, at the summit, it unites with the crown chakra, symbolizing the god Shiva. The coupling of the deities is thus made complete.

Another path toward this union is the Tantrika rite of *chakra-puja*, in which several couples participate in sexual rites. Partners are chosen at random, and according to the

A symbol for spiritual fulfillment in the Tantrika art of Tibet, this sixteenth century sculpture depicts the perfect coupling of the male and female.

This Shri yantra, or mandala, which dates from about 1700, was used as a meditation device by Tantrikas to focus their energies. The yantra symbolizes the continuous process of generation.

teachings of the Tantrikas, sex is performed as a sacred ritual, without the ordinary encumbrances of love or even passion.

The Theosophists did not embrace Tantrika sexual methodology. But Charles Leadbeater, a Theosophist leader, was intrigued with Tantrika sex, as well as with the sect's other rituals and beliefs. He based his book, *The Chakras*, on the Hindu notions—given special emphasis in Tantra—of the subtle body and its seven energy centers, and he managed to introduce those ideas into Theosophy's eclectic mystical stream.

Leadbeater was introduced to Tantra in 1915 by a former pupil who had joined a sect that was known as the Ordo Templi Orientis (Order of the Templars of the East), whose pursuits featured Tantrika sex.

While still in her teens, she became obsessed with Anglo-Catholicism; it therefore seemed only natural that at age twenty she should determine to marry the Reverend Frank Besant, an Anglican clergyman. But life as the wife of the vicar of Sibsey was not for Annie Besant. As a friend put it, "She could not be the bride of Heaven, and therefore became the bride of Mr. Frank Besant. He was hardly an adequate substitute." In 1873, after six years of domestic unhappiness, the two were separated.

nnie Besant went into full-throttle reverse, becoming an active atheist in the freethinking National Secular Society and rising rapidly in its ranks. As a fledgling feminist, she was the first Englishwoman to publicly advocate the use of contraceptives, and in 1877, she was arrested on charges of selling "obscene literature"—to wit, a birth-control booklet.

A few years afterward, Besant enlisted in the Fabian Society at the behest of her friend and fellow socialist George Bernard Shaw, the writer who later described her as a woman "who always came into a movement with a bound, and was preaching the new faith before the astonished spectators had the least suspicion that the old one was shaken." That being the case, it was in perfect character that Mrs. Besant, in 1889, suddenly proclaimed that she had become a Theosophist.

The conversion came after she had written a favorable review of *The Secret Doctrine,* which led to a meeting with HPB. Madame Blavatsky had a keen eye for promising recruits, and once she had signed Besant up, she promoted her rapidly through the ranks of the Esoteric Section. Said HPB of her protégée: "She is not psychic or spiritual in the least—all intellect." Besant differed from Blavatsky in another respect; she was a known for her probity, a reputation she valued highly.

Before Blavatsky died, she made it known that she wanted Annie Besant to succeed her as secretary of the Theosophical Society and head of the elite Esoteric Section, which had become the core of power within the larger organization. One person to whom HPB expressed her wishes was William Quan Judge, an Irish-born New York lawyer who was by then managing Theosophical affairs in the United States. But Judge had plans of his own.

"Do nothing till I arrive," he cabled Besant on learning of HPB's death, and he immediately left for England. Once there, he set forth a scheme that would divide authority in the Esoteric Section between Besant in England and himself in America. While Besant was mulling over his proposal, she was astonished to find in a drawer a note from one of the Mahatmas, Morya. It was written in what appeared to be the same hand as letters received during Blavatsky's time, with the same kind of crayon, on the same rice paper. The message was direct: "Judge's plan is right."

Guided, it seemed, by the Master's words, Annie Besant agreed to William Judge's proposal. When Madame Blavatsky was still alive, the Mahatmas had stated flatly that the letters would cease with her death. Loyal Theosophists had taken this to mean that the Masters would not communicate through anyone else; Blavatsky's critics had interpreted it as a clear confirmation that she actually wrote the letters herself.

Missives from the Mahatmas continued to arrive, however, although the means of their delivery is not completely clear; they were variously said to flutter down from the ceiling, to appear in unexpected places when no one was present, or to arrive by ordinary mail. At first, Annie Besant and the others who were aware of the letters kept the entire matter confidential.

But some four months after HPB's death, in a large hall crowded with admirers as well as reporters from virtually every London paper, Annie Besant decided to make a startling announcement. If Blavatsky was a fraud, she said, so was she—for she, too, had received letters from the "unseen world."

"You have never known me to tell a lie to you," she said. "My worst public enemy has never cast a slur upon my integrity. I tell you that since Madame Blavatsky left I have had letters in the same handwriting as the letters which she received. Unless you think dead persons can write, surely that is a remarkable feat."

Her words caused an international sensation. Annie Besant was a public figure of considerable stature. Although her embrace of Theosophy had been difficult for some of her supporters to swallow, she still possessed credibility far in excess of any ever enjoyed by the more unorthodox Blavatsky. Her statement provoked jeers from some quarters but made others wonder whether perhaps Blavatsky herself had been unfairly judged by the Society for Psychical Research. London papers were swamped by letters from their readers about Besant's revelation, while press clippings on the subject flooded into the Theosophical Society's offices from all over the world—initially at the rate of around a hundred a day, slowing later to a mere trickle of a thousand or so articles a month.

Theosophy and the Mahatmas were, in short, all the rage again—in fact, bigger than ever. The *Times* of London at first tried to maintain decorum by ignoring the whole subject, but by October the newspaper was compelled by unflagging public interest to cover it. Even William Gladstone, Britain's former and future prime minister, got involved. Pressed by the leader of a workingmen's club for an opinion, Gladstone said he could not positively say that Spiritualism and Theosophy were not possible, but on the other hand he did not see why people in workingmen's clubs should discuss such topics.

A serialized novel called *Morial the Mahatma* boosted the circulation of the popular magazine in which it appeared. An enterprising milliner soon had a Mahatma hat on the market, priced at three shillings, and fashionable Londoners greeted one another with a new, cheery salutation: "How's your karma today?" Although much of the publicity was skeptical or jocular, leaders of the Theosophical Society agreed that it was good for Theosophy, since it provided a wider audience for Theosophical ideas than the organization had ever before experienced.

Within two years, however, Theosophists developed serious doubts about the affair. It was whispered within the society that the letters were fakes. Eventually, Annie Besant herself spoke it aloud. "When I publicly said that I had received . . . letters in the writing H. P. Blavatsky had been accused of forging," she stated, "I referred to letters given to me by Mr. Judge, and, as they were in the well-known script, I never dreamed of challenging their source. I know now that they were not written or precipitated by the Master; they were done by Mr. Judge." Judge, apparently, had discovered Blavatsky's supplies of crayons and rice paper and the seal of the Mahatmas when he visted London after her death, and he had taught himself to credibly mimic the handwriting.

By then an open struggle for control of the Esoteric Section was under way. In November of 1894, Judge said the Mahatmas had instructed him by letter to remove Besant from office and take charge himself because Besant was controlled by "Dark Powers." Olcott sided with Besant and demanded Judge's resignation. In 1895, Judge led nearly all of the eighty-five U.S. chapters out of the fold and established a separate organization named the Theosophical Society in America. Besant soon struck back. In 1897, she embarked on a speaking tour of the United States. By the time Besant finished the tour, thirty-seven new Theosophical Society chapters, all of them loyal to the administrative headquarters in Adyar, had been formed.

 enry Steel Olcott died in 1907, and Annie Besant assumed the position of president. Once at the society's helm in Adyar, she devoted her energies to the service of India's people and did so with her customary intensity. Besant tried to stir the people to a new sense of national pride with a series of lectures entitled "Wake Up, India." On a more practical level, she established a Theosophic Order of Service whose branches, before long, extended throughout much of India, engaging in all manner of humanitarian work, from women's suffrage and care for the blind to prison and hospital reform.

Besant also became deeply involved in Indian education: Largely because of her endeavors, the Central Hindu

College was formed. In its classrooms, many of the men who would eventually shape India's independent destiny, including Mahatma Gandhi and Jawaharlal Nehru, absorbed a great deal of their education about Hindu culture and Hindu traditions.

During World War I, Besant became a champion of Indian self-government. In 1916, she founded the Home Rule League as an auxiliary to the Indian National Congress, the native political party founded in 1885 to foster economic reform and to move India toward independence from her British rulers. Later Besant purchased a daily newspaper in Madras, changed its name to *New India,* transformed it into the country's largest Anglo-Indian publication, and was so vociferous in her criticism of British rule that colonial authorities placed her under house arrest. Even Gandhi, who was sometimes critical of Theosophy, recognized that An-

nie Besant had ''made Home Rule a *mantrum* [precept] in every cottage.''

In 1917, with Gandhi and other Indian leaders on the dais, Mrs. Besant, then seventy years of age, was inaugurated as president of the Indian National Congress—an office that, though mostly honorary, was the highest the Indian people then had within their power to bestow.

Yet for all her humanitarian successes, the long Theosophical Society administration of Annie Besant was marked by bitter dissension. Part of her trouble arose in the person of Charles W. Leadbeater, a former Anglican priest who was expelled from the Theosophical Society in 1906 because of a scandal involving some American boys he tutored. His transgression, apparently, was telling the youths that it was all right to masturbate.

Annie Besant was charmed by Leadbeater, and soon

Crowds cheer a triumphant Annie Besant in the streets of Madras, India, in 1917 after her release from British internment. Besant's advocacy of Indian self-rule had prompted the British to jail her, but the move brought such public outcry that she was freed after three months.

after becoming the society's president, she produced a letter from the reliable Koot Hoomi with assurances that "no mistake was made by Mr. Leadbeater in the nature of the advice he gave his boys." Leadbeater was reinstated in the society—and he soon involved Annie Besant in an undertaking that eventually would break her heart.

Leadbeater became entranced by a fourteen-year-old Brahman boy named Jiddu Krishnamurti, the son of an Indian clerk and Theosophist. The Englishman was convinced that he had discovered in the boy the conduit for a great new teacher. Jiddu would have a function akin to that of channelers, as his counterparts would be called a half century later, and the source of his message would be a fresh incarnation of the Messiah. The wisdom that Jiddu would deliver, according to Leadbeater, would lead humanity in its evolution to the new root-race described in Theosophical teachings. At Leadbeater's urging, Annie Besant talked the boy's father into letting her adopt Jiddu. As a vehicle for the young Krishnamurti's eventual mission, she established a new organization, the Order of the Star in the East.

Within the Theosophical Society, the whole affair brought furious recriminations. Many Theosophists felt that Besant and Leadbeater were trying to create a new church—the last thing Blavatsky had in mind when she founded the movement, so inimical did she find the establishment aspect of organized religion. One leading Theosophist, Rudolf Steiner, a distinguished literary scholar and head of the society's German branch, went so far as to withdraw his allegiance and found his own Anthroposophical Society, which still exists today as one of Theosophy's several offshoots.

Despite such opposition, Besant and Leadbeater persisted in their purpose for several years, imparting their purported occult knowledge to Krishnamurti and grooming

Mourners gather at Adyar in 1933 to witness the Hindu cremation rites for the Theosophist and humanitarian Annie Besant. Her former colleague Charles Leadbeater (in robes at center) lit the pyre.

him for his role as mouthpiece for the Messiah. The young man sometimes accompanied Annie Besant on various speaking tours. But although some Indian believers prostrated themselves before him, Jiddu Krishnamurti was developing his own serious doubts about his destiny. Finally, in 1929, as he appeared before Besant and 3,000 others at a Theosophist summer camp, Krishnamurti renounced his nascent linkup with the divine, dissolved the Order of the Star in the East, rejected all organized religious sects, and followed an independent life as a lecturer and educator until his death in 1986.

Annie Besant was never quite the same after the repudiation by Krishnamurti. Forsaking her crusades, she stayed close to the Adyar headquarters for most of her remaining days. Upon her death in 1933 at age eighty-five, she was cremated according to Hindu rite—with Charles W. Leadbeater on hand to put a torch to her pyre.

The Theosophical Society still survives, with its headquarters in Adyar. After Krishnamurti's defection, its membership plummeted from its 1920s peak of 45,000. It gradually inched back up to its current level of some 35,000, although the schisms dividing its various branches never completely healed. Still, the society today is as active as ever in its programs for social welfare and its promotion of a universal human brotherhood.

Thoughts on the Astral Plane

Charles Leadbeater believed he could tell a lot about people by reading the energy emanating from their bodies. This energy, he claimed, manifested itself in two ways—as auras and thought forms.

According to Leadbeater, an aura was the outer part of a cloudlike bioenergetic field surrounding the physical body. This field consisted of a person's "higher bodies," including a "mental" body and an "astral" body. As one became more highly evolved and focused on "pure and sublime topics," he maintained, the aura reflected the mental body's beautiful colors. When the astral body was fully enlightened, strong, clear colors appeared in the aura; while undesirable characteristics showed themselves as dull greens, browns, and reds.

Leadbeater also claimed he could see thoughts in auras. Each thought, he said, appeared both as a vibration in the astral body and as a separate form. If a thought was simple, it produced only one rate of vibration. But a wave of emotion could cause the astral body to agitate violently and the aura to flush a brilliant blue or scarlet.

But few emotions were pure, Leadbeater found. Affection, for example, was usually tinged with pride, selfishness, jealousy, or sexual passion. Its radiating vibration was therefore com-

Leadbeater believed that energy flowed into the physical, mental, and astral bodies through seven "force-centers" called chakras. He described the chakras as saucerlike wheels that rotate as energy races through them. In an undeveloped person, he claimed, the chakras moved sluggishly; in a more evolved being, they glowed and pulsed "with living light."

plex and its aura multicolored. Leadbeater worked out correspondences for colors and emotions: black for ha-

tred; red for anger; clear brown for avarice; dull brown-gray for selfishness; deep, heavy gray for depression; pale gray for fear, and brownish green for jealousy. Crimson and rose meant affection, deep orange showed pride and ambition, yellow signaled intellect, and blue denoted religious feeling.

Leadbeater believed thoughts not only affected the aura, but could assume a separate form of their own. He claimed there were three types of thought forms. One variety, caused by thoughts of another place, could allegedly make the thinker's image appear in that location. This image, Leadbeater said, was sometimes mistaken for the thinker's astral body or ghost.

The second type of thought form assumed the image of another person or an object— a friend, a house, or a landscape, perhaps. These forms could float as tiny images before their originator.

Leadbeater's third type of thought form was emotional. A thought of love or concern, for example, would supposedly float to the loved one and enter his or her aura; there it would remain, acting much like the person's guardian angel.

Leadbeater described auras and thought forms for an artist, whose interpretations are shown on the opposite page.

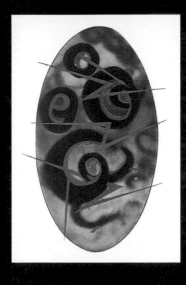

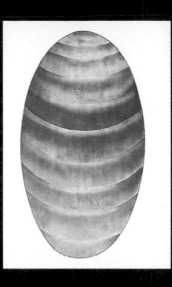

"Fiery arrows of uncontrolled anger" and heavy black coils "lit up from within by the lurid glow of active hatred," mark the aura (far left) of an individual who is in the midst of a terrible rage, claimed Leadbeater. A sudden wave of fear (center), he believed, would suffuse the astral body with a gray mist and violently vibrating horizontal lines. Static, dull gray lines resembling a cage, Leadbeater wrote, are the sign of a deep depression. A less serious level of gloom, he explained, would manifest itself in only "a few bars of depression" or a gray fog of despair.

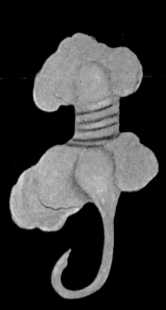

The eye-shaped thought form (above) of a losing gambler reveals, stated Leadbeater, depression, selfishness, and fear. Above it, a winning gambler's thought form signals pride and greed. A thought form of jealousy appears snakelike (above, right). And the thought forms of two mourners at a funeral supposedly display a sharp contrast in emotions—one mourner feels selfish grief (far right), while the other one (near right) shows sympathy and faith.

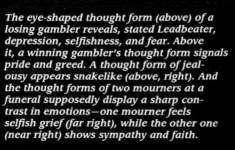

34

The second most prominent occult society of the era, the Order of the Golden Dawn, was much smaller than the Theosophical Society, never counting many more than 300 members at any one time, but its influence was far greater than its numbers might have suggested. Founded three years before HPB's death, the new organization was established at least partly as a Western reaction to the Theosophical Society's orientalism. Though draped in Egyptian trappings, the Golden Dawn had Greco-Roman underpinnings and evoked the Christian fraternity of the Rosicrucians. All its founding members, in fact, were Rosicrucians and Freemasons. The Golden Dawn also stressed the kind of elaborate secret rituals that HPB, with her notions of Indian simplicity, abhorred; meetings of the Theosophical Society were conducted according to procedures no more mysterious than *Robert's Rules of Order.*

The full name of the new group was the Hermetic Order of the Golden Dawn, but to maintain secrecy its members publicly referred to it as the GD. Like many things about the Golden Dawn, its origins are clouded in dispute. According to the order's own lore, it began in 1880, when the Reverend A. F. A. Woodford, an Anglican clergyman who was also a Mason, was browsing through a London bookstall and happened upon a batch of manuscripts, written in cipher and apparently of impressive antiquity. By 1887, the manuscripts had found their way into the hands of Dr. William Wynn Westcott, a physician who had won appointment as a North London coroner. He was also a practicing Freemason, a member of the Rosicrucian Society of England, and a Theosophist.

hile leafing through the manuscripts, Westcott supposedly found a letter, written in German, advising anyone who desired further information to contact Sapiens Dominabitur Astris—Latin for "the wise one will be ruled by the stars"—and subsequently known in Golden Dawn circles as SDA. The letter said SDA could be reached through a certain Fräulein Anna Sprengel, for whom a German address was thoughtfully provided. A lively correspondence was soon under way. When deciphered, the manuscripts were found to contain notes and diagrams that outlined, in bareboned fashion, five rituals for an occult society. Before long, instructions came from SDA for Westcott to see to it that the skeleton was fleshed out into fully developed rituals and to induct some initiates—or so went the official story. Evidence strongly suggests, however, that the cipher manuscripts, far from being rooted in antiquity, were written sometime after 1870, probably by Westcott himself.

There seems little doubt that SDA and Fräulein Sprengel were fictional characters and that their communications were Westcott forgeries; once the Golden Dawn was fairly well started, Westcott announced the sad demise of Anna Sprengel, and Sapiens Dominabitur Astris disappeared along with her. And Westcott is known to have spread false information about the Hermetic Students of the GD, as he then termed it, in order to make it appear "a very ancient" society, when in fact he was just then lining up its first initiates.

Why William Wynn Westcott, a respectable public official, would indulge in such fraudulent behavior remains one of many mysteries surrounding the Golden Dawn. British historian Ellic Howe may have discovered an answer almost a century later, however, while delving into the society's old papers. Howe showed a handwriting expert several documents penned by Westcott. The graphologist insisted that the papers could not all have been written by the same person; the handwriting styles were too different. When convinced by other evidence that one man indeed had written all the documents, the graphologist concluded that Westcott clearly was a case of multiple personality.

Another possible explanation—and one that might also illuminate the motives of some other Victorian occultists—is that Westcott may not have taken the whole business completely seriously and thus saw no offense in his little deceptions. (He definitely was not in it for the money; each member paid only two shillings and sixpence a year in dues, and the order's outlay for incense, ritual wine, stationery, and similar items just about balanced its meager

The Mystic Soldier

John Frederick Charles Fuller, a British soldier who would later become known as a brilliant military strategist and a fascist, had always been interested in the occult. When he was posted to India early in this century, that interest developed into a full-blown passion.

While in India, Fuller studied Hindu sacred writings, became acquainted with Indian holy men, and developed an interest in yoga. He also began corresponding with British eccentric Aleister Crowley *(see pages 112-123),* a former Golden Dawn member who was in Darjeeling in 1905.

Crowley had announced a contest with a £100 prize for the best essay on his own writings. Fuller entered the contest, writing an essay that lauded Crowley as a godlike genius and predicted that "Crowleyanity" would become the new religion of humankind.

Since his was the only entry, Fuller won. (He might well

JOHN FREDERICK CHARLES FULLER

have won in any case, given his fawning tone toward the megalomaniac Crowley.) He never received the prize, however, since Crowley was almost always without funds, but the two men became friends, even collaborating in 1909 on an occult journal called the *Equinox.*

Fuller was also an accomplished artist, and Crowley called on him to design artwork for a temple to be used by the Argentinum Astrum, Crowley's splinter group from the Golden Dawn. For the design *(below),* Fuller drew from Tantrika teachings to depict the polarity between the "female" zodiacal circle and the "male" forces of the physical world.

Fuller broke with Crowley after a dispute over the *Equinox* and turned his energies full-time to his military career. He never abandoned the occult, however. He authored a book on yoga in 1925 and one on the Cabala in 1937.

income.) Perhaps, just perhaps, Westcott and some others involved in the era's secret societies viewed their activities at least partly as a kind of game, an opportunity to dream up and recite portentous-sounding mumbo jumbo while swirling about in hooded robes, to share secret words and signs with an exclusive band of pals—purposes not at all dissimilar to those of American college students who were forming and joining secret fraternities during the same period.

Certainly there was a sense of almost childish excitement about the entire enterprise, as Alfred Edward Waite, a distinguished scholar of the occult who was present, recalled a number of

decades later: "In Theosophical and kindred circles, the rumours of an Occult Order making great pretences were abroad in those days. Obscure persons were placing cryptic sigils [seals] after their names in unexpected communications, as if to test whether I was already a member. Dark hints were conveyed in breathless murmurs . . . something to do with this darkly glittering business. The name of Wynn Westcott . . . loomed remotely."

If indeed Westcott was in it mainly for the fun and entertainment, the young Scotsman to whom he assigned the task of fleshing out the rituals, Samuel Liddell Mathers, would prove to be driven by less playful gods. At first Mathers seemed to be harmless enough. A. E. Waite dismissed him as a buffoonish magician and described him, not too flatteringly, as "a strange person, with rather fishlike eyes."

W. B. Yeats, who abandoned Theosophy in favor of the Golden Dawn, commented that Mathers had "much learning but little scholarship." Having spent years poring over thick, arcane tomes in the British Museum reading room and being possessed of a natural theatrical flair for ornate costumes and ceremony, Mathers, at Westcott's request, worked up a set of impressive rituals and splendid regalia for the order. He later became less cooperative, however, gradually elbowing Westcott aside and growing more and more the autocrat himself.

Mathers was peculiar in the extreme. According to his wife, Moina, who was better known in the Golden Dawn as Vestigia, neither she nor Mathers had anything "whatever to do with any sexual connection—we have both kept perfectly clean." He could be charming. Yeats liked spending

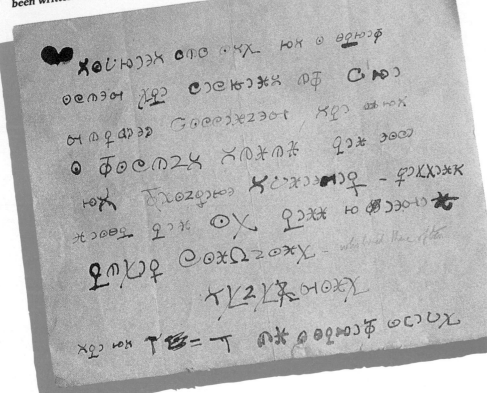

Mathers chose for his own the Gaelic for "royal is my tribe." Within the Order of the Golden Dawn Mathers insisted, in his own words, on "complete and absolute submission."

"I do not care one atom what you *think,*" he told a member who dared to question his authority. "I refuse absolutely to permit open criticism of, or any argument concerning my action . . . from you or any other member." Unfortunately for Mathers, the members of the Golden Dawn were a fairly independent lot. The order's rolls—listing members in five different temples, from London to Edinburgh to Paris—included many talented people, the occasional recognized genius, and some who simply enjoyed too much money or celebrity to kowtow comfortably.

In retrospect, W. B. Yeats, who in 1923 was awarded the Nobel Prize for literature, was undoubtedly the order's most illustrious initiate. The poet had a lifelong romance with the occult. Since childhood, he had read Irish stories of ghosts and sorcery, and in adolescence had sought out people who "try to communicate with evil powers." As a youth, he had attended a gathering where a hooded sorcerer—working with a censer, daggers, a human skull, and other appropriate implements—slit the throat of a black cockerel and drained its blood into a bowl as incantations were murmured. Yeats did not see serpents appear, as others in the room said they did, but he sensed himself being surrounded by evil black clouds so threatening that he felt he had to struggle to avoid being overcome. As a member of the Theosophical Society's Esoteric Section, he had joined Annie Besant in experiments in which, he wrote to a friend, "a needle suspended from a silk thread under a glass case has moved to and fro and round in answer to my will, some experiments too of still stranger nature."

time with him and on some evenings would join the Matherses for a strange game of four-player chess that pitted Yeats and Vestigia as partners against Mathers and a spirit. Mathers would stare intently at his partner's empty chair before making the spirit's move.

athers's megalomania was rarely restrained by the boundaries of reality. Active in a Celtic fringe group whose goal was to restore the House of Stuart to the throne of an independent Scotland, he added a Scottish patronymic to his name, at first calling himself Samuel Liddell MacGregor Mathers and later escalating to Count MacGregor de Glenstrae, a title that owed less to *Burke's Peerage* than to his own vivid imagination. According to some who knew him, he claimed at various times to be James IV—not killed at the Battle of Flodden in 1513, as was generally believed, but surviving as an immortal adept. Yeats said that Mathers "imagined a Napoleonic role for himself" in a Europe transformed by the return of the Jacobites and "even offered subordinate posts to unlikely people." Each member of the Golden Dawn was identified by a personal motto:

several years. Yeats said that she had "three great gifts, a tranquil beauty . . . an incomparable sense of rhythm and a beautiful voice." She also had a finely honed wit. Although others frequently get credit for the quip, it apparently was Florence Farr who declared at the time of Oscar Wilde's trial—a slander case involving Wilde's homosexuality—"I don't care what they do, as long as they don't do it in the street and frighten the cab horses."

Like Yeats, Farr was no mere dabbler in magic. For a period in the 1890s, she was praemonstratrix, the principal ritual instructor, of London's Isis-Urania Temple of the Golden Dawn; and she is on record on one occasion as raising a spirit named Taphthartharath by boiling a pickled snake in a "hell broth" of magic ingredients. The vision of the beautiful actress, dressed in white robe and yellow sash and carrying a dagger as she attends the magical brew, becomes a virtual epiphany of the Golden Dawn when the other participants around the cauldron are added to the scene: a painter, a stockbroker, and an electrical engineer, all similarly costumed and bearing swords, candle, chain, and lamp. Shaw said that his mistress was "in violent reaction against Victorian morals, especially sexual and domestic morals." Her rebellious temperament cannot have made Mathers's would-be authoritarianism easier.

Neither did the equally rebellious nature of another well-known member, Annie Horniman. Horniman, the daughter of a rich and famous tea importer, was in fact a particularly sharp thorn in Mathers's side because she was as wealthy as he was impecunious. A generous woman, she was devoted to the stage and would be remembered outside the Golden Dawn as the builder of Dublin's famous Ab-

For three decades, Yeats was so deeply involved in both the magic and the politics of the Golden Dawn and its numerous successor organizations that it is difficult to understand how he had the time to write. He declared magic to be, "next to poetry, the most important pursuit of my life" and evidently saw no conflict between his art and his immersion in occult matters. When reproved by a friend for his mystical interests, Yeats said that he "could not have written a single word" of some of his works "if I had not made magic my constant study."

"The mystical life is the centre of all that I do and all that I think and all that I write," he proclaimed.

Another famous artist in the Golden Dawn was the actress Florence Farr, who starred in plays by Henrik Ibsen and George Bernard Shaw and was Shaw's mistress for

bey Theatre. She got Mathers a job as curator of her father's private museum and later extended an annual stipend to Mathers and his wife, who happened to be her old schoolmate. All this was fine at first, but eventually the Matherses, who at the time were living the high life in Paris at her expense, became so extravagant and demanding that Annie Horniman put her financial foot down. The result was a major ruckus in the Golden Dawn.

Other notables in the GD included writer Algernon Blackwood, known for his occult stories; astronomer William Peck, who was head of the Edinburgh observatory; and psychoanalyst and novelist Dion Fortune, whose books often dealt with the supernatural. Fortune eventually founded her own occult society, the Fraternity of the Inner Light, which is still in existence today. Another GD member, A. E. Waite—the scholar who recalled the "darkly glittering" rumors of the order's founding—has been described as one of the few people of modern times to write intelligently about the Cabala.

Mathers's most important tool in his continual struggle to control the members was his alleged exclusive relationship with the Secret Chiefs of the order. These were immortal, superhuman teachers somewhat similar to the Theosophists' Mahatmas. In Mathers's day, only he and his wife claimed to hear from them, and he guarded his presumed connection jealously. "I can tell you *nothing*," he stated in an 1896 manifesto concerning the Secret Chiefs. "I know not even their earthly names. I know them only by certain secret mottoes. I have but very rarely seen them in the physical body; and on such rare occasions *the rendezvous was made astrally by them.*" Just being in the presence of

these adepts, he said, was like being close to "a flash of lightning," except that the experience was sustained rather than momentary. "I cannot conceive a much less advanced initiate being able to support such a strain, even for five minutes, without death ensuing," Mathers smugly declared.

By his account, the Secret Chiefs delivered to him all of the ancient wisdom and rituals that he then passed on to the Golden Dawn. He said they communicated with him by clairvoyance, by devices similar in principle to Ouija boards, by "Direct Voice audible to my external ears and those of Vestigia," and by showing him old books to copy. "The strain of such labour has been, as you can conceive, enormous," he said, especially the ordeal of receiving instructions for one secret ritual that was particularly rigorous, "which I thought would have killed me, or Vestigia, or both."

In 1892, Mathers relocated to Paris and, purportedly under the

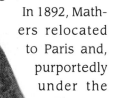

A. E. Waite, leader of the Golden Dawn's mystical faction in its waning years, controlled the Isis-Urania Temple in London from 1903 until it closed in 1914. Waite authored many books on the occult, including the Pictorial Key to the Tarot. He also designed the Golden Dawn Tarot cards, the deck most commonly used today.

Moina Mathers, dressed to perform
the rites of Isis in this 1900 photograph,
continued to lead a group of loyal
followers after her husband's death in 1918.

guidance of the Secret Chiefs, founded a second, or inner, order of the Golden Dawn. With the establishment of this elite cadre, which Mathers called the Order of the Rose of Ruby and the Cross of Gold (*Ordo Rosae Rubeae et Aurea Crucis*, or simply the RR et AC), the GD was effectively transformed into an academy for magicians. The Golden Dawn member who had already passed the relatively simple examinations for the order's four outer grades was faced with a daunting task. He had to pass five separate examinations just to enter the RR et AC. Once he had his foot in the door, so to speak, he had to pass eight more tests to attain the state of *theoricus adeptus minor*—an adept of the inner order. There were an additional five grades beyond that, but hardly anyone besides Mathers and Westcott scaled those heights. With the RR et AC up and running under Mathers's leadership, Westcott's outer order became little more than an empty shell. Even Westcott himself belonged to the inner group.

The rituals of the new core order were marvelous Mathers creations. For example, in the initiation rite of the RR et AC, the candidate entered an eight-foot-high, seven-sided vault of the adepts, its walls covered with Cabalistic symbols in colors of occult significance. The vault accommodated at least four persons, along with an altar—and a coffin in which reposed the body of Christian Rosenkreutz, usually portrayed by Mathers or Westcott. (If nothing else, this colorful rite served Mathers well by ridding him of Westcott once and for all. The idea of one of their coroners imitating a corpse and lying in a coffin apparently did not appeal to London authorities, who, once they heard about it, took the necessary steps to force Westcott's withdrawal from the Golden Dawn.) The dramatic climax to the initiation rite was a terrible vow of secrecy, the violation of which would result in "a deadly and hostile current of will set in motion by the Secret Chiefs of this Order, by which I might fall slain and paralyzed."

During this ritual the candidates pledged to apply themselves to "the Great Work, which is to purify and exalt my Spiritual nature, that with the Divine aid, I may . . . attain to be more than human . . . and that in this event I will not abuse the Great Power entrusted to me."

The magic through which initiates used the great power was concocted from a number of sources in addition to the Secret Chiefs. It was drawn from the work of John Dee, the occult-minded seventeenth-century mathematician and astrologer who had advised Queen Elizabeth I, and from two hoary French manuscripts: *The Sacred Magic of Abra-Melin the Mage*, a quietly mystical treatise that Mathers purportedly had discovered and translated, and *The Clavicula of Solomon the King*, a medieval primer instructing magicians to wear peculiar clothing and to employ geometric figures, swords, wands, and chants that took hours to utter.

Mathers was not the sole originator of Golden Dawn magic rituals; at least one, the ceremony used by actress Florence Farr to call forth the spirit Taphtharharath, was written by a twenty-three-year-old electrical engineer named Allan Bennett, who was one of those joining Farr in its use. It required a lot of preparation and assembling of

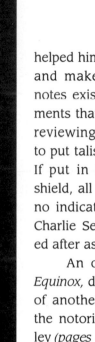

props: The gum ammoniac and coriander seed were easy enough to obtain, but Bennett had to write to a friend to get hold of a snake pickled in spirits. The ritual itself was long and included some powerful threats that could be used by the magus of art (in this case, Florence Farr) if Taphthartharath should be slow to answer the summons. "I curse and blast Thee, O Thou Spirit," she declaimed. "I consign Thee unto the lowest Hell of Abaddon."

Presumably the spirit did appear at last—at least to the satisfaction of the participants, although there is no record of what it looked like or whether it could be seen in the purely physical sense at all. After being constrained to "teach us all the Mysteries of the Hidden Arts and Sciences," Taphthartharath was allowed to slink back to its usual abode, with instructions to return "hastily when we invoke and call Thee."

Sometimes Golden Dawn magic was used for medical purposes. Annie Horniman was asked by a member of lesser grade to do something for "poor little Charlie Sewell," a child with epilepsy. Horniman undertook to investigate the problem "in the astral plane."

"Went through the golden Hexagram and red Cross," she reported later. There, in the astral plane, she could see that the astral version of the boy had a "whirling black and blue ball following him, attached to his head by a string." She put a talisman on his breast and made some banishment signs. "The ball which was alive seemed to die and the string withered," she wrote. Next she saw that his home environment was "full of black imps, like flies," so she helped him to hold her sword and make more signs. Her notes exist, along with comments that Mathers wrote on reviewing them—"Not wise to put talisman *on* his breast. If put in front of him as a shield, all right." But there is no indication as to whether Charlie Sewell's illness abated after astral treatment.

An occult journal, the *Equinox,* did report the results of another case. It involved the notorious Aleister Crowley *(pages 112-123),* a brilliant but dark-spirited protégé of Mathers's who would become a destructive factor in the Golden Dawn. Crowley—who, incidentally, published the *Equinox*—supposedly made a talisman known as a "Flashing Tablet of The Eagle Kerub of Jupiter" to cure a fellow member's mother, who was seriously ill. Because the member failed to obey Crowley's instructions to "feed the talisman with incense, and water it with dew," it at first almost killed the old woman, who "was seized with a violent series of fits." After the member correctly reconsecrated the talisman, however, her mother "speedily recovered the whole of her former strength, and survived to the ripe old age of ninety-two." Or so, at least, the *Equinox* reported.

Despite their pledge "not to abuse the Great Power," initiates were occasionally accused of using magic maliciously. On one occasion, Bennett and Crowley became convinced that W. B. Yeats was wielding black magic to attack Crowley because—their reasoning takes the breath away—he was jealous of Crowley for being a better poet. So they conducted an unspecified ritual to counter his supposed attack. The presumed duel must have been a draw because no damage was reported by either side. Another incident involved a glass rod belonging to Bennett that supposedly was invested with powerful magic. A Theosophist acquaintance of Bennett's, who poked fun at the notion of the "magical blasting rod," is said to have suddenly found himself paralyzed by the device he had mocked. According to the story, he was unable to move for fourteen hours.

In the 1920s, Dion Fortune said she came under a brutal occult assault from Vestigia Mathers, punishment for writing some articles of which Mrs. Mathers disapproved. Fortune claimed to have first developed a "general sense of vague uneasiness" that "gradually matured into a definite sense of menace and antagonism." Then the faces of demons began to appear to her in flashes. Next, the story

goes, her neighborhood was invaded by black cats, so numerous that the caretaker next door pushed "bunches of black cats off doorstep and window-sill with a broom, and declared he had never in his life seen so many." When Fortune encountered "a gigantic tabby cat, twice the size of a tiger," on her own stairwell, she knew she had to fight back—even though the giant cat disappeared as she stared at it. She claimed she journeyed to the astral plane, where she engaged in a titanic struggle with Vestigia Mathers. Finally, with the help of the Secret Chiefs, Dion Fortune prevailed, and the attack ended—although she later found her back "was scored with scratches as if I had been clawed by a gigantic cat."

A few years later, a young woman by the name of Netta Fornario, who belonged to an offshoot sect of the Golden Dawn and had dealings with Vestigia Mathers, was found dead on the beach of the Scottish isle of Iona. She was naked except for a black cloak—the uniform of the Golden Dawn officer known as the hiereus. Around her neck was a silver chain that had turned black, and in her lifeless hand she held a large knife. A local doctor said Fornario died of heart failure. Dion Fortune insisted otherwise. The body was extensively scratched, she claimed, a sure sign that the young woman had been victimized by Vestigia Mathers on the astral plane.

Long before Dion Fortune's astral battle with Vestigia Mathers, earthly clashes of both philosophy

Florence Farr, a celebrated actress and the mistress of George Bernard Shaw, became a Golden Dawn devotee in the late nineteenth century. Farr, author of a book entitled Egyptian Magic, applied her considerable talents toward helping to instruct members in carrying out the order's rituals, which resembled theatrical productions.

and personality within the Golden Dawn fragmented the order into a number of successor sects. The most devastating schism resulted from the struggle of wills between Mathers in Paris and the members of the Isis-Urania Temple in London. Mathers alienated many of the members in 1896 by expelling Annie Horniman from the organization. His ostensible reason was insubordination—she had refused to sign a pledge of complete submission to his edicts—but he undoubtedly was also reacting to Horniman's having recently stopped his £200-a-year allowance.

But the final rupture between Mathers and the London members was precipitated by the introduction of Aleister Crowley into the Golden Dawn. Crowley, who was already hard at work on his reputation as the world's wickedest man, was admitted to the outer order in 1898 and soon cast his spell on Mathers, who rapidly promoted him. Crowley's behavior, however, was too outrageous for most of the London members, who disapproved of his blatant sexual activities. In January of 1900, the Isis-Urania Temple refused to obey an instruction from Mathers to initiate Crowley into the second order, the RR et AC. Mathers was livid. He invited Crowley to Paris and initiated him in that city.

By March of 1900, Mathers and Golden Dawn officers in London were exchanging allegations and threats. Mathers sent an edict removing Florence Farr from her post as local head of the second order and another one abolishing a London committee that was considering the validity of his leadership. He threatened to smite the insurgents with a "Punitive Current" generated by the Hidden and Secret Chiefs. Then he dispatched none other than Aleister Crowley to suppress the rebellion.

The result was a near-farcical confrontation that has been called the Battle of Blythe Road. On April 17, Crowley and another member loyal to Mathers broke into the order's London headquarters, located at 36 Blythe Road, and seized the property. Before long, Florence Farr and others opposing Mathers arrived. They enlisted the aid of a constable, who ejected the invaders. Farr's supporters then quickly changed the locks.

On April 19, Crowley reappeared in Blythe Road—in a getup that must have astonished the neighbors. He was clad in Highland dress, wore a black mask of Osiris over his face, and carried a dagger. The rebels got rid of him by again calling the police. Crowley returned to Paris, where he found Mathers shaking some dried peas in a sieve and calling upon the demons Beelzebub and Typhon-Set to work their malevolent might against those who opposed him.

The demons apparently let him down. The Londoners expelled Mathers, who therewith largely vanished from the annals of the Golden Dawn. Little is known of his fate thereafter. He died in France in 1918.

With its despotic bête noir out of the way, the Isis-Urania Temple tried to remake itself under Yeats's energetic leadership, but infighting hampered his efforts from the outset. After about two years, the temple split along factional lines: Members whose main orientation was mysticism kept control of the temple under the leadership of A. E. Waite, while Yeats and others who were interested mostly in magic realigned themselves as a splinter sect called the Stella Matutina, or Morning Star. Meanwhile, several temples that remained loyal to the departed Mathers took to calling themselves the Alpha and Omega, a GD spinoff that proved to be short-lived.

The Stella Matutina limped along into the 1930s, although Yeats himself, fed up with nonstop bickering in the faltering organization, withdrew from an active role in 1923. Still, he kept in touch with his old companions in sorcery. Some years after putting all remnants of the Golden Dawn behind him, Yeats observed that although few "who belonged at all intimately to our circle abandoned the study . . . the lives of most in so far as they are known to me have been troubled & unhappy" because of their participation. And yet, he apparently felt that familiarity with the occult was worth the price in pain. "You have made the darkness your enemy," he once wrote, in a passage that can be read as a challenge from those who embrace the mystic's lot to those who reject it. "We—we exchange civilities with the world beyond."

From Theosophy to Modern Art

Within a decade of its founding in New York City in 1875, the Theosophical Society and its teachings had circled the globe and become an international force in the spiritual movement. Along the way, Theosophy helped spawn a revolution in the world of art.

Led initially by Helena P. Blavatsky, the much-traveled Russian adventuress, the Theosophists took their name and their goal from the Greek words for divine wisdom. They sought to attain such wisdom through inquiry into the laws of the universe, which for them included spiritual as well as physical realms. In their research they found affinities and common symbols in all the world's religions, and in their publications—usually illustrated with occult imagery—they advanced ancient revelations of Hinduism and Buddhism as solutions to modern questions. Among the most influential Theosophical books were Blavatsky's *The Secret Doctrine* and Annie Besant's and Charles W. Leadbeater's *Thought-Forms*—one of several illuminated bibles of the creed. Britishers Besant and Leadbeater, writing in India, inspired similar works by other Europeans, such as Germany's Rudolf Steiner.

Theosophy's mystical symbolism and its belief in a higher reality were particularly appealing to the four European painters whose works appear on the following pages. Working independently in Amsterdam, Munich, Paris, and Moscow, each set out to transmute the ethereal into the visual with brush and palette. Each began with recognizably natural forms that evolved ultimately into nonobjective imagery. Reaching for the sublime, these pioneers of abstract painting helped lay the paving stones of modern art.

Theosophy Finds an Artistic Apostle in the Netherlands

In Devotion, painted in 1908, a young woman seeks mystical, cosmic oneness by meditating on a flower. This early Theosophy-inspired painting was too representational to satisfy Mondrian's purpose of portraying the concept of devotion rather than the act.

Dying Chrysanthemum displays the aura that is supposedly given off by all living things. Theosophists saw plants as exemplifying the stages of death and rebirth in the transmigration of souls.

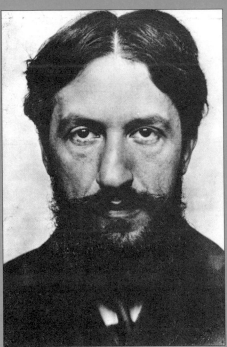

Piet Mondrian in 1910

Piet Mondrian, a Dutch painter born in 1872, was more directly involved with Theosophy than any of the other pioneers of abstract art. He first studied the works of Helena Blavatsky in the early 1900s. He also acquired a book of Rudolf Steiner lectures that he annotated and kept until his death. Mondrian joined the Theosophical Society in 1909.

Geometric forms were already emerging in Mondrian's work when he moved to Paris in 1910, bent on finding a medium of pure form to represent the higher universal truths he was finding in Theosophy.

Returning to Amsterdam in 1914, Mondrian and a friend founded the de Stijl circle of artists and architects. But he remained restless, living again in Paris, then London, and finally New York, where—still seeking to limn the ethereal—he died in 1944.

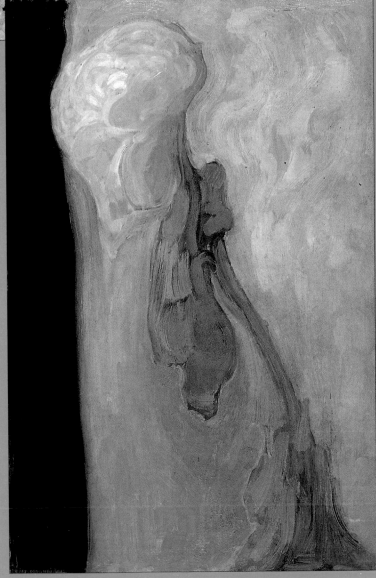

Male and female symbols contend with each other in the erect trees and horizontal ground planes of Woods near Oele. When he created the work in 1908, Mondrian was still striving to evoke abstract concepts, like the Theosophical notion of duality, through natural, recognizable forms. But it hints at an emerging fascination with pure geometry.

The six-foot-high triptych Evolution, painted in 1910 and 1911, is a Theosophical vision of the human progression from earthly body (left panel) through astral body (right panel) to divine insight (center). Each flower, triangle, and circle has an occult meaning. The stars in the far right panel, formed by joined triangles, are ancient symbols found at the center of the Theosophical Society's emblem.

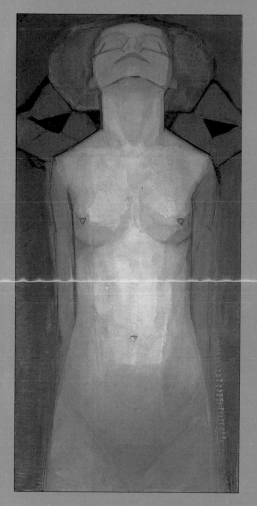
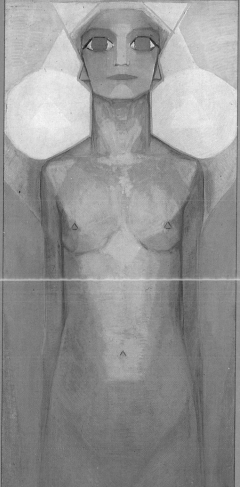
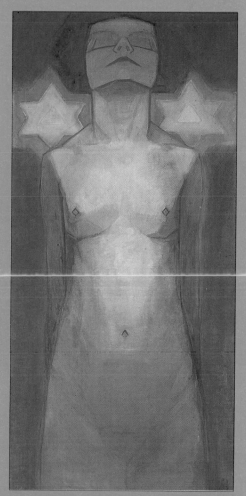

159

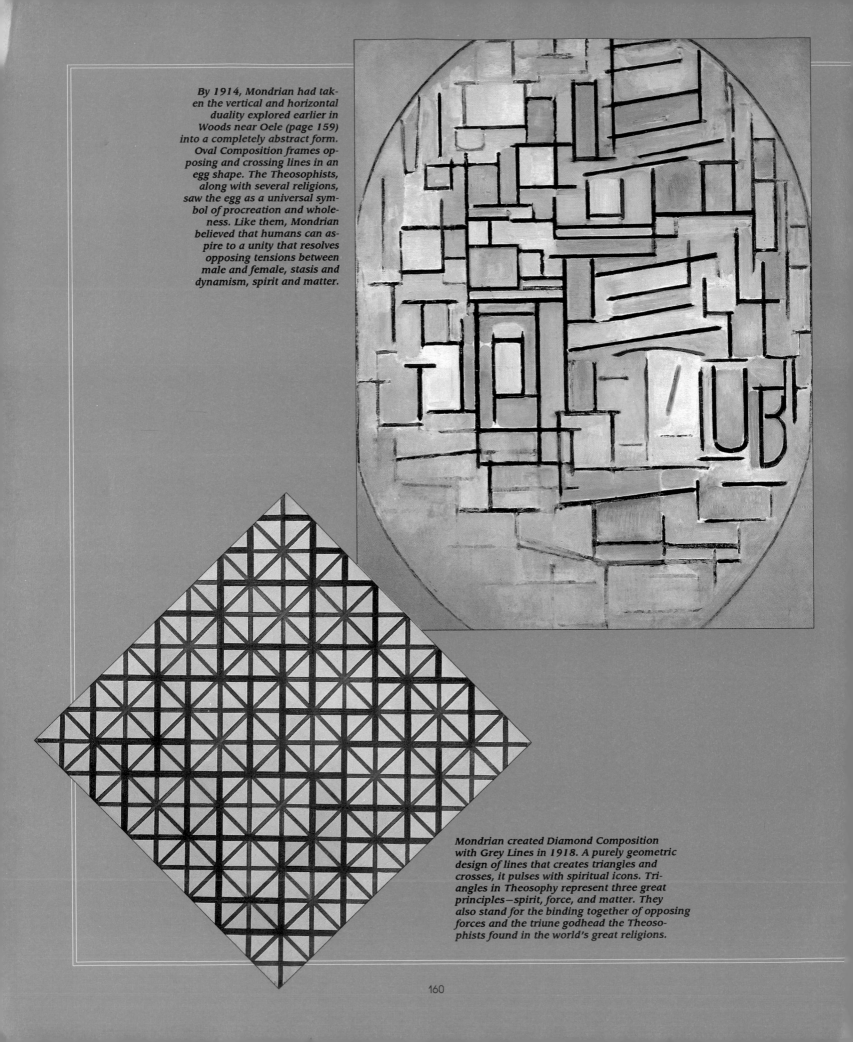

By 1914, Mondrian had taken the vertical and horizontal duality explored earlier in Woods near Oele (page 159) into a completely abstract form. Oval Composition frames opposing and crossing lines in an egg shape. The Theosophists, along with several religions, saw the egg as a universal symbol of procreation and wholeness. Like them, Mondrian believed that humans can aspire to a unity that resolves opposing tensions between male and female, stasis and dynamism, spirit and matter.

Mondrian created Diamond Composition with Grey Lines in 1918. A purely geometric design of lines that creates triangles and crosses, it pulses with spiritual icons. Triangles in Theosophy represent three great principles—spirit, force, and matter. They also stand for the binding together of opposing forces and the triune godhead the Theosophists found in the world's great religions.

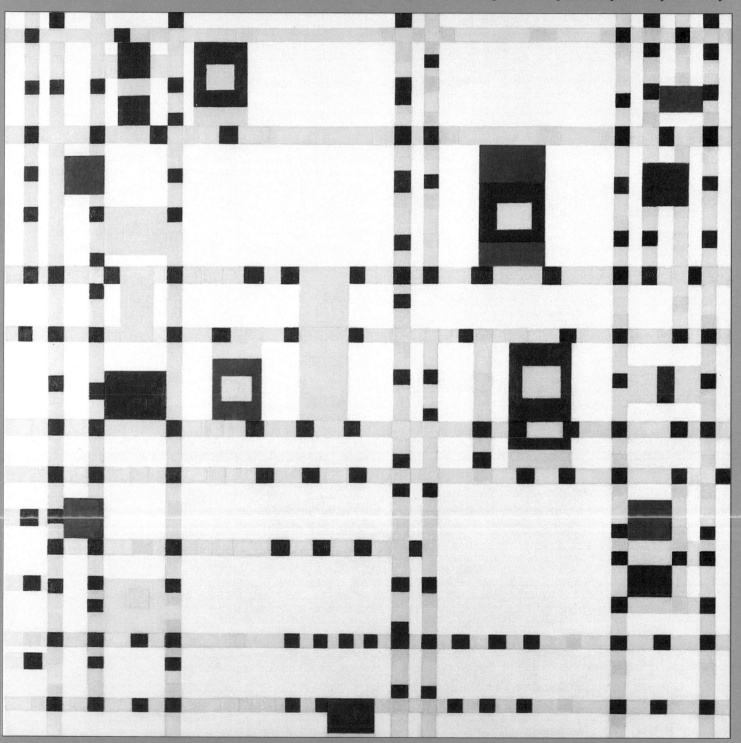

Broadway Boogie Woogie, Mondrian's last completed painting, captures the 1940s rhythm and beat of New York City. By then, Mondrian was using only the three primary colors plus black in what he called his form-giving mathematics; the style became known as neoplasticism. By whatever name, Mondrian's ultimate visualization of the Theosophists' higher reality was too abstract for them to recognize or accept as an expression of their beliefs.

Thought Vibrations Become Art in Germany

Author-painter Wassily Kandinsky

Wassily Kandinsky was born in Moscow in 1866 to a prosperous family. Well-educated and widely traveled, he developed an early fondness for music and painting. When he was almost thirty, he gave up a legal and academic career to pursue his abiding interest in art. He went to Munich and immersed himself in the new aesthetic currents of Impressionism and Art Nouveau, then traveled to Paris in the first decade of the new century. There, he steeped himself in the spiritual, reading Blavatsky and Steiner and poring over illustrations in the books of Besant and Leadbeater.

By 1910, Kandinsky was experimenting with nonobjective painting. His struggle to express visual forms in an abstract way was documented in his book *Concerning the Spiritual in Art,* published in 1912.

Meditation as spiritual training intrigued him. He embraced and extended the Theosophical belief that a work of art is shaped by the artist's thought vibrations, which in turn are transmitted by the work to the viewer. Kandinsky passed on his ideas as a painter and teacher at Germany's Bauhaus school from 1922 to 1933. He died in France in 1944.

Kandinsky's belief in the occult notion of a "spiritual atmosphere," filled with unseen thoughts and feelings, is the basis for Lady in Moscow, painted in 1912. On a material plane, the viewer sees a woman and, beside her, a dog on a table. On a spiritual plane appear manifestations of thoughts and feelings— hers or someone else's. A dark form threatens to block out health-giving rays of the sun at the top of the picture. The rosy thought form at right suggests love and goodwill in Theosophical terms, using Leadbeater's notion of meaningful color.

Black Spot I, painted immediately after Lady in Moscow, visualizes the same situation on a completely spiritual and nonobjective plane, depicting what a spiritually initiated viewer might see. The same menacing, dark form seems to move toward a light source above it, but the human figures and the carriage from the earlier painting are merely suggested by abstract forms.

Tension in Red, painted in 1926, shows Kandinsky's fascination with the occult notion of synesthesia—an overlapping of the senses wherein, through concentration, one is able to taste colors, for instance, or feel sounds. Here, the viewer is meant to experience the vivid red as a physical sensation of tension.

A Czech Artist As Spiritual Medium

As a child in Czechoslovakia, where he was born in 1871, Frantisek Kupka was apprenticed to a saddler who also happened to be a spiritualist. When he entered art school in Vienna, his familiarity with the occult made him receptive to Theosophy and other spiritual ideas astir in that cosmopolitan capital. He paid the tuition for his first semester with money earned as a medium at séances.

To sharpen Kupka's presumed spiritual powers, fellow mystic and artist Karl Diefenbach tutored him in vegetarianism, daily nude exercise outdoors, meditation, and musical accompaniment to his painting sessions. Nude exercise once got Kupka jailed in Munich for indecency. Nevertheless, he continued the practice until his death in Paris in 1957.

Frantisek Kupka in 1919

In *The Beginning of Life*, Kupka uses an oriental symbol of creation to represent cosmic birth or spiritual awakening. The lotus is rooted dccp in water while its flower thrives in the sun, symbolizing the life-giving duality of water and fire in both Hinduism and Theosophy. The repeated circles in this 1900 work foreshadow Kupka's later focus on geometric forms.

The Dream, painted between 1906 and 1909, draws on Kupka's rich inner life. He apparently believed that mediumistic powers enabled him to grasp the essence of reality.

In Piano Keys—Lake, painted in 1909, the artist explored the Theosophical symbolism of vertical planes. Fingers strike an A-major chord at the lower right, and the music catapults the keys—which are vertical symbols for humankind—from the darkness of the water into the enlightenment of the sun-drenched sky. Vertical lines also represent the Theosophical philosophy of ascendancy to higher understanding. Frantisek Kupka intended the paired meanings to symbolize humanity's evolution toward true spirituality.

Vertical forms continued to dominate Kupka's painting as he moved toward abstraction. Kupka, like the Theosophists, was drawn to oriental religions, and in this work, produced in 1920, the forms suggest rows and rows of Hindu temples leading upward to truer knowledge. After his death, his widow said the initial inspiration for the painting had been a stack of jam pots glistening in the sun. Madame Kupka shared many of her husband's beliefs, including a faith in the transference of energy. She claimed that when he worked too hard, it was she who felt tired.

In Animated Oval (Birth), completed in 1912, Kupka used the egg shape to symbolize the generation of life. During this period, the artist began to describe his way of painting as Orphism. He had been trying for years to create with paint the emotions musicians produce with sound, and he believed that the images of the Greek hero-musician Orpheus that appear on ancient friezes and vases came as close as he could imagine to "something between sight and hearing."

The Russian Dawn of Nonobjective Art

The Russian artist Kazimir Malevich, like a number of poets and painters working in Moscow early in the twentieth century, was captivated by mystical philosophies based on yoga. One particularly appealing idea was that humankind would someday be united in a single utopian language of understanding.

In order to give form to his vision of unity, Malevich tried to move from figures of the third dimension to the geometry of a mystical fourth, a notion found in the writings and drawings of Russian Theosophist P. D. Ouspensky as well as the American architect-philosopher Claude Bragdon. From his conviction that the individual can rise to cosmic consciousness, Malevich invented the term *suprematism* to describe his work. He died at the age of fifty-seven in 1935, the year socialist realism began eroding Russian artistic expression.

Painted in 1908, Woman in Childbirth shows the remnants of realism in Malevich's highly symbolic early period. The figure is clearly recognizable as a woman, although she has a symbolic function in representing purity and transcendence.

In 1915, Malevich switched to a completely abstract style and founded his own artistic movement under the name suprematism. This 1918 work, titled Suprematist Painting, represents a body passing into the fourth dimension.

Kazimir Malevich in 1927

In these three paintings—all examples of the approach Malevich called suprematism—the artist wanted to negate the rational world in order to transcend it. He regarded the works as aids to attaining a state where the mind can glimpse an ultimate reality.

BIBLIOGRAPHY

Allen, Paul M., comp. and ed., with Carlo Pietzner, *A Christian Rosenkreutz Anthology*. Blauvelt, N.Y.: Rudolf Steiner, 1968.

Allsopp, Fred W., *Albert Pike: A Biography*. Little Rock, Ark.: Parke-Harper, 1928.

Art of the Invisible (exhibition catalog). England: Bede Gallery, Tyne & Wear, 1977.

Bakhtiar, Laleh, *Sufi: Expressions of the Mystic Quest*. London: Thames and Hudson, 1976.

Bennett, Olivia, *Annie Besant*. London: Hamish Hamilton, 1988.

Besant, Annie, and C. W. Leadbeater, *Thought-Forms*. Wheaton, Ill.: Theosophical Publishing House, 1925.

Birks, Walter, and R. A. Gilbert, *The Treasure of Montsegur: A Study of the Cathar Heresy and the Nature of the Cathar Secret*. Wellingborough, Northamptonshire, England: Aquarian Press, 1987.

Bischoff, Erich, *The Kabbala*. York Beach, Me.: Samuel Weiser, 1985 (reprint of 1910 edition).

Blau, Joseph Leon:
The Christian Interpretation of the Cabala in the Renaissance. Port Washington, N.Y.: Kennikat Press, 1965.
The Story of Jewish Philosophy. New York: Random House, 1962.

Brothwell, Don, *The Bog Man and the Archaeology of People*. London: British Museum Publications, 1986.

Burman, Edward:
The Assassins. Wellingborough, Northamptonshire, England: Aquarian Press, 1987.
The Templars: Knights of God. Wellingborough, Northamptonshire, England: Aquarian Press, 1986.

Camp, L. Sprague de:
The Fringe of the Unknown. Buffalo, N.Y.: Prometheus Books, 1983.
The Ragged Edge of Science. Philadelphia: Owlswick Press, 1980.

Campbell, Bruce F., *Ancient Wisdom Revived: A History of the Theosophical Movement*. Berkeley, Calif.: University of California Press, 1980.

Carpenter, William A., *The Exemplar: A Guide to a Mason's Actions*. Philadelphia: The Right Worshipful Grand Lodge of Free & Accepted Masons of Pennsylvania, 1985.

Castell, F. de P., *The Genuine Secret in Freemasonry Prior to A.D. 1717*. London: A. Lewis, 1930.

Cavendish, Richard, *A History of Magic*. New York: Taplinger, 1977.

Cavendish, Richard, ed.:
Man, Myth & Magic. New York: Marshall Cavendish, 1983.
Mythology: An Illustrated Encyclopedia. London: Orbis, 1980.

Chadwick, Nora K., *The Druids*. Cardiff, Wales: University of Wales, 1966.

Chippindale, Christopher, *Stonehenge Complete*. Ithaca, N.Y.: Cornell University Press, 1983.

Coil, Henry Wilson, Sr., *Freemasonry through Six Centuries*. Ed. by Lewis C. "Wes" Cook. Vol. 1. Richmond, Va.: Macoy Publishing and Masonic Supply, 1967.

Cook, Roger, *The Tree of Life: Image for the Cosmos*. New York: Avon, 1974.

Coxhead, David, and Susan Hiller, *Dreams*. New York: Crossroad, 1976.

Cyr, Donald L., ed., *Stonehenge Viewpoint*. Santa Barbara, Calif.: Stonehenge Viewpoint, 1985.

Daraul, Arkon, *A History of Secret Societies*. Secaucus, N. J.: Citadel Press, 1961.

Demott, Bobby J., *Freemasonry in American Culture and Society*. Lanham, Md.: University Press of America, 1986.

Denslow, William R., *10,000 Famous Freemasons*. 4 vols. Reprinted from the Transactions of the Missouri Lodge of Research for the Educational Bureau of the *Royal Arch Mason Magazine* (Trenton, Mo.), 1957-1961.

Douglas, Charlotte, *Swans of Other Worlds: Kazimir Malevich and the Origins of Abstraction in Russia*. Ann Arbor, Mich.: University Microfilms International, 1976.

Edwardes, Michael, *The Dark Side of History: Magic in the Making of Man*. New York: Stein and Day, 1977.

Ellwood, Robert S., Jr., *Religious and Spiritual Groups in Modern America*. Englewood Cliffs, N.J.: Prentice-Hall, 1973.

Epstein, Perle, *Kabbalah: The Way of the Jewish Mystic*. Garden City, N.Y.: Doubleday, 1978.

Eschebach, Hans, *Pompeji*. Leipzig, East Germany: VEB E. A. Seemann, 1978.

Faÿ, Bernard, *Revolution and Freemasonry 1680-1800*. Boston: Little, Brown, 1935.

Ferguson, John, *Encyclopedia of Mysticism and Mystery Religions*. New York: Crossroad, 1982.

Forbes, Esther, *Paul Revere & the World He Lived In*. Boston: Houghton Mifflin, 1942.

Franco, Barbara, *Fraternally Yours: A Decade of Collecting* (exhibition catalog). Lexington, Mass.: Scottish Rite Masonic Museum, June 1985-January 1986.

Frank Kupka (exhibition catalog). Cologne, West Germany: Galerie Gmurzynska, February-April 1981.

Frothingham, Richard, *History of the Siege of Boston, and of the Battles of Lexington, Concord, and Bunker Hill*. Boston: Little, Brown, 1873.

Gilbert, R. A.:
"Freemasonry & the Hermetic Tradition." *Gnosis*, winter 1988.
The Golden Dawn and the Esoteric Section. London: Theosophical History Centre, 1987.
The Golden Dawn Companion. Wellingborough, Northamptonshire, England: Aquarian Press, 1986.

Godwin, Joscelyn, *Robert Fludd: Hermetic Philosopher and Surveyor of Two Worlds*. London: Thames and Hudson, 1979.

Gomes, Michael, *The Dawning of the Theosophical Movement*. Wheaton, Ill.: Theosophical Publishing House, 1987.

Gould, Robert Freke, *The Concise History of Freemasonry*. New York: Macoy Publishing & Masonic Supply, 1924.

Grant, Michael, *Cities of Vesuvius: Pompeii and Herculaneum*. New York: Macmillan, 1971.

Grant, Michael, ed., *Greece and Rome*. London: Thames and Hudson, 1986.

Gray, Nicolete, *Jacob's Ladder: A Bible Picture Book from Anglo-Saxon and 12th Century English MSS*. London: Faber and Faber, 1949.

Guirdham, Arthur, *The Great Heresy*. Jersey, Channel Islands, England: Neville Spearman, 1977.

Guitton, Jean, *Great Heresies and Church Councils*. Transl. by F. D. Wieck. New York: Harper & Row, 1965.

Guthrie, W. K. C.:
The Greeks and Their Gods. Boston: Beacon Press, 1950.
Orpheus and Greek Religion. New York: W. W. Norton, 1966.

Halevi, Z'ev ben Shimon, *Kabbala: Tradition of Hidden Knowledge*. New York: Thames and Hudson, 1980.

Hall, Manly Palmer:
The Adepts in the Western Esoteric Tradition. Los Angeles: Philosophical Research Society, 1949.
Collected Writings of Manly P. Hall. Vol. 1. Los Angeles: Philosophical Research Society, 1958.
An Encyclopedic Outline of Masonic, Hermetic, Quabbalistic and Rosicrucian Symbolical Philosophy. San Francisco: H. S. Crocker Co., 1928.
The Phoenix. Los Angeles: Philosophical Research Society, 1960.
The Rosicrucians and Magister Christoph Schlegel: Hermetic Roots of America. Los Angeles: Philosophical Research Society, 1986.

Hamill, John, *The Craft: A History of English Freemasonry*. Wellingborough, Northamptonshire, England: Aquarian Press, 1986.

Hare, Harold Edward, and William Loftus Hare, *Who Wrote the Mahatma Letters?* London: Williams & Norgate, 1936.

Harper, George Mills, *Yeats's Golden Dawn*. Wellingborough, Northamptonshire, England: Aquarian Press, 1974.

Hartmann, Franz, *Personal Christianity, A Science: The Doctrines of Jacob Boehme*. New York: Macoy, 1919.

Heckethorn, Charles William, *The Secret Societies of All Ages and Countries*. Vol. 1. New Hyde Park, N.Y.: University Books, 1965.

Helms, L. C., *A Modern Mason Examines His Craft: Fact vs. Fiction*. Richmond, Va.: Macoy Publishing & Masonic Supply, 1981.

Hemleben, Johannes, *Rudolf Steiner: A Documentary Biography*. Transl. by Leo Twyman. East Grinstead, Sussex, England: Henry Goulden, 1975.

Higgins, Godfrey, *The Celtic Druids*. Los Angeles: Philosophical Research Society, 1977.

Hoffman, Edward, *The Way of Splendor: Jewish Mysticism and Modern Psychology*. Boulder, Colo.: Shambhala, 1981.

Holmes, Edmond, *The Albigensian or Catharist Heresy*. London: Williams and Norgate, 1925.

Holroyd, Stuart, *Magic, Words, and Numbers*. Garden City, N.Y.: Doubleday, 1976.

Howe, Ellic, *The Magicians of the Golden Dawn: A Documentary History of a Magical Order 1887-1923*. New York: Samuel Weiser, 1972.

Jinarajadasa, C., ed., *The Golden Book of the Theosophical Society*. Adyar, Madras, India: Theosophical Publishing House, 1925.

Johnson, George, *Architects of Fear: Conspiracy Theories and Paranoia in American Politics*. Los Angeles: Jeremy P. Tarcher, 1984.

Judah, J. Stillson, *The History and Philosophy of the Metaphysical Movements in America*. Philadelphia: Westminster Press, 1967.

Kandinsky, Wassily, *Concerning the Spiritual in Art*. Transl. by M. T. H. Sadler. New York: Dover Publications, 1977.

Kelly, Clarence, *Conspiracy against God and Man*. Belmont, Mass.: Western Islands, 1974.

Kerr, Howard, and Charles L. Crow, eds., *The Occult in America: New Historical Perspectives*. Urbana, Ill.: University of Illinois Press, 1983.

King, Francis:
The Magical World of Aleister Crowley. London: Weidenfeld and Nicolson, 1977.
Witchcraft and Demonology. New York: Exeter Books, 1987.

Kinney, Jay:
"The Gnosis Interview: J. Gordon Melton." *Gnosis*, spring/summer 1987.
"The Tree of Knowledge of Good and Evil." *Gnosis*, fall/winter 1985.

Knight, Stephen, *The Brotherhood: The Secret World of the*

Freemasons. London: Granada, 1984.

Knight, Thomas A., *The Strange Disappearance of William Morgan.* Cleveland, Ohio: Central Publishing House, 1932.

Knightley, Thomas, *Secret Societies of the Middle Ages.* London: Charles Knight, 1837.

Lamy, Lucie, *Egyptian Mysteries.* Transl. by Deborah Lawlor. New York: Crossroad, 1981.

Langguth, A. J., *Patriots: The Men Who Started the American Revolution.* New York: Simon and Schuster, 1988.

Larson, Bob, *Larson's Book of Cults.* Wheaton, Ill.: Tyndale House, 1982.

Leadbeater, Charles Webster:
Ancient Mystic Rites. Wheaton, Ill.: Theosophical Publishing House, 1986.
The Chakras. Wheaton, Ill.: Theosophical Publishing House, 1987 (reprint of 1927 edition).
Man: Visible and Invisible. Wheaton, Ill.: Theosophical Publishing House, 1987 (reprint of 1925 edition).
A Textbook of Theosophy. Adyar, Madras, India: Theosophical Publishing House, 1971 (reprint of 1912 edition).

Lennhoff, Eugen, *The Freemasons.* Transl. by Einar Frame. London: A. Lewis, 1978.

Lepper, John Heron, *Famous Secret Societies.* London: Sampson Low, Marston, 1932.

Lévi, Éliphas, *The History of Magic.* Transl. by Arthur Edward Waite. Los Angeles: Borden, no date.

Lewis, Bernard, *The Assassins: A Radical Sect in Islam.* New York: Oxford University Press, 1967.

Lewis, H. S., "The Authentic and Complete History of the Ancient and Mystical Order Rosae Crucis." *The Mystic Triangle,* January 1928.

Lutyens, Mary:
Krishnamurti: The Years of Awakening. London: Hutchinson Group, 1984.
Krishnamurti: The Years of Fulfilment. London: Hutchinson Group, 1985.

McIntosh, Christopher:
Eliphas Lévi and the French Occult Revival. London: Hutchinson Group, 1972.
The Rosicrucians: The History, Mythology and Rituals of an Occult Order. Wellingborough, Northamptonshire, England: Thorsons Publishing Group, 1987.

MacKenzie, Norman, ed., *Secret Societies.* New York: Holt, Rinehart and Winston, 1967.

Manns, Peter, *Martin Luther: An Illustrated Biography.* Transl. by Michael Shaw. New York: Crossroad, 1982.

Markham, James M., "Spain's Freemasons, Legalized, Fight among Themselves." *The New York Times,* September 21, 1979.

Martensen, Hans L., *Jacob Boehme.* Transl. by T. Rhys Evans. London: Rockliff, 1949.

Masonic Symbols in American Decorative Arts (exhibition catalog). Lexington, Mass.: Scottish Rite Masonic Museum and Library, 1975-1976.

Matthews, John, *The Grail: Quest for the Eternal.* New York: Crossroad, 1981.

Meade, Marion, *Madame Blavatsky: The Woman behind the Myth.* New York: G. P. Putnam's Sons, 1980.

Meyer, Marvin W., ed., *The Ancient Mysteries: A Sourcebook.* San Francisco: Harper & Row, 1987.

Miller, Edith Starr (Lady Queenborough), *Occult Theocrasy.* Hawthorne, Calif.: The Christian Book Club of America, no date.

Morley, John, *Death, Heaven and the Victorians.* London: Studio Vista, 1971.

Mylonas, George E., *Eleusis and the Eleusinian Mysteries.* Princeton, N. J.: Princeton University Press, 1961.

Naudon, P., *Geschichte der Freimaurerei.* Frankfurt, West Germany: Propyläen Verlag, 1982.

Nethercot, Arthur H.:
The First Five Lives of Annie Besant. Chicago: University of Chicago Press, 1960.
The Last Four Lives of Annie Besant. Chicago: University of Chicago Press, 1963.

Norton-Taylor, Duncan, and the Editors of Time-Life Books, *The Celts* (The Emergence of Man series). New York: Time-Life Books, 1974.

O'Donnell, Elliott, *Strange Cults and Secret Societies of Modern London.* New York: E. P. Dutton, 1935.

Olcott, Henry Steel:
Inside the Occult: The True Story of Madame H. P. Blavatsky. Philadelphia: Runny Press, 1975.
Old Diary Leaves. Adyar, Madras, India: Theosophical Publishing House, 1941.

Oldenbourg, Zoé, *Massacre at Montségur: A History of the Albigensian Crusade.* Transl. by Peter Green. New York: Random House, 1961.

Oppenheim, Janet, *The Other World: Spiritualism and Psychical Research in England, 1850-1914.* Cambridge: Cambridge University Press, 1985.

Partner, Peter, *The Murdered Magicians: The Templars and Their Myth.* Wellingborough, Northamptonshire, England: Aquarian Press, 1987.

The Paul Revere Memorial Association, *Paul Revere—Artisan, Businessman, and Patriot: The Man behind the Myth* (exhibition catalog). Lexington, Mass.: Museum of Our National Heritage, April 1988-March 1989.

Paul Revere's Boston: 1735-1818 (exhibition catalog). Boston: Museum of Fine Arts, Boston, April-October 1975.

Piet Mondrian 1872-1944 (exhibition catalog). New York: Solomon R. Guggenheim Museum, 1971.

Piggott, Stuart, *The Druids.* London: Thames and Hudson, 1968.

Poncé, Charles, *Kabbalah.* San Francisco: Straight Arrow Books, 1973.

Powell, Neil, *Alchemy, the Ancient Science.* Garden City, N.Y.: Doubleday, 1976.

Purce, Jill, *The Mystic Spiral: Journey of the Soul.* London: Thames and Hudson, 1974.

Ransom, Josephine, comp., *A Short History of the Theosophical Society.* Adyar, Madras, India: Theosophical Publishing House, 1938.

Rawson, Philip:
The Art of Tantra. London: Thames and Hudson, 1973.
Tantra: The Indian Cult of Ecstasy. New York: Avon, 1973.

Réau, Louis, *Iconographie de l'Art Chrétien.* Paris: Presses Universitaires de France, 1956.

Roberts, Allen E., *Freemasonry in American History.* Richmond, Va.: Macoy Publishing & Masonic Supply, 1985.

Roberts, J. M., *The Mythology of the Secret Societies.* New York: Charles Scribner's Sons, 1972.

Robertson, Sandy, *The Aleister Crowley Scrapbook.* London: W. Foulsham, 1988.

Robison, John, comp., *Proofs of a Conspiracy against All the Religions and Governments of Europe Carried on in the Secret Meetings of Free Masons, Illuminati, and Reading Societies.* London: 1798.

Rosicrucian Digest, November 1977.

Rutherford, Ward, *The Druids and Their Heritage.* London: Gordon & Cremonesi, 1978.

Ryan, Charles J., *H. P. Blavatsky and the Theosophical Movement.* Ed. by Grace F. Knoche. Pasadena, Calif.: Theosophical University Press, 1975.

Scholem, Gershom:
Kabbalah. New York: Dorset Press, 1974.
On the Kabbalah and Its Symbolism. Transl. by Ralph Manheim. New York: Schocken Books, 1965.

Sharkey, John, *Celtic Mysteries.* New York: Thames and Hudson, 1975.

Shepard, Leslie, ed., *Encyclopedia of Occultism & Parapsychology.* Vol. 1. Detroit, Mich.: Gale Research, 1984.

Shumaker, Wayne, *The Occult Sciences in the Renaissance: A Study in Intellectual Patterns.* Berkeley, Calif.: University of California Press, 1972.

Smith, David, *A People and a Proletariat: Essays in the History of Wales 1780-1980.* London: Pluto Press, 1980.

Spence, Lewis, *The History and Origins of Druidism.* New York: Rider, 1950.

Supreme Grand Lodge of A.M.O.R.C., *The Rosicrucians (AMORC).* San Jose, Calif.: Supreme Grand Lodge of A.M.O.R.C., 1966.

Symonds, John, *The Great Beast: The Life of Aleister Crowley.* London: Rider, 1951.

Symonds, John, and Kenneth Grant, eds., *The Confessions of Aleister Crowley: An Autohagiography.* New York: Hill and Wang, 1970.

Tansley, David V., *Subtle Body: Essence and Shadow.* New York: Thames and Hudson, 1977.

The Theosophical Society, *The Theosophical Movement, 1875-1950.* Los Angeles: Cunningham Press, 1951.

Thorndike, Joseph J., Jr., ed., *Mysteries of the Past.* New York: American Heritage, 1977.

Tillett, Gregory, *The Elder Brother: A Biography of Charles Webster Leadbeater.* London: Routledge & Kegan Paul, 1982.

Tompkins, Peter, *The Magic of Obelisks.* New York: Harper & Row, 1981.

Trowbridge, W. R. H., *Cagliostro.* New Hyde Park, N.Y.: University Books, 1961.

Trythall, Anthony John, *'Boney' Fuller: Soldier, Strategist, and Writer 1878-1966.* New Brunswick, N.J.: Rutgers University Press, 1977.

Vivian, Herbert, *Secret Societies Old and New.* London: Thornton Butterworth, 1927.

Waite, Arthur Edward:
The Brotherhood of the Rosy Cross. New Hyde Park, N.Y.: University Books, 1961.
The Holy Kabbalah. New Hyde Park, N.Y.: University Books, 1960.

Webb, James, *The Flight from Reason.* London: MacDonald, 1971.

Weber, Julius A., comp., *Religions and Philosophies in the United States of America.* Los Angeles: Wetzel, 1931.

Weisberger, Edward, ed., *The Spiritual in Art: Abstract Painting 1890-1985* (exhibition catalog). Los Angeles and New York: Los Angeles County Museum of Art Abbeville Press, 1986.

Wernick, Robert, "What Were Druids like, and Was Lindow Man One?" *Smithsonian,* March 1988.

Westwood, Jennifer, ed., *The Atlas of Mysterious Places.* New York: Weidenfeld & Nicolson, 1987.

Whalen, William J., *Minority Religions in America.* New York: Society of St. Paul, 1981.

Williams, Gertrude Marvin:
The Passionate Pilgrim: A Life of Annie Besant. New York: Coward-McCann, 1931.
Priestess of the Occult: Madame Blavatsky. New York: Alfred A. Knopf, 1946.

Wilson, Colin, *Aleister Crowley: The Nature of the Beast.* Wellingborough, Northamptonshire, England: Aquarian Press, 1987.
Wilson, Peter Lamborn, *Angels.* New York: Pantheon Books, 1980.
Witten, Laurence C., II, and Richard Pachella, comps., *Al-* chemy and the Occult. New Haven, Conn.: Yale University Library, 1977.
Wosien, Maria-Gabriele, *Sacred Dance: Encounter with the Gods.* New York: Avon, 1974.
Wright, Dudley, *Druidism: The Ancient Faith of Britain.* Totowa, N. J.: Rowman and Littlefield, 1974 (reprint of 1924 edition).
Yates, Frances A.:
Giordano Bruno and the Hermetic Tradition. New York: Random House, 1964.
The Occult Philosophy in the Elizabethan Age. London: Routledge & Kegan Paul, 1979.

PICTURE CREDITS

The sources for the illustrations in this book are listed below. Credits from left to right are separated by semicolons; credits from top to bottom are separated by dashes.

Cover: Art by Bryan Leister. 1, 3, and initial alphabet constructed and photographed by John Drummond. 6-9: Art by Bryan Leister. 11: From *Secret Teachings of All Ages,* by Manly P. Hall, © The Philosophical Research Society. 12: Scala, Florence, courtesy Museo Archeologico Nazionale, Naples. 13: Emmett Bright, courtesy Musei Vaticani, Rome. 14: G. Nimatallah/Ricciarini, Milan, courtesy Museo Archeologico Nazionale, Naples. 15: Sonia Halliday Photographs, Weston Turville, Buckinghamshire. 16: Scala, Florence, courtesy Musei Vaticani, Rome. 17: Biblioteca Apostolica Vaticana, Rome. 18: Harold Chapman, from *Celtic Mysteries,* by John Sharkey, Thames and Hudson, New York, 1979. 19: Ira Block, courtesy Silkeborg Museum, Denmark. 20: Courtesy The Danish National Museum, Copenhagen. 21: National Museum of Wales (Welsh Folk Museum), Cardiff. 22: Michael Holford Photographs, Loughton, Essex. 23: Courtesy of the Royal Ontario Museum, Toronto. 25, 26: Courtesy the Trustees of the British Library, London. 27: Badische Landesbibliothek, Karlsruhe. 28: The Oriental Institute, University of Chicago. 29: G. Sansoni, Florence, courtesy Biblioteca Nazionale Centrale, Florence. 30: Jean Dieuzaide, Toulouse. 31: Lauros-Giraudon, Paris. 32: Bibliothèque Nationale, Paris. 33: Ara Guler/Topkapi Palace Museum Library, Istanbul. 34: Courtesy the Trustees of the British Library, London. 35: The Bodleian Library, Oxford—courtesy the Trustees of the British Library, London. 36: Jean-Loup Charmet/Explorer Archives, Paris. 37: Giraudon, Paris. 38: Bibliothèque Nationale, Paris. 39: Courtesy the Trustees of the British Library, London. 40: Courtesy National Museum, New Delhi. 41-43: Courtesy the Trustees of the British Library, London. 44, 45: Aldus Archive, courtesy Mrs. M. Sleeman, London; from *Secret Societies,* edited by Norman MacKenzie, Aldus Books Limited, London, 1967—India Office Library, London. 47: From *Magic, the Western Tradition,* by Francis King, Thames and Hudson, London. 48: Archive für Kunst und Geschichte, West Berlin. 49: Bildarchiv Preussischer Kulturbesitz, West Berlin. 52: Roger Viollet, Paris. 53: Ullstein Bilderdienst, West Berlin; Granger Collection. 54: The Ashmolean Museum, Oxford. 55: From *A Christian Rosenkreutz Anthology,* compiled and edited by Paul Marshall Allen, Rudolf Steiner Publications, 1968. 56: Courtesy the Trustees of the British Library, London. 57: Detail from a portrait of Francis Bacon, courtesy the National Portrait Gallery, London. 58, 59: Courtesy the Trustees of the British Library, London. 60, 61: From *Robert Fludd,* by Joscelyn Godwin, Thames and Hudson, London, 1979—Ann Ronan Picture Library, Taunton, Somerset/E. P. Goldschmidt and Co., Ltd. (6). 62: The Beinecke Rare Book and Manuscript Library, Yale University. 65: Aldus Archive, London. 66, 67: Jean-Loup Charmet, Paris. 69: Bibliotheca Philosophica Hermetica, Amsterdam. 70, 71: Courtesy the AMORC Rosicrucian Order. 73: John Miller/Museum of Our National Heritage, Lexington, Mass. 74, 75: Museum of Fine Arts, Boston; American Antiquarian Society, Worcester, Mass.—Museum of Fine Arts, Boston; Library of Congress. 76: Museum of Fine Arts, Boston, except bottom right, Museum of Our National Heritage, Lexington, Mass. 77: American Antiquarian Society, Worcester, Mass.—Granger Collection. 78: Museum of Fine Arts, Boston—Yale University Art Gallery. 79: From *Histoire Pittoresque de la Franc-Maçonnerie,* by F. T. B. Clavel, Pagnerre, Paris, 1844—from *Robert Mills: Architect of the Washington Monument,* by H. M. Pierce Gallagher, Library of Congress, 1935. 80, 81: Larry Sherer, courtesy the U.S. Naval Academy Museum; courtesy the Grand Lodge of Free and Accepted Masons of Pennsylvania—Metropolitan Museum of Art, gift of John Bard, 1892 (72.6), Jean Antoine Houdon; Cliché de la Réunion des Musées Nationaux, Paris; courtesy the U.S. Naval Academy Museum. 82, 83: Courtesy the Grand Lodge of Masons in Massachusetts, Boston; Alexandria-Washington Lodge No. 22, A.F. & A.M., Alexandria, Va.; The Bostonian Society/Old State House—Chicago Historical Society. 85: Art by John Drummond from a photo by Erich Lessing, courtesy Historisches Museum, Vienna. 86: Courtesy the Trustees of the British Library, London. 87: Erich Lessing, Kunsthistorisches Museum, Vienna. 88: From *Geschichte der Freimaurerei,* by Paul Naudon, Propylaen, Munich, 1982. 90: Courtesy the National Portrait Gallery, London. 91: Courtesy the United Grand Lodge of England, London. 92: Deutsches Freimaurer Museum, Bayreuth, Fotostudio Schmidt. 93: Erich Lessing, courtesy Historisches Museum, Vienna. 94, 95: G. Nimatallah/Ricciarini, Milan. 97: Bibliothèque Nationale, Paris. 98: Roger Viollet, Paris. 99: Roger Viollet, Paris—Bibliothèque Nationale, Paris. 100: David Doody, courtesy University Archives, Swem Library, College of William and Mary, Williamsburg, Va. 101: From *Histoire Pittoresque de la Franc-Maçonnerie,* by F. T. B. Clavel, Pagnerre, Paris, 1844. 102: Library of Congress. 103: Bibliothèque Nationale, Paris. 104: Museum of Our National Heritage, Lexington, Mass. 105: Library of the Supreme Council, Washington, D.C. 106: From *Robert Mills: Architect of the Washington Monument,* by H. M. Pierce Gallagher, Library of Congress, 1935. 107: Larry Sherer, National Archives Neg. No. 42 MJB—Larry Sherer, National Archives Neg. No. 111-SC-106655. 108, 109: The Bettmann Archive. 110: Bob East, Hagen's Studio, Spokane. 111: The Bettmann Archive; Wide World Photos; Robert E. Perry Collection, © 1988 National Geographic Society. 112: Edward Owen, courtesy the Library of the Supreme Council, Washington, D.C. 113: Harry Price Library, University of London. 114: Hulton Picture Library, London. 115: Private Collection; Hulton Picture Library, London. 116: Hulton Picture Library, London. 117: Hulton Picture Library, London (2); Harry Price Library, University of London (2). 118: Hulton Picture Library, London. 119: Private Collection—Hulton Picture Library, London (2). 120: Private Collection. 121: Private Collection (2)—Hulton Picture Library, London; Harry Price Library, University of London. 122: Hulton Picture Library, London. 123: Hulton Picture Library, London—courtesy of the Boleskine Collection. 125: From *The Golden Dawn,* by Israel Regardie, Llewellyn Publications, St. Paul, Minn., 1986. 126: From *The Phoenix,* by Manly P. Hall, © The Philosophical Research Society, 1960; from the Collection of Manly P. Hall, courtesy the Philosophical Research Society. 127: Courtesy the Temple of the People, Halcyon, Calif. 130: Courtesy The Archives, The Theosophical Society, Pasadena, Calif.—R. A. Gilbert, Bristol, England. 132, 133: Courtesy The Archives, The Theosophical Society, Pasadena, Calif. 136, 137: The Bettmann Archive; The Theosophical Society, Adyar, Madras, India; courtesy The Archives, The Theosophical Society, Pasadena, Calif. (2)—Mary Evans Picture Library, London. 138: Thames and Hudson, London, Collection Sven Gahlin, London. 139: Werner Forman Archive, London/Philip Goldman Collection; John Webb, Surrey. 142: The Theosophical Society, London. 143: Gregory Tillet's Private Collection, copied by James Pozarik. 144: Mary Evans Picture Library, London. 145: From *Man Visible and Invisible,* by Charles W. Leadbeater, reprint, The Theosophical Publishing House, Quest Books, Wheaton, Ill., 1987 (3)—from *Thought Forms,* by Annie Besant and Charles W. Leadbeater, reprint, The Theosophical Publishing House, Quest Books, Wheaton, Ill., 1986 (3). 147: Special Collections and Archives, Rutgers University Libraries—Mary Evans Picture Library, London. 148: R. A. Gilbert, Bristol, England. 149: Hulton Picture Library, London. 150: Ellic Howe, London. 151-153: R. A. Gilbert, Bristol, England. 154: BBC Hulton Picture Library/The Bettmann Archive. 155: Hulton Picture Library, London—Ellic Howe, London. 158-160: Haags Gemeentemuseum, © Stichting Beeldrecht, Estate of Piet Mondrian/VAGA, New York, 1988. 161: Piet Mondrian, *Broadway Boogie-Woogie,* 1942-43. Oil on canvas 50x50, Collection, Museum of Modern Art, New York, given anonymously, Estate of Piet Mondrian/VAGA, New York, 1988. 162: Musée National d'Art Moderne, Centre National d'Art et de Culture Georges-Pompidou, Paris; Städtische Galerie im Lenbachhaus, Munich, © ARS, N.Y./ADAGP, 1988. 163: State Russian Museum, Leningrad, © ARS, N.Y./ADAGP, 1988—Wassily Kandinsky, *Tension in Red,* 1926 Collection, Solomon R. Guggenheim Museum, New York, photo by Robert E. Mates, © ARS, N.Y./ADAGP, 1988. 164: The Narodni Galerie, Prague, © ARS, N.Y./ADAGP, 1988; Photo Architect/Vanek, Prague. 165: Musée National d'Art Moderne, Centre National d'Art et de Culture Georges-Pompidou, Paris, © ARS, N.Y./ADAGP, 1988—courtesy Museum Bochum, West Germany, © ARS, N.Y./ADAGP, 1988. 166: The Narodni Galerie, Prague, © ARS, N.Y./ADAGP, 1988. 167: Musée National d'Art Moderne, Centre National d'Art et de Culture Georges-Pompidou, Paris, © ARS, N.Y./ADAGP, 1988—courtesy The Joseph H. Hazen Collection, © ARS, N.Y./ADAGP, 1988. 168: *Woman in Childbirth,* by Malevich, © 1981, George Costakis—*Catalogue of the Galerie Gmurzynska,* Cologne, 1978; Stedelijk Museum, Amsterdam. 169: The Los Angeles County Museum of Art. Purchased with funds provided by Kay Sage Tanguy, Rosemary B. Baruch, and Mr. and Mrs. Charles Boyer; Stedelijk Museum, Amsterdam—Ahmet and Mica Ertegun.

ACKNOWLEDGMENTS

The editors wish to thank the following individuals and institutions for their valuable assistance in the preparation of this volume:

Dorothy Abbenhouse, The Theosophical Society in America, Wheaton, Illinois; Inge Baum, Supreme Council, Washington, D.C.; Professor Hans Bender, Institut für Grenzgebiete der Psychologie und Psychohygiene, Freiburg, West Germany; Bibliotheca Philosophica Hermetica, Amsterdam, the Netherlands; Jessica Boissel, Documentation des Collections, M.N.A.M., Centre Pompidou, Paris; Alice Buse, Philosophical Research Society, Los Angeles; Donna Cleinmark, The Theosophical Society in America, Wheaton, Illinois; Joe A. Diele, Tokyo, Japan; Hilary Evans, London; Professor Yukio Fujino, Tokyo, Japan; Leif Geiges, Staufen, West Germany; Music Department, Colgate University, Hamilton, New York; Haags Gemeentemuseum, The Hague; Joseph H. Hazen, New York, New York; Heidi Klein, Bildarchiv Preussischer Kulturbesitz, West Berlin; Gabrielle Kohler-Gallei, Archiv für Kunst und Geschichte, West Berlin; Florence de Lussy, Conservateur, Département des Manuscrits, Bibliothèque Nationale, Paris; Dominique Morillon, Bibliothècaire Adjointe, Département des Manuscrits, Bibliothèque Nationale, Paris; Richard Morris, Los Angeles County Museum of Art, California; Eleanor O'Keeffe, London; Klaus Präkelt Pressestelle, Stadt Bochum, Bochum, West Germany; Floren L. Quick, Yokosuka, Japan; Chris Rawlings, British Library, London; Pietro Saja, Cefalù, Italy; Herbert Schneider, Freimaurer Museum, Bayreuth, West Germany; Society for Psychical Research, London; Dr. Gerhard Stamm, Badische Landesbibliothek, Karlsruhe, West Germany; Stedelijk Museum, Amsterdam, the Netherlands; Dr. Rolf Streichardt, Institut für Grenzgebiete der Psychologie und Psychohygiene, Freiburg, West Germany; Theosophical Society, London; Maurice Tuchman, Los Angeles County Museum of Art, California; Kirby Van Mater, Theosophical Society, Pasadena, California.

INDEX

Time-Life Books Inc.
is a wholly owned subsidiary of
TIME INCORPORATED

FOUNDER: Henry R. Luce 1898-1967

Editor-in-Chief: Jason McManus
Chairman and Chief Executive Officer: J. Richard Munro
President and Chief Operating Officer: N. J. Nicholas, Jr.
Editorial Director: Ray Cave
Executive Vice President, Books: Kelso F. Sutton
Vice President, Books: Paul V. McLaughlin

TIME-LIFE BOOKS INC.

EDITOR: George Constable
Executive Editor: Ellen Phillips
Director of Design: Louis Klein
Director of Editorial Resources: Phyllis K. Wise
Editorial Board: Russell B. Adams, Jr., Dale M. Brown,
Roberta Conlan, Thomas H. Flaherty, Lee Hassig, Donia
Ann Steele, Rosalind Stubenberg
Director of Photography and Research:
John Conrad Weiser
Assistant Director of Editorial Resources: Elise Ritter Gibson

PRESIDENT: Christopher T. Linen
Chief Operating Officer: John M. Fahey, Jr.
Senior Vice Presidents: Robert M. DeSena, James L. Mercer,
Paul R. Stewart
Vice Presidents: Stephen L. Bair, Ralph J. Cuomo, Neal
Goff, Stephen L. Goldstein, Juanita T. James, Hallett
Johnson III, Carol Kaplan, Susan J. Maruyama, Robert
H. Smith, Joseph J. Ward
Director of Production Services: Robert J. Passantino
Supervisor of Quality Control: James King

Editorial Operations
Copy Chief: Diane Ullius
Production: Celia Beattie
Library: Louise D. Forstall

Library of Congress Cataloging in Publication Data
Ancient wisdom and secret sects / the editors of Time-
Life Books.
   p.   cm.—(Mysteries of the unknown)
Bibliography: p.
Includes index.
ISBN 0-8094-6348-2.   ISBN 0-8094-6349-0   (lib. bdg.)
1. Occultism—History.   2. Cults—History.
I. Time-Life Books.   II. Series.
BF1505.S43 1989
135′.4—dc19   88-38892 CIP

MYSTERIES OF THE UNKNOWN

SERIES DIRECTOR: Russell B. Adams, Jr.
Series Administrator: Myrna Traylor-Herndon
Designer: Herbert H. Quarmby

Editorial Staff for *Ancient Wisdom and Secret Sects*
Associate Editors: Sarah Schneidman (pictures);
Janet Cave, Laura Foreman, Jim Hicks (text)
Assistant Designer: Susan Gibas
Copy Coordinators: Mary Beth Oelkers-Keegan,
Jarelle S. Stein
Picture Coordinator: Richard A. Karno
Researchers: Constance Contreras, Sarah D. Ince, Christian
D. Kinney, Sharon Obermiller, Elizabeth Ward
Editorial Assistant: Donna Fountain

Special Contributors: Christine Hinze (London, picture
research); Denise Dersin (lead research); Lesley Coleman,
Mark A. Galan, Ruth J. Moss, Patricia A. Paterno, Evelyn
Prettyman, Linda Proud, Jeremy Ross, Jacqueline L.
Shaffer (research); Champ Clark, George Daniels, Lydia
Preston Hicks, Peter Kaufman, Ellen Klavan, Richard D.
Kovar, John I. Merritt, Wendy Murphy, Judy L. Pedersen,
Sandra Salmans, Moira Saucer, Nancy Shuker, John
Tompkins, Ann Waldron, Ricardo Villlaneuva (text); John
Drummond (design); Hazel Blumberg-McKee (index)

Correspondents: Elisabeth Kraemer-Singh (Bonn), Vanessa
Kramer (London), Maria Vincenza Aloisi (Paris), Ann
Natanson (Rome).
Valuable assistance was also provided by Dr. Karel
Ornstein (Amsterdam); Mehmet Ali Kislali (Ankara); Mirka
Gondicas (Athens); Angelika Lemmer (Bonn); Nihal
Tamraz (Cairo); Judy Aspinall (London); Arti Aluwalia
(New Delhi); Elizabeth Brown, Christina Lieberman (New
York); Mieko Ikeda (Tokyo); Ann Wise (Rome); Traudl
Lessing (Vienna).

The Consultants:
Marcello Truzzi, the general consultant for the series, is a
professor of sociology at Eastern Michigan University. He
is also director of the Center for Scientific Anomalies
Research (CSAR) and editor of its journal, the *Zetetic
Scholar.* Dr. Truzzi, who considers himself a "constructive
skeptic" with regard to claims of the paranormal, works
through the CSAR to produce dialogues between critics
and proponents of unusual scientific claims.

Robert A. Gilbert, an antiquarian bookseller in his native
Bristol, England, studied psychology and philosophy at the
University of Bristol, from which he was graduated with
honors. His writings on the history of occultism include
numerous articles and books, among them *The Golden
Dawn Companion.*

John Melton Gordon is director of the Institute for the
Study of American Religion in Santa Barbara, California,
and the author of numerous books, among them
Paganism, Magic and Witchcraft and *Biographical Dictionary of American Cult and Sect Leaders.*

John M. Hamill is a widely recognized authority and
frequent writer on the history and development of English Freemasonry. He currently serves as librarian and
curator of the Library and Museum of the Grand Lodge
of England.

Other Publications:

AMERICAN COUNTRY
VOYAGE THROUGH THE UNIVERSE
THE THIRD REICH
THE TIME-LIFE GARDENER'S GUIDE
TIME FRAME
FIX IT YOURSELF
FITNESS, HEALTH & NUTRITION
SUCCESSFUL PARENTING
HEALTHY HOME COOKING
UNDERSTANDING COMPUTERS
LIBRARY OF NATIONS
THE ENCHANTED WORLD
THE KODAK LIBRARY OF CREATIVE PHOTOGRAPHY
GREAT MEALS IN MINUTES
THE CIVIL WAR
PLANET EARTH
COLLECTOR'S LIBRARY OF THE CIVIL WAR
THE EPIC OF FLIGHT
THE GOOD COOK
WORLD WAR II
HOME REPAIR AND IMPROVEMENT
THE OLD WEST

*For information on and a full description of any of the
Time-Life Books series listed above, please call 1-800-
621-7026 or write:*
Reader Information
Time-Life Customer Service
P.O. Box C-32068
Richmond, Virginia 23261-2068

This volume is one of a series that examines the history
and nature of seemingly paranormal phenomena. Other
books in the series include:

Time-Life Books Inc. offers a wide range of fine record-
ings, including a *Rock 'n' Roll Era* series. For subscription
information, call 1-800-621-7026 or write Time-Life
Music, P.O. Box C-32068, Richmond, Virginia 23261-2068.